WORKING WITH PLYWOOD, including Indoor/Outdoor Projects

Other TAB books by the author:

No. 872 *Wood Heating Handbook*
No. 892 *Do-It-Yourselfer's Guide To Chainsaw Use and Repair*
No. 949 *Do-It-Yourselfer's Guide To Auto Body Repair and Painting*
No. 1074 *How To Build Your Own Vacation Home*

WORKING WITH PLYWOOD, including Indoor/Outdoor Projects

by Charles R. Self

TAB BOOKS

BLUE RIDGE SUMMIT, PA. 17214

FIRST EDITION

FIRST PRINTING—AUGUST 1979

Copyright © 1979 by TAB BOOKS

Printed in the United States of America

Library of Congress Cataloging in Publication Data

Self, Charles R.
    Working with plywood, including indoor/outdoor projects.
 	
    Includes index.
    1. Woodwork. 2. Plywood. I. Title.
TT191.S44   674'.834   79-12563
ISBN 0-8306-9786-1
ISBN 0-8306-1144-4 pbk.

Cover photos of standard plywood courtesy of American Plywood Assn. and of redwood plywood courtesy of California Redwood Assn. Art on pages courtesy of American Plywood Assn.

Preface

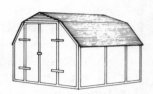

Wood is one of nature's greatest gifts to mankind. With it we can heat ourselves, shelter ourselves, and often even clothe ourselves. Wood provides chemicals for use as disinfectants and in other ways. The variations in the use of wood are close to infinite, and we discover more of them just about every day. As population around the world continues to expand, much faster than we have been able to expand the growth of harvestable wood in just about any country (those Middle Eastern deserts were not always sandy wastes—many at one time were finely wooded slopes, and became deserts because of intemperate wood cutting), the pressures on today's woodland will increase, though in many cases such pressures are already extreme.

With present and increasing demands for wood as a shelter building material, fuel, and a source of other materials such as alcohol, the cropping of woodlands in the United States must increase. In many cases, proper woodlot or forest management would increase annual yields by a great many percentage points. Small forest areas, particularly in the East, are seldom managed so that their yields are anywhere near the maximum possible. Basically, often all that is done in such areas is to interfere with certain natural processes to the extent that forest growth is badly slowed. Deformed, or wolf, trees sometimes come close to being the predominant crop, while useful varieties and shapes of trees are unable to grow properly.

Economics has a lot to do with this lack of management. It is only a very infrequent stand of timber a few dozen acres in size that can produce enough income to interest professional foresters, or others who will do anything but clearcut. They turn what might have someday been a fine, producing forest area into a pasture or hayfield. With hay prices today, a 50-acre hayfield, assuming variables such as weather don't bite back, is almost a gold mine if the land is at all productive. In this area, three annual cuttings of alfalfa hay will often produce 2,000 bales per acre, at $3 a bale. Of course, that's not the whole story. It never is. For the past couple of years, hay farmers have lost their shirts as the rains didn't come. And there is fertilizer to buy and equipment to run and maintain. But 50 acres of alfalfa hay in a year like this one could possibly gross the farmer $300,000. No tree farm could come close over many years, unless it were a solid stand of black walnut.

The small farmer with a 50 or 60-acre tree lot is usually better off to either financially cut pulpwood, or sell pulpwood for stumpage, than to hope and work on the basis that 20 years from now he might have a fine stand of veneer grade poplar, oak, birch or whatever. While pulpwood is essential to many industries (you wouldn't be able to read this book without it), most times the trees cut are immature. Too often they are clear cut, so that no trees remain to grow to full size.

The increasing price of wood products over the next decade or two may just turn the entire situation around, but by that time we can't really be sure there will even be enough woodland left to produce our basic needs. Wood prices, for all kinds of wood, have risen wildly in the past ten years, as has most everything else. A 2x4 that used to cost about 80¢ is now up around $1.50 or more. Usually more. And it is smaller. Clear pine for building cabinets and shelves is now just about impossible to find in many areas, while number two pine costs something like six times what I paid for clear pine 12 years ago.

Still, because of their workability and versatility, wood products continue to be used, and the use increases even though the prices rise beyond points we would have thought insane only 15 years ago. The reasons are quite simple: wood is still abundant; it is still relatively cheap as a building material; it offers great strength for weight; it is easily formed into a fantastic variety of shapes; durability of many types of wood is excellent and can rather cheaply be made even greater; wood is easily joined, both to more wood, or to other materials. Put succinctly, there just is no other building material that offers all of wood's advantages, at wood's price. No matter whether you are building a new barn, a desk or bookshelves, it is just about the finest, cheapest choice you can make.

And to all that, we can add wood's greatest beauty. As an example, consider a table I own. The cherry is in widths no longer to be found, about 2 feet across the top, with each drop leaf about 2 feet wide. The table was built, according to a professional estimator, about 1795. There is not a thing wrong with that table, except for a need to have the joints reglued, a job I'll finish this winter. The finish on the wood is nothing more than wax, but you can lose yourself in its depths. If the wood to build this antique could be found today, the actual cost of a reproduction would probably be higher than the value the older table has, if all work were done by hand.

Is there a cure for the coming shortage of wood? Sure. There are a dozen cures, maybe more, but most are not workable. Fewer people and more forests is the surest repair for the situation, but that just isn't likely. Better forest management in areas where forests are small in acreage will provide some help. Faster growing varieties of trees will also help, and are being developed by the large lumber companies.

One present wood that does a great deal for the overall situation, and will continue to do so, is plywood. Today's plywood is nothing like the cheap efforts of fifty years ago, the veneer quality junk that makes some moderately old furniture about the worst possible buy in the world. I don't care if you need to build a barn for horses or cattle, a cattle rack for a pick-up truck, or a sea-going replica of a World War II PT boat. Today any plywood you need, for nearly any purpose, is readily available. And it is durable under any condition the manufacturer lists it as being useful for.

Plywood is also stronger than plain wood. It can be shaped. It can be veneered. It can be made with marine glue, exterior glue, or interior glue, in decreasing order of cost. It can be made with a final laminate of furniture quality wood of just about any kind you can imagine (and probably a lot you can't imagine, as the stuff comes in some truly exotic woods, which are also available as solid wood, and are totally unaffordable until made into plywood). Plywood can be made cheaply enough to floor, roof, side and panel an entire house, or it can be made expensively enough to make the entire DuPont family shudder. Versatility is great, as plywood is used for floors, roofing, siding, wall decoration, cabinets, shelves, large and small boats, the occasional airplane (probably the most famous of which is Howard Hughes' misnamed Spruce Goose), sheds, barns, beer coolers, home bars, etc. The list can be nearly endless. You'll find more than a few of the possibilities covered in this book with plans supplied by the American Plywood Association.

When plywood is made, the largest portion of the tree is used. Cutting down on waste is another fine way of keeping up with demand, without wasting any increase in forest growth we're able to get in the next few years.

Plywood may be the most popular form of wood in the future. It is certainly close to it now, if not already there, and most do-it-yourselfers will be well served by having a good idea of how to work with most forms of this material that provides natural strength and beauty, combined with man-made strength and economy.

Charles Self

Contents

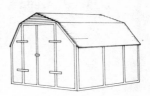

The Tale of a Tree's Unwinding

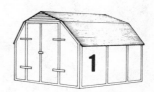

1

The simplicity, or seeming simplicity, of a sheet of plywood belies some of the complexities in its manufacture, from the instant the logger pulls the starter cord on his chainsaw to the time you nail (or glue) the final panel in place.

Most of our modern plywood comes from trees raised on tree farms, where the companies follow a planned routine of patient planting, thinning and fertilization, as well as keeping up a constant war on harmful insects and diseases. Trees are a basic, renewable resource anyway, and the careful cultivation of tree crops speeds the renewal (as does experimentation with many varieties to locate the fastest growing types).

The tree is felled and limbed, thereby becoming a log, which is cut to transportable lengths and removed to the mill. The wood form never really changes, as the veneering process does nothing more than arrange the wood in a more efficiently used form, with each layer at right angles to the layer above and the layer below (Figs. 1-1 and 1-2).

The log is placed on what amounts to a huge turning lathe, with a knife blade pressed against the wood (Fig. 1-3). The log turns, and the knife peels off thin sheets. Bark is removed and used for garden mulch or fuel. Some industries have been working to use wood as a fuel in their plants, and in such cases large amounts of bark and sawdust are commonly used, rather

Fig. 1-1. The first bite of the saw at the mill starts the process which will end with your sheet of plywood

than logs, since it can be packed into the furnaces better than logs (Fig. 1-4). As the peeling goes on, the veneer strips are examined for knots and other faults. These are cut out (such chips can be used as pulp to make paper or particleboard). When the log is peeled as far as possible, the remaining core can be cut into 2 × 4's. As you can see, what waste there is from any tree turned into plywood is absolutely minimized.

In the mill the veneer sheets are called plies, and are next coated with adhesive and joined under pressure. In correctly made plywood, the bond between the plies is as strong as, sometimes even stronger than, the plies themselves (Figs. 1-5, 1-6, 1-7).

The plies are laid up in many ways, but always with an odd number of layers in each final sheet. Basically, there are two methods of laying up the plies in everyday use now. One method will have four plies, in three layers because the two center plies will have their grain running in the same direction. The next method has five plies and five layers since each ply is

Fig. 1-2. The first step nears completion

Fig. 1-3. The log must now be peeled to uniform

Fig. 1-4. High speeds produced fast work

cross laminated (cross laminating is simple because the top ply has its grain running the long way of the sheet, the next ply has its grain running across the sheet, the third has its grain running the long way, and so on, to produce a sheet of very great strength).

If we go back in history, we find that some form of veneering has been used for many, many centuries. Modern plywood, though, came into being in the very early 1900's, with the first being made in 1905. By 1910 several mills had started production, and by 1925 production had hit 153 million square feet per year. Today, plants can produce that amount in just a few days!

Uniform grade marking entered the picture in 1933 when the Douglas Fir Plywood Association came into existence (grade marking remains, though in a much more sophisticated manner, and the old DFPA now exists as the American Plywood Association). Look for the APA stamp on plywood you buy, and you'll be assured it is made to match the grade marks.

Waterproof glues entered the picture in 1934, and widely increased the use of plywoods. By 1940, plywood was in use for subflooring, paneling, cabinets and many other jobs. Production had passed a billion square feet by the year's end. By 1060, plywood production had passed the seven billion square foot mark, and that figure today is more than doubled again.

Originally all plywood was manufactured in the West, and the predominating wood was Douglas fir. Today plywood is made in many areas, and Southern pine is becoming an important species in its manufacture. In total, though, over 70 species of wood are now used to make plywood.

As plywood developed into an immense industry, the techniques for growing trees began to keep pace with the need for more and more wood. As we have already said, the manufacturers formed tree farms, protecting seedlings and growing trees from disease and insects. Genetic selection began to play an important part as foresters selected trees for fast, straight growth, and soil analysts began checking to see which type of tree grows best in what type of soil. Tree nurseries

Fig. 1-5. Plywood sheets are nearly ready to go

now supply over a billion seedlings each year to replace harvested trees, and the companies with tree farms plant more than a half million acres annually to keep the cycle going.

Even during the tree farming process, we see savings reflected. As the trees grow, they have to be thinned for best growth rates. These cut down small trees then become 2 × 4's, wood chips for particleboard, or pulp for paper. A further benefit of tree farms is the fact that certain sections are opened to the public as recreation areas, with picnic and camping and hiking sites available.

The effort at using all of the tree has extended even to the point of development of a thinner saw blade for the mill so that the narrower kerfs will produce less sawdust!

With all of this work to produce a versatile building material, some of us could end up a bit confused as to the types and standards for a particular job. While all plywood is of the flat panel type, built of sheets of veneer and glued together under pressure, there are a great many differences in plywood types, finishes, purposes, cost and final appearance. It is quite possible to waste a great deal of cash using the wrong plywood for the job. That waste could come just as easily from buying too cheap a grade of plywood as from buying too expensive a grade. For example, trying to get by with interior glue sheathing on a house may work for a short time, but the first or second time a bit of moisture penetrates the siding and reaches your sheathing, the plies are going to begin to delaminate. The wasted money here can be a tremendous amount, for the only cure is stripping all the siding off, ripping the sheathing plywood off and then installing exterior glue sheathing plywood. By the same token, the use of furniture grade, or marine glue, plywood as exterior sheathing is a waste of money, as is the use of plywood with an A (sanded and clear) face for underlayment for floors.

Fortunately, the American Plywood Association grading system tells just about all you'll ever need to know about any particular piece of plywood. The grading system is not extremely simple—it can't be with the wide variety of plywoods on the market—but it is basically understandable to anyone. New parts even include structural spacing recommendations for home and other construction uses.

Veneer grades start with A: the surface is smooth and paintable. Neatly made repairs (plugs or patches) are permitted, and a natural finish can be used in applications where a perfect surface is not essential. Grade B offers a solid surface veneer which may have circular plugs and a few tight knots. Grade C allows knotholes to 1 inch in diameter, with most limited to ½ inch or less. Limited splits are allowed. This is the minimum veneer quality permitted in exterior plywood grades. Grade C plugged (abbreviated plgd) is a better C grade for many uses where a smooth surface is desirable, as splits are limited to ⅛ of an inch, and knotholes and borer holes may not be larger than a quarter by half an inch. Class or grade D allows knots and knotholes to 2½ inches width, though under certain conditions they may go to a half inch larger. Some splits are permitted.

Basic plywood grades come in two types, interior and exterior. Plywood is graded for both sides, and also has a rating for inner plies. The top exterior grade is A-A, with

Fig. 1-6. The plywood is cut to final size

interior plies graded C. This is used in outdoor applications where both sides of the panel will be visible, and appearance is important. Grade A-B, with internal plies C, is used where the looks of one side of the panel is of less importance, but still needs to be fairly good looking. A-C is used where only a single side of the panel will show such as on siding, or soffits. Grade B-C is for use where the looks of one side is of some importance, but not really needed as decoration. This grade is extremely useful for construction of farm buildings, garden sheds and so on. Grade C-C plugged offers one side or face plugged and is often used as a base for tile or linoleum floors subject to frequent wettings, or for walls to be covered with other materials. Grade C-C is unsanded and is used for rough construction where appearance is of little importance. Grade B-B Plywood is specifically made to be used as concrete form construction material, and can be used and re-used until the wood simply wears out. There are at least four other exterior plywood grades of interest to the amateur builder or workman. Type 303 (Registered Trademark) siding is just that. The panels have a variety of surface textures or grooves or patterns, and veneer grades will be C or better, with uses extending from siding to fences to outdoor screening and fences. Grade T1-11 (Registered Trademark) is a special paneling of ⅝-inch thickness with deep parallel grooves and is used as a finish siding, with or without (usually without, but often as a replacement siding) sheathing. The surface can be had in a variety of textures. MDO plywood offers a B face veneer, as well as a B back veneer, and is short for medium density overlay. The surface forms just about an ideal base for almost all paints, so this grade is very useful as siding, built-in cabinets and for use in signs. HDO is similar to MDO, except that the face veneer may be either A or B grade, as may the back. The center plies can be C or C plugged, and the surface is extremely hard so no painting is needed. For us, its greatest uses would be in cabinet building and counter tops (Fig. 1-8).

Interior types of plywood offer pretty much the same grades as do exterior types, with different glues used, and with the internal plies usually of D grade rather than C. Grade A-A with D inner plies is for cabinet doors and furniture where both sides will be visible. Grade A-B has a solid and smooth

Fig. 1-7. The final product rolls off the mill machines

back of slightly lesser attractiveness than A grade. Grade A-D interior is the general grade rating for indoor paneling of many types where the back will be invisible. Grade B-D is the type of plywood you would need for the back portions of built-in furniture or desks, or cabinets, where the face will not be seen, or at least not often. Unsanded C-D interior plywood is often used for subflooring and, whenever needed, interior sheathing of walls, usually temporary. It is one of the cheapest grades of plywood you can buy, but comes in extremely handy at times. Underlayment grade is C-plugged on the face, with a D back and C or D inner plies. It is used as underlayment where a smooth surface is absolutely essential to a good job (this often is the case when rubber or plastic tile comprise the finish floor, as these materials will, sooner or later, conform to any irregularities in the underlayment).

To add a bit more to the possible confusion, or to, we hope, clarify things more, the type of wood used in the plywood is classified by species of tree. Each classification, and there are five basic ones, consists of a group of species considered to be closely related. Group 1 includes Douglas fir,

INTERIOR TYPE

Use These Terms When You Specify Plywood	Description and Most Common Uses	Typical Grade-trademarks	Veneer Grade Face	Veneer Grade Back	Veneer Grade Inner Plies	Most Common Thicknesses (inch) (2) (3)				
C-D INT-APA (1) (4)	For wall and roof sheathing, subflooring, industrial uses such as pallets. Usually supplied with exterior glue; sometimes with interior glue. Product Standard has provision for intermediate glue, but availability is currently limited. Specify exterior glue for best durability in longer construction delays and for treated wood foundations.	C-D 48/24 APA INTERIOR P.S. 1-000	C	D	D	5/16	3/8	1/2	5/8	3/4
STRUCTURAL-I C-D INT APA (4) and STRUCTURAL II C-D INT-APA (4)	Unsanded structural grades where plywood strength properties are of maximum importance: structural diaphragms, box beams, gusset plates, stressed-skin panels, containers, pallet bins. Made only with exterior glue. See (5) for Group requirements.	STRUCTURAL I C-D 32/16 APA INTERIOR P.S. 1-000 EXTERIOR GLUE	C	D	D	5/16	3/8	1/2	5/8	3/4
C-D PLUGGED INT-APA (1) (5)	For built-ins, wall and ceiling tile backing, cable reels, walkways, separator boards. Not a substitute for Underlayment, as it lacks Underlayment's punch-through resistance. Touch-sanded.	C-D PLUGGED GROUP 2 APA INTERIOR P.S. 1-000	C Plgd.	D	D	5/16	3/8	1/2	5/8	3/4
2-4-1 INT-APA (1) (6)	"Heavy Timber" roof decking and combination subfloor-underlayment. Quality base for resilient floor coverings, carpeting, wood strip flooring. Use 2-4-1 with exterior glue in areas subject to moisture. Unsanded or touch-sanded as specified.	2-4-1 GROUP 1 APA INTERIOR P.S. 1-000	C Plgd.	D	C & D	1-1/8"				

	Unsanded grade with waterproof bond for subflooring and roof decking, siding on service and farm buildings, wood foundations, crating, pallets, pallet bins, cable reels.	C	C	C	5/16	3/8	1/2	5/8	3/4
C-C EXT-APA (4)									
STRUCTURAL I C-C EXT-APA (4) and STRUCTURAL II C-C EXT-APA (4)	For engineered applications in construction and industry where full Exterior type panels are required. Unsanded. See (5) for Group requirements.	C	C	C	5/16	3/8	1/2	5/8	3/4

(1) Can be manufactured with exterior or intermediate glue (check dealer for availability of intermediate glue in your area).

(2) All grades can be manufactured tongue-and-grooved in panels 1/2" and thicker.

(3) Panels are standard 4x8-foot size. Other sizes available.

(4) Grade-trademarked with Identification Index shown in guide below.

(5) Can be manufactured in Structural I (all plies limited to Group 1 species) and Structural II (all plies limited to Group 1, 2, or 3 species).

(6) Available in Group 1, 2, or 3 only.

Identification indexes for unsanded grades

Panels thicker than 7/8 inch shall be identified by Group.

Thickness (inch)	C-C EXTERIOR C-D INTERIOR			STRUCTURAL I C-D & C-C STRUCTURAL II (b) C-D & C-C	STRUCTURAL II C-D & C-C
	Group 1 Group 2(a)	Group 2 or 3 Group 4(a)	Group 4	Group 1	Group 2 or 3
5/16	20/0	16/0	12/0	20/0	16/0
3/8	24/0	20/0	16/0	24/0	20/0
1/2	32/16	24/0	24/0	32/16	24/0
5/8	42/20	32/16	30/12	42/20	32/16
3/4	48/24	42/20	36/16	48/24	42/20
7/8	-	48/24	42/20	-	48/24

(a) Panels conforming to special thickness provisions and panel construction of Paragraph 3.8.6 of PS 1.

(b) Panels manufactured with Group 1 faces but classified as STRUCTURAL II by reason of Group 2 or Group 3 inner plies.

Typical grade-trademark

Grade of veneer on panel face
Grade of veneer on panel back

C-D (APA)
32/16
INTERIOR
PS 1-74   000
EXTERIOR GLUE

Identification Index
Designates the type of plywood
Exterior or Interior
Product Standard governing manufacture
Type of glue used
Mill number

Fig. 1-8. Here are plywood types, a typical trademark and identification indexes for unsanded grades

Western Larch, Southern pines and the birches, while Group 2 has Port Orford cedar, cypress, black maple, and Western white pine. Figure 1-9 will show the rest of the groups. In the case of decorative uses, of course, you will need to not only know the group, but the specific wood being used in order to do the best job possible.

We have covered exterior and interior plywoods, with a note that the basic difference is in the types of glues used but this in not totally true. Generally, interior type plywood is not as strong as exterior, though the glue grade may be changed to meet conditions of internal dampness. Interior grades of plywood start with that made with interior glue only. This should not be subjected to extremes of humidity or dampness over any prolonged period of time. Interior plywood with intermediate glue (abbreviated IMG) has an adhesive that is more resistant to molds, bacteria and dampness. Interior grades are also made with exterior glue, which is waterproof. Still, these interior grades are never the total equivalent of similar exterior grades of plywood, and will not last as long under extreme conditions. Figures 1-10 and 1-11 show how some of the grade markings are applied, always on the back ply or veneer.

Of less interest to home workshops are the engineered grades of plywood, as they are most often used where absolute maximum strength is required. Still, we will occasionally have need of gusset plates (possibly you'll want to make up roof trusses to use when building a new home, garage or barn) or you may find a need to form a box beam to support a heavy load. Too, these engineered grades come with an identification index that shows what on center distance is correct for a particular grade and thickness, which means these panels are exceptionally easy to use for roofing, decking and subflooring. There are four basic engineered plywood grades. Structural I and II each come in either C-C or C-D appearance grades. Structural I grades may be made only with woods listed in Group one species, while Structural II grades may be made with Group one, two or three woods. All Structural I and II plywood is made with exterior glue only.

C-D Sheathing grade is an interior type of sheathing made with either intermediate or fully waterproof adhesive. These

Group 1	Group 2		Group 3	Group 4	Group 5
Apitong [(a)(b)]	Cedar, Port Orford	Maple, Black	Alder, Red	Aspen	Basswood
Beech, American	Cypress	Mengkulang [(a)]	Birch, Paper	Bigtooth	Fir, Balsam
Birch	Douglas Fir 2 [(c)]	Meranti, Red [(a)(d)]	Cedar, Alaska	Quaking	Poplar, Balsam
Sweet	Fir	Mersawa [(a)]	Fir, Subalpine	Cativo	
Yellow	California Red	Pine	Hemlock, Eastern	Cedar	
Douglas Fir 1 [(c)]	Grand	Pond	Maple, Bigleaf	Incense	
Kapur (a)	Noble	Red	Pine	Western Red	
Keruing (a) (b)	Pacific Silver	Virginia	Jack	Cottonwood	
Larch, Western	White	Western White	Lodgepole	Eastern	
Maple, Sugar	Hemlock, Western	Spruce	Ponderosa	Black (Western Poplar)	
Pine	Lauan	Red	Spruce	Pine	
Caribbean	Almon	Sitka	Redwood	Eastern White	
Ocote	Bagtikan	Sweetgum	Spruce	Sugar	
Pine, Southern	Mayapis	Tamarack	Black		
Loblolly	Red Lauan	Yellow Poplar	Engelmann		
Longleaf	Tangile		White		
Shortleaf	White Lauan				
Slash					
Tanoak					

(a) Each of these names represents a trade group of woods consisting of a number of closely related species.
(b) Species from the genus Dipterocarpus are marketed collectively. Apitong if originating in the Philippines; Keruing if originating in Malaysia or Indonesia.
(c) Douglas fir from trees grown in the states of Washington, Oregon, California, Idaho, Montana, Wyoming, and the Canadian Provinces of Alberta and British Columbia shall be classed as Douglas fir No. 1. Douglas fir from trees grown in the states of Nevada, Utah, Colorado, Arizona and New Mexico shall be classed as Douglas fir No. 2.
(d) Red Meranti shall be limited to species having a specific gravity of 0.41 or more based on green volume and oven dry weight.

Fig. 1-9. Here are wood species used in plywoods

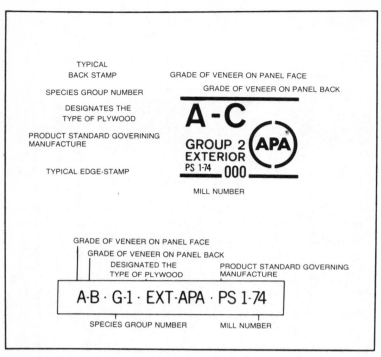

Fig. 1-10. American Plywood Association (APA) grade marks

panels are unsanded, and are considered close to ideal for such things as subflooring, wall sheathing and roof decking where the final cover may get a delayed application, allowing a fair amount of moisture to hit the panels during construction.

C-C Exterior is used when C-D Sheathing will not be good because of constant moisture problems.

The Identification Index on engineered grades of plywood offers a help to both the professional and amateur builder. Simply put, they tell you just how far apart you can space rafters or floor joists when using a particular grade and thickness of plywood. The first number (numbers, as you see in Fig. 1-12, are listed with a slash between them) shows how many inches apart the rafters can be, while the second number shows the spacing for floor joists. Thus a 24/0 rating would mean that you could use the particular panel for rafters only, with spacing up to 24 inches on center. A 32/16 rating means the panel can be used for both flooring and roofing, with the floor joist spacing half of the rafter spacing of 32 inches on center.

PARTICLEBOARD

Particleboard is not strictly plywood, but is often used in certain areas to replace or supplement plywood, so it is of some importance that it be covered in a book on working with plywood in the interests of completeness. Particleboard is the general term used to describe a panel made from wood pieces or particles, combined with a synthetic resin or some other adhesive or binder and bonded together under heat and pressure in a special press. In the process, the particles are tightly bound together. Other materials can be added to remove or add certain qualities to the particleboard.

Hardboard is a specific kind of particleboard. The hot press operates to combine the particles, which may also include materials other than wood chips and pieces, to a density of 31 pounds per cubic foot or more. The addition of other materials will be indicated, and will add one or more of the following characteristics: stiffness, hardness, ease of finish for different types of finishes, resistance to abrasion, resistance to moisture, added overall strength, durability and ease of use.

Medium density fiberboard is a dry formed panel product. The hot press forms these at no more than 50 pounds per cubic foot density, and, again, no less than 31 pounds per cubic foot. In this case, almost the entire interfiber bond is created by the addded binder.

In general, particleboards of all types are made up of what would otherwise be waste products from other areas of the

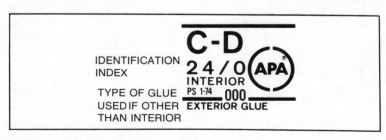

Fig. 1-11. APA engineered grade marks

wood industry. This can include sawdust, chips, and other types of residue.

Fillers for particleboard vary greatly, but most are added in the following forms, which meet, to varying degrees, the need for rendering the board smooth enough for easy finishing, while keeping shrinkage of the finished product to a minimum.

Ultraviolet cured polyester fillers offer good workability, and excellent filling, with good adhesion to most types of wood used in the panels. Sanding qualities are excellent. Cost of the filler itself is not extremely high, but the cost to us is a bit more because the manufacturer needs special equipment to dry the panels.

Water base emulsion type fillers offer good workability, good sanding properties, rapid drying with no special equipment, and the possibility of pigmentation to just about any color anyone might want. In addition chemical resistance is quite good, the cost is low and painting is easy. The surfaces are liable to be less even because the water in the filler has a tendency to cause swelling. Surface particles must be fine.

Lacquer based fillers offer excellent sanding, extremely quick drying with no special equipment, and easy panel pigmentation. Filling is not as good as with other fillers used in most cases, and cost is high, while the fast drying limits the workability of the finished panel. Chemical resistance is not as good as with other kinds of particleboard.

Polyurethane based fillers offer fine workability, good sanding properties, fair drying speed with conventional methods, and maximum hardness if properly cured at the factory. The cost per gallon of the filler tends to be quite high and the drying period for proper curing is long, both of which add to the cost of the finished panels.

Particleboard of various kinds can be used in many areas to replace plywood, though many of us are probably most familiar with particleboard as underlayment for floors to be finished with other materials, and as backing for the unseen portions of many kinds of furniture.

Floor underlayment is generally 42-44 pounds per cubic foot in density, with a sanded finish (usually done with an 80 grit paper). Defect toleration is greater than in other areas of

UA

Guide to engineered grades of plywood for floors

Specific grades and thicknesses may be in locally limited supply.
See your dealer for availability before specifying.

Use these terms when you specify plywood	Description and Most Common Uses	Typical Grade-trademarks	Veneer Grade Face	Back	Inner plies	Most Common Thicknesses (inch) (a)					
Interior Type						1/4	5/16	3/8	1/2	5/8	3/4
C-D INT-APA (c) (b)	For subflooring. Also available with intermediate glue or exterior glue. Specify intermediate glue if moderate construction delays are expected, exterior glue for better durability in somewhat longer construction delays.	C-D 32/16 APA INT-APA 000 / C-D 32/16 APA INT-APA 000 EXTERIOR GLUE	C	D	D		5/16	3/8	1/2	5/8	3/4
STRUCTURAL I C-D INT-APA STRUCTURAL II C-D INT-APA	Unsanded structural grades where plywood strength properties are of maximum importance: structural diaphragms, stressed-skin panels. Made only with exterior glue.	STRUCTURAL I APA INT-APA 000 EXTERIOR GLUE	C (e)	D (f)	D (f)		5/16	3/8	1/2	5/8	3/4
UNDERLAYMENT INT-APA (c) (h)	For underlayment or combination subfloor-underlayment under resilient floor coverings, carpeting in homes, apartments, mobile homes. Specify exterior glue where moisture may be present, such as bathrooms, utility rooms. Touch-sanded. Also available with tongue and groove.	UNDERLAYMENT GROUP 2 APA INT-APA 000	C Plugged	D	C & D (g)	1/4		3/8	1/2	5/8	3/4
2-4-1 INT-APA (b) (d)	Combination subfloor-underlayment. Quality base for resilient floor coverings, carpeting, wood-strip flooring. Use 2-4-1 with exterior glue in areas subject to moisture. Unsanded or touch-sanded as specified. Also available with tongue and groove.	2-4-1 GROUP 1 APA INT-APA 000	C Plugged	D	C & D	1-1/8"					
Exterior Type						1/4	5/16	3/8	1/2	5/8	3/4
C-C EXT-APA (c)	Unsanded grade with waterproof bond for subflooring.	C-C 32/16 APA EXT-APA 000	C	C	C		5/16	3/8	1/2	5/8	3/4
UNDERLAYMENT C-C Plugged EXT-APA (c) (h) C-C PLUGGED EXT-APA (c) (h)	For underlayment or combination subfloor-underlayment under resilient floor coverings where severe moisture conditions may be present, as in balcony decks. Touch-sanded. Also available with tongue and groove.	UNDERLAYMENT GROUP 2 APA EXT-APA 000 C-C PLUGGED	C Plugged	C	C (g)	1/4		3/8	1/2	5/8	3/4

(a) Panels are standard 4 x 8-foot size. Other sizes may be available.
(b) Also available with exterior or intermediate glue.
(c) Available in Group 1, 2, 3, 4, or 5.
(d) Available in Group 1, 2, or 3 only.
(e) Special improved C grade for structural panels.
(f) Special improved D grade for structural panels.
(g) Ply beneath face a special C grade which limits knotholes to 1 inch. For interior UNDERLAYMENT only, ply beneath face may be D grade provided faces are Group 1 or 2 and 1/6 inch thick.
(h) Also available in Structural I (all plies limited to Group 1 species) and Structural II (all plies limited to Group 1, 2, or 3 species).

Fig. 1-12. Engineered floor plywood grades

particleboard manufacturing in terms of sanding skips and streaks.

Industrial board quality particleboard comes in a variety of densities, with the breaking point considered to be 50 pounds per cubic foot. Above that is medium density. Then comes high density paneling or boards. Edge tightness and finish of the overall panel is better than with underlayment grades, with thicknesses generally within .005 inches overall.

Your selection will depend on the use which you intend for the particleboard. Certainly it will be a waste of your hard-earned cash these days to use industrial quality panels for underlayment for a bathroom or kitchen tile floor. You would find it as big a waste of money to specify underlayment grade for use in visible, to be painted, shelving or countertops that need to have plastic laminates contact cemented to an extremely smooth surface.

HARDWOOD PLYWOOD

In addition to the plywood and particleboard types already covered, the home furniture maker will be interested in varieties of hardwood plywoods and veneered particleboards. Generally, these panels or boards come in veneers of exotic and beautiful woods of many types. Lately it seems there is no type of wood you cannot get in furniture quality veneers. Whether you wish to use domestic white oak Japanese ash, Carpathian elm, olive, French walnut or ebony, you can find a source of the plywood somewhere, usually locally through a lumberyard or lumber dealer.

Hardwood plywood is made in exterior and interior types, just as the softwood plywoods are in thicknesses ranging from an eighth of an inch on up to an inch. Type I uses exterior glue for applications in areas where there is a lot of moisture. Type II uses a water resistant glue and is for use in moderate moisture areas, indoors. Type III uses moisture resistant glue, for indoors use in standard applications where exposure to moisture is infrequent and light. Type IV, or Technical Type I uses waterproof glue, as in Type I, but varies in thicknesses and ply designs for special uses.

Appearance grading starts with Premium #1, which uses only select, matched veneers, with no great color contrasts. It is the most expensive. Good grade # 1 is next with no great color contrasts and no great grain contrasts. Sound grade # 2 will allow some surface defects of grain matching and color contrasts. Utility grade #3 will have some tight knots, color streaks and, possibly, some small splits. From this point, you have back grade panels with greater surface defects, and SP grade which must be custom made and is supremely expensive (Fig. 1-13).

If we haven't lost you yet in our tale of the versatility and availability of plywood, let's take a quick look at the next style—wall paneling. The varieties of panels for interior walls are great, ranging from pressed photographs of wood grain over inexpensive hardboard to actual exotic wood veneers such as pecan over light plywood cores and backs. Generally this type of paneling is not meant to be structural, serving totally as decorative, easily cared for wall coverings that almost never need replacing, repainting or refinishing.

Selection depends on your own tastes, the total cost to allow for the job, and the need for any other special qualities. Damp basements will obviously require a different sort of glue than will dry living rooms or dining rooms, while kitchens using paneling will require a different surface finish to allow a great amount of surface wiping for removing greasy residues.

Paneling is made in so many varieties it would be a bit futile here to try and list them all. Simply check the stores with which you are used to dealing to locate the variety you wish to use. Expect to pay anywhere from about $4 per panel for the photo overlay types on up past $30 per panel for more or less exotic woods with a real wood surface and a clear plastic finish for use in kitchens.

If you are using a great many of the panels, or just a small number to make one wall an accent, check the grain patterns on the panels to be delivered to you. You may wish to match or mix grain swirls and colors, and this process will ease things for you. Have the dealer set aside the packages to be delivered. Take them with you if at all possible as this lessens the chance of getting your panels mixed up with someone else's. Some dealers don't like this selection process, while others

	Grade Designation(2)	Description and Most Common Uses	Typical Grade-trademarks	Face	Back	Inner plies	1/4	5/16	3/8	1/2	5/8	3/4
Interior Type	N-N, N-A, N-B INT-APA	Cabinet quality. For natural finish furniture, cabinet doors, built-ins, etc. Special order items.	NN G1 INT APA PS1 74 / NA G2 INT APA PS1 74	N	N,A, or B	C						3/4
	N-D-INT-APA	For natural finish paneling. Special order item.	ND G3 INT APA PS1 74	N	D	D	1/4					
	A-A INT-APA	For applications with both sides on view. Built-ins, cabinets, furniture and partitions. Smooth face; suitable for painting.	A A G4 INT APA PS1 74	A	A	D	1/4		3/8	1/2	5/8	3/4
	A-B INT-APA	Use where appearance of one side is less important but two smooth solid surfaces are necessary.	A B G4 INT APA PS1 74	A	B	D	1/4		3/8	1/2	5/8	3/4
	A-D INT-APA	Use where appearance of only one side is important. Paneling, built-ins, shelving, partitions, and flow racks.	A-D GROUP INTERIOR PS1 000	A	D	D	1/4		3/8	1/2	5/8	3/4
	B-B INT-APA	Utility panel with two smooth sides. Permits circular plugs.	B B G1 INT APA PS1 74	B	B	D	1/4		3/8	1/2	5/8	3/4
	B-D INT-APA	Utility panel with one smooth side. Good for backing, sides of built-ins. Industry: shelving, slip sheets, separator boards and bins.	B-D GROUP 3 INTERIOR PS1 000	B	D	D	1/4		3/8	1/2	5/8	3/4
	DECORATIVE PANELS—APA	Rough-sawn, brushed, grooved, or striated faces. For paneling, interior accent walls, built-ins, counter facing, displays, and exhibits.	DECORATIVE HI G1 INT APA PS1 74	C or btr.		D		5/16	3/8	1/2	5/8	
	PLYRON INT-APA	Hardboard face on both sides. For counter tops, shelving, cabinet doors, flooring. Faces tempered, untempered, smooth, or screened.	PLYRON INT APA PS1 74			C & D				1/2	5/8	3/4
	A-A EXT-APA	Use where appearance of both sides is important. Fences, built-ins, signs, boats, cabinets, commercial refrigerators, shipping containers, tote boxes, tanks, and ducts. (4)	A A G1 EXT APA PS1 74	A	A	C	1/4		3/8	1/2	5/8	3/4
	A-B EXT-APA	Use where the appearance of one side is less important. (4)	A B G1 EXT APA PS1 74	A	B	C	1/4		3/8	1/2	5/8	3/4

Exterior Type [1]

Type	Use	Grade stamp	Face	Back	Inner	1/4	3/8	1/2	5/8	3/4
A-C EXT-APA	Use where the appearance of only one side is important. Soffits, fences, structural uses, boxcar and truck lining, farm buildings, Tanks, trays, commercial refrigerators. [4]	A-C GROUP 1 APA EXTERIOR PS 1-74 000	A	C	C	1/4	3/8	1/2	5/8	3/4
B-B EXT-APA	Utility panel with solid faces. [4]	B-B G1 EXT APA PS 1-74	B	B	C	1/4	3/8	1/2	5/8	3/4
B-C EXT-APA	Utility panel for farm service and work buildings, boxcar and truck lining, containers, tanks, agricultural equipment. Also as base for exterior coatings for walls, roofs. [4]	B-C GROUP 2 APA EXTERIOR PS 1-74 000	B	C	C	1/4	3/8	1/2	5/8	3/4
HDO EXT-APA	High Density Overlay plywood. Has a hard, semi-opaque resin-fiber overlay both faces. Abrasion resistant. For concrete forms, cabinets, counter tops, signs and tanks. [4]	HDO 60/60 B-B PLYFRM EXT APA PS 1-74	A or B	A or B or C	C or C plgd		3/8	1/2	5/8	3/4
MDO EXT-APA	Medium Density Overlay with smooth, opaque, resin-fiber overlay one or both panel faces. Highly recommended for siding and other outdoor applications, built-ins, signs, and displays. Ideal base for paint. [4]	MDO B-B G4 EXT APA PS 1-74	B	B or C	C		3/8	1/2	5/8	3/4
303 SIDING EXT-APA	Proprietary plywood products for exterior siding, fencing, etc. Special surface treatment such as V-groove, channel groove, striated, brushed, rough-sawn. [6]	303 SIDING 16 oc GROUP 1 APA EXTERIOR PS 1-74 000	(5)	C	C		3/8	1/2	5/8	
T 1-11 EXT-APA	Special 303 panel having grooves 1/4" deep, 3/8" wide, spaced 4" or 8" o.c. Other spacing optional. Edges shiplapped. Available unsanded, textured, and MDO. [6]	303 SIDING 16 oc T1-11 GROUP 1 APA EXTERIOR PS 1-74 000	C or btr.	C	C				5/8	
PLYRON EXT-APA	Hardboard faces both sides, tempered, smooth or screened.	PLYRON EXT APA PS 1-74	C					1/2	5/8	3/4
MARINE EXT-APA	Ideal for boat hulls. Made only with Douglas fir or western larch. Special solid jointed core construction. Subject to special limitations on core gaps and number of face repairs. Also available with HDO or MDO faces.	MARINE A-A EXT APA PS 1-74	A or B	A or B	B	1/4	3/8	1/2	5/8	3/4

(1) Sanded both sides except where decorative or other surfaces specified.
(2) Available in Group 1, 2, 3, 4, or 5 unless otherwise noted.
(3) Standard 4x8 panel sizes, other sizes available.
(4) Also available in Structural I (all plies limited to Group 1 species) and Structural II (all plies limited to Group 1, 2, or 3 species).
(5) C or better for 5 plies, C Plugged or better for 3-ply panels.
(6) For finishing recommendations, see form V307.
(7) For strength properties of appearance grades, refer to "Plywood Design Specification," form Y510.
(8) Stud spacing is shown on grade stamp.

Fig. 1-13. A guide to appearance plywood grades

31

are satisfied to let you go through the entire stock on hand as long as it doesn't add to their handling costs. Others will simply let you make the selection and then send off the first package of the product that comes to hand.

When the panels arrive, do a check on them and make sure the truck driver doesn't leave until the check is completed. Look for edge damage (the panels are thin and prone to this), and look for surface mars, especially on the top and bottom panels in any group delivered. Insist on replacements, and have the driver sign the damage statement. If this isn't possible, refuse the load. This is decorative material and you can only protect yourself in this manner.

Plywood Workshops 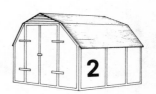 2

In general, any workshop set up for handling most any kind of woodworking can also be used for working with plywood. Most of the changes needed are generated simply because of the size of the sheets usually involved (4 by 8 feet and larger), and by specialized layout and edge treatment methods.

Workshops are so highly individual that giving a tool and layout combination for one is almost certain to leave out much of what the next person needs, or to include tools of little or no interest to another. The basic home workshop, for plywood, may include nothing more than a hand drill and drill bits, some kind of electric circular saw (you can even get by with a hand saw here, but after a half dozen long cuts on a full sheet of plywood, I'll make a substantial bet that 99 out of 100 people will head for the local hardware store and opt for power sawing), a square, hammer, screwdrivers, and a pencil, plus a good quality 8-feet or longer rule or tape measure.

The deluxe home workshop could include so many items the total tool cost alone could exceed $5,000, and might even approach twice that. Consider a top quality table saw, a radial arm saw, a jigsaw, a band saw, a drill press, a lathe (maybe even two if you do a lot of different kinds of turning), jointers, shapers and planers, belt and disc sanders and bench grinders. All of these are considered stationary tools. Moving into the portable tool list we see circular saws, saber saws, drills, routers, various sanders and hand grinders of several kinds.

Also we must consider storage for tools and accessories, lighting, floor space needed for particular jobs, smaller tools such as chisels, hammers, chalk lines, and varied other tools of one kind or another.

Probably the best starting point is to describe the various tools, their uses alone and in combination, and then recommend a basic workshop set up for the beginner, with another for the intermediate woodworker and a final shop for the expert.

CIRCULAR SAWS

Second only to the electric drill in popularity is the circular saw. The Skil Corporation made history when they first introduced this tool. They are almost in danger of having their corporate name become a generic term, as most circular saws today seem to be called Skil-saws, whether they are made by Sears, Black & Decker, Rockwell or another company (Fig. 2-1).

While the great accuracy possible with stationary saws such as the bench and radial arm types are not quite attainable with circular saws, a properly used saw will provide more of that accuracy than most of us have ever seen. Much of the accuracy comes from technique in use. Simply put, mark lines as close to exactly as possible, use jigs when possible, and keep the work steadily supported all during work time.

In most cases, the home workshop will be best served with a circular saw blade diameter from 6½ to 7¼ inches. Personally, my preference goes to the larger size, since you then have a greater cutting depth capacity, so that it is possible to work with full size 2 x 4 framing timbers as well as with sheet material. Check any saw you are purchasing for weight and feel. There is a great variation in weights among circular saws with the same size blades. And if you think of going to over-sized blades, such as the readily available 10¼ inchers, reconsider. Mine weighs 18½ pounds, and is almost never used inside. It was bought to work with post and beaming framing timbers, and serves the purpose well, but is just about useless for other jobs because of that great weight.

Fig. 2-1. One of the handiest tools in anyone's shop is the circular saw. Here's one with an extra carbide-tipped combination blade (courtesy Rockwell International).

When using a circular saw, place the bulk of the saw, whenever possible, on the portion of the work that is best supported. This provides greater steadiness and, thus more accuracy when making the cut. Grip the saw firmly, with both hands, and make sure all guide marks line up. If you are cutting a piece of wood where one face is more important than another, place the face that is to show down. The circular saw blade cuts on the up stroke (it turns counterclockwise) and will leave the smoothest cut on that underside. Keep cutting speed as steady as possible: too fast a speed often leaves burn marks, but too slow a speed can do the same. A steady speed, suited to the thickness and density of the material being cut, will provide the smoothest, straightest cut line or kerf. Suiting the speed of the cut to the material being cut is something you must learn through experience as every saw is different. In fact, the same saw will react in different ways depending on the type of blade in use and the sharpness of that blade.

Make your actual cut on the waste side of the material. The saw kerf has a definite width, varying with the blade in use, so cutting on the good side of the wood will leave you a hair or so short on your measurements.

Whenever possible, use a guide to keep your cut in line. Free hand cutting will suffice for a great many jobs, but guides of many kinds are available for cutting just about any width stock, and good ones provide much greater trueness than does freehand cutting.

Before starting your cut, allow the blade to get up to full speed. This is especially important in heavy material, but also cuts down on splintering in lighter material, as well as cutting down on possible saw kickback.

Select the saw blade for the job, and change blades as you change jobs. There are, basically, about six different kinds of circular saw blades. Most new circular saws come with a combination blade, used for making rip, cross and miter cuts. The planer blade is a good addition, as it will also make the above three cuts, but also provides a very clean edge so that little or no sanding is required. A flooring blade is generally used where old flooring is being used again, or taken up, as it is specially built to take an occasional contact with a nail. The plywood blade has many teeth, smaller than those on many blades, and gives a smoother cut with fewer splinters, no matter the direction of the cut in relation to the surface veneer (the blade still cuts up, though, so the good side remains down). The cut-off blade is used to make relatively short crosscuts for final trims to size. The rip blade is used for extensive ripping where a combination blade would dull too quickly or tear up the work too much. When changing blades, make sure the saw is unplugged.

SABER SAWS

Saber saws sometimes seem like an indispensable tool for work on large panels. In no way can they replace a good circular saw, either in cut speed or cut accuracy—especially on long cuts. But for internal cuts of many kinds, and for cutting circles and special designs, this tool is just about impossible to beat.

Prices can range about a bit, though not quite as widely as they usually do with circular saws (the variation in circular saws depends not only on saw size, but on overall construction and type of drive). A standard cut-off saw might sell for as little as $35, while a gear driven 240-volt builder's saw, with the same size (7¼ inch) blade, will run as much as $200 or more. Most saber and jig saws for the home shop will run under $75, though there are some available for as much as $200 in commercial duty models.

Stroke length on saber saws will vary with price and the power of the motor. Stroke length and power affect cut speed more than any other factor. Top of the line models will have a stroke length of 1 inch or so, with at least a quarter horsepower motor. Generally these more powerful saws will also offer a selection of speeds for use in different kinds of material. Make sure whatever kind you buy has a tilt base, as sooner or later this will come in quite handy (Fig. 2-2).

Specialty blades are available for saber saws. In fact, specialty blades could be said to be the name of the game here, as correct blade selection will do everything from providing a smoother cut to giving longer blade life. Most plywood blades for saber, jig and reciprocating saws will have taper ground teeth, with 10 of these to the inch. For extremely smooth cuts in plywood, look for a blade with 12 to 14 teeth per inch and a taper grind. The greater number of smaller teeth slows down the cut speed but immeasurably cuts down on the amount of

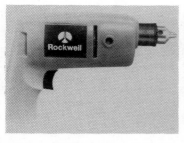
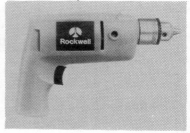
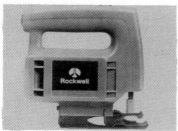

Fig. 2-2. Electric drills and sanders cut way down on the amount of time needed for projects (courtesy Rockwell International).

finish sanding needed to get an acceptable edge. If you wish, you can select saber saw blades to cut everything from thin wood veneers to various metals, and there is even a special knife blade for cutting materials such as leather, cork and styrofoam.

Selecting the number of teeth, and the grind of the back of the blade, is not the only job. If you are making wide cuts, select a wider blade (possibly as wide as ½ inch), while for those designs where sharp curves are needed look for the narrow ¼ inch blades. Blade lengths also vary: they may be as short as 3 inches or as long as 6 inches. The lower powered your saber saw is, the shorter your blade should be (Fig. 2-3).

Like the circular saw, the saber saw cuts on the up stroke, so the finish face of the work should be on the under side if you need a clean edge.

Reciprocating saws differ from saber saws in that most of the work with them is done with the blade on a horizontal plane, instead of the vertical. Blade length will be greater too, usually starting at no less than 6 inches and going to as much as a foot. Stroke lengths will also be longer. And the saws tend to cost more.

Basically, the reciprocating saw is a heavier duty saw than is the saber saw, though if you intend to do a lot of heavy paneling work you might wish to replace the saber saw with this tool. Generally, for our purposes as covered in this book, a good quality saber saw will be more than sufficient for all uses.

ELECTRIC DRILLS

Electric drills are ubiquitous. They are without a doubt the most popular hand tool to be found, and have improved in quality and features strongly in the past two decades, while the basic drill has come down in price—a strange reversal, these days, that the choice could cause problems. A basic ¼ inch drive electric drill may well retail for a few cents under 10 bucks these days. My first basic drill cost me more than $25 about 20 or so years ago. Still, a look at an only slightly outdated Skil Corporation price list shows that we'd have little or no problem in spending as much as $110 for the same size drill today (that's a builder's model 240 volt drill, though, and

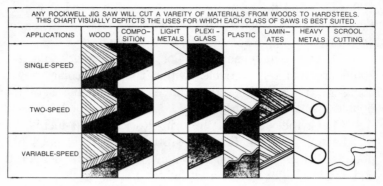

APPLICATIONS	WOOD	COMPO-SITION	LIGHT METALS	PLEXI-GLASS	PLASTIC	LAMIN-ATES	HEAVY METALS	SCROOL CUTTING
SINGLE-SPEED								
TWO-SPEED								
VARIABLE-SPEED								

ANY ROCKWELL JIG SAW WILL CUT A VAREITY OF MATERIALS FROM WOODS TO HARDSTEELS. THIS CHART VISUALLY DEPITCTS THE USES FOR WHICH EACH CLASS OF SAWS IS BEST SUITED.

Fig. 2-3. Matching the jig saw to the job is a good idea because it extends uses (courtesy Rockwell International).

not really needed by us). More practical drill chuck sizes in my opinion are ⅜-inch models, and the new models could have you spending as much as $140 for a two speed hammer drill. Half-inch hammer drills (these are kits with a fair to middling number of accessories) could easily run costs up to $200.

As you can see, a fairly careful examination of your needs is a prerequisite to getting the tool you need at a cost you can, or wish, to pay. A quick check of the newest Rockwell Buyer's Guide shows 15 different electric drills ranging from the cordless ¼ inch on up to various ½ inch models. Of these, eight are ⅜-inch models offering just about anything the home workshop could ever need, from a simple single speed, non-reversing model to a hammer drill that converts with a simple twist of a special collar.

As a personal taste item, I tend to prefer the reversing variable speed models, in heavy duty capacities. I have seldom had a need for a full power ½-inch drill, while I have burned out several ¼-inch models. Variable speeds allow work in many different materials, and also, sometimes, allow starting the hole in metal without center punching. The reversible feature allows the use of several accessories (screwdriver tips, socket driver tips, etc.) as well as providing us a chance to back out of a hole when the drill bit becomes jammed up. Such a drill, in commercial duty size and drawing 3.25 amperes, should cost right around $50 now and in the near future. A slightly heavier duty model (4.0 amps) might cost as much as

$30 more, and the extra power is seldom needed at home. Fancier models (Rockwell's 4190 hammer drill, for instance) will draw 4.0 amperes, and can cost as much as $100.

There are different types of variable speed controls: some are infinitely variable (within their particular range) using the trigger, while others have control knobs. Look for double insulation, or three wire construction.

Check the weight of the drill. Rockwell's ⅜-inch 4176 weighs four pounds, but the 4190 hammer drill goes 8½ pounds. (These are shipping weights, so the final delivered and in use weight will be a bit lighter.)

Operation of any electric drill starts with a firm grip. First, you must make sure the chuck has a firm grip on the tool being used (whether it is a drill bit, wire brush or other accessory). Always use the chuck key and never buy an electric drill of any kind that clamps down on the bits without a chuck key. Then you need to have a firm grip on the tool to prevent its spinning in the hold, around the workpiece, or slipping loose and smacking you in the wrist.

The chuck key should be taped to the drill cord as close to the plug as you can get it. This key forces you to unplug the tool whenever you are changing bits or tightening up on bits and is a safety feature.

There are so many jobs an electric drill can do, and so many accessories to help you with those jobs, that your best bet is to gain experience in scrap material with each job and accessory. To attempt to describe them here would lengthen the book to little purpose, especially since most of us have at least a small amount of experience in their use simply because the tools are so helpful and plentiful.

The accessories only begin with drill bits, wire brushes, and polishing heads and pads. You also have sanding drums, Surform rasps, plug cutters, countersinks, screwdriver and nut drive bits, cut-off wheels, grinding wheels, various rotary rasps and files, molding cutters, lawnmower sharpeners, hole saws, circular saw heads, saber saw heads, liquid pumps, paint mixers, and so on. By the time you read this, someone will probably have come up with half a dozen more, with two or three to come before you can finish the book (Figs. 2-4 and 2-5).

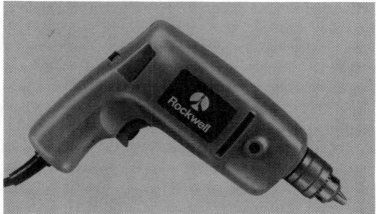

Fig. 2-4. These two are basics. No home shop should be without them (courtesy Rockwell International).

ROUTERS

Routers are often considered tools that provide decorative carvings, or insets for inlays, and decorative edges on panels and other pieces of wood. Fortunately, this is an oversimplification, and the tool is becoming more and more popular as time goes on. This tool with one or more accessories can allow the rank novice to produce dovetail joints that will be the envy of many professionals. It trims edges to a degree of

41

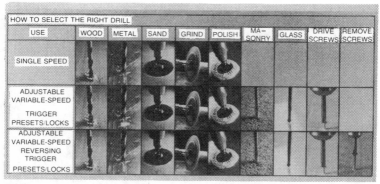

HOW TO SELECT THE RIGHT DRILL									
USE	WOOD	METAL	SAND	GRIND	POLISH	MA- SONRY	GLASS	DRIVE SCREWS	REMOVE SCREWS
SINGLE SPEED									
ADJUSTABLE VARIABLE-SPEED TRIGGER PRESETS/LOCKS									
ADJUSTABLE VARIABLE-SPEED REVERSING TRIGGER PRESETS/LOCKS									

Fig. 2-5. Again, matching the drill to the job is an aid in getting the most for your money (courtesy Rockwell International).

perfection otherwise impossible (especially those on laminated countertops), and allows just about anyone to become a journeyman woodcarver with little practice and a few special templates or jigs.

A router is not much more complex looking than is an electric drill. The motor sits on a baseplate with a couple of knoblike handles projecting, while underneath and in the center of the baseplate you'll find a collet style chuck to accept router bits (Fig. 2-6). Simple, right. It sure is, until you begin to think of the variety of bits available, and the different sizes of routers to be found. Routers are high speed machines, with the lower price models generally turning about 20,000 rpm, or a bit less (don't judge any router totally on its speed, as many other factors come into play in getting a smoothly finished job). A half horse power router (about the minimum for good work in heavy stock) with a no load speed of 28,000 rpm shows in the Rockwell catalog for about $50. For those who wish to get fancier, and do heavier or more constant work, a 1½ horsepower router with a 22,000 rpm speed will cost about $110. For those who wish to go really crazy, Stanley is now producing a production line product line with routers going as high as $500, suggested retail!

In most cases, the home shop will do as well with a half horsepower router as with a one and a half, but there are intermediate models to be found. These might be of use if you are doing a lot of routing (Fig. 2-7).

Router bits come either separately or in sets, with the sets cutting the cost per bit, but often offering bits you may well never use.

As a general recommendation, I would suggest that you start with a straight bit, used for basic stock removal, slotting, grooving and rabetting. Sizes range from about ⅛-inch in width to ¾ of an inch, with depths to 1 inch. Then go to a dovetail bit of the size you're most like to use (generally, you'll find dovetail bit widths of ¼ and ½ inches). After that, the mortise bit for dados, rabbets and hinge butt mortising would probably be handy, with sizes ranging from about ½ inch wide and 9/16 inches deep to ¾ inches wide. From there, you get to consider such times as bead bits, corner round bits, rabbetting bits, V groove bits, core box bits, cover bits, 45° bevel chamfer bits, and the various plastic laminate trimming bits, as well as at least two dozen others.

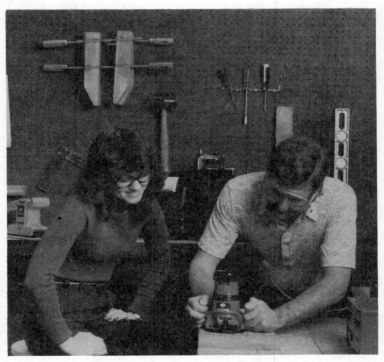

Fig. 2-6. Routers may not be essential, but they will make extra projects easy to do and speed up many jobs in the home.

In addition to all the bits, there are various hinge butt template kits, dovetail template kits, grinding wheels, and so on. Since a single carbide tipped bit could run you as much as $25, it's easy to see the need for care in selection (most bits, even carbide tipped ones, are cheaper than that, with many costing only about $4).

If you are cutting many laminates, I would suggest the carbide tipped bits be used here since there is a fair amount of abrasive material present in many laminates. You could find yourself spending most of your working time sharpening standard bits.

Using the router requires a bit of practice, and a sharp eye for a few details. Direction of cut is clockwise, so that for the smoothest edges and neatest overall work, not to mention general working ease, you should do your job, whenever you can, from left to right to allow the bit to pull the tool along the cut. Make sure any job you're working on is secure. Rough cuts will result if the work slips around or wobbles a lot.

Use edge guiders whenever you can, as these are great aids to a neat cut. Some are available for certain circular and curved cuts, too. Make sure design layout is complete and well outlined on the work. Use templates wherever possible, such as in making dove tail joints for drawers, or mortising for hinges on a door.

Consider special accessories, such as a lathe turning accessory. These are available from several sources and can greatly add to various furniture designs (turned legs for chairs, as an example, with each being identical to the other).

As you go along, a number of other ideas will come to you on router use. Have fun, for this tool added to a moderately equipped home workshop will possibly allow more creativity and fun than any other, once you've mastered the basics and picked up a few extra bits, and one or two templates. Sooner or later you'll come up with an elaborately inlaid or carved piece, which might even have some practical application around the house or garage.

SANDERS

In this portion, we'll consider only sanders that are suitable for general use with wood, which eliminates all rotary

Fig. 2-7. A good router need not be an extreme expense. Over the years you're likely to find you have invested much more money in router bits than in the original tool (courtesy Rockwell International).

sanders of any kind. Wood should be sanded, in almost every instance, with the grain or very close to with the grain, if the results are to be at all attractive and the finish is to be easily applied. That leaves use of belt and pad sanders only, and not all of them. For finishing work, pad sanders with orbital action do not generally do as fine a job as do straight line sanders. If the orbit is small enough, and some are, the finish will be nearly as fine as you would get with a straight line sander, though. And some orbital sanders can be adjusted to work in a straight line, which allows use of the orbital feature for final buffing of the finish or wax.

Belt sanders are more powerful machines than are orbital sanders, and are designed to remove more material more quickly. Like all other power tools, belt sanders will vary in price, often widely. I have seen prices as low as $110 for a commercial duty belt sander and as high as $300. The difference in such sanders is most often the horsepower (indicated often by the amperage of the motor) and the belt speed. Less expensive models will turn a belt speed of 900 SFPM, (surface feet per minute) while more powerful (the 900 SPFM models are actually very powerful) sanders can hit a rate of 1300 SPFM. The basic advantage of the higher speed belt is the greater rapidity with which wood is removed. It may or may not offset the increased cost of the tool.

Generally, a home shop sander with a 3 inch by 21 inch belt traveling about 900 feet per minute will be more than sufficient for anything almost any of us will want to do. To cut down on mess, you will probably want to get a belt sander with a dust collector bag. This doesn't totally cut down on sanding dust flying around, but it sure makes a difference.

Check sander weight, too. While a more powerful machine is often heavier, the difference needn't always be great. Rockwell's number 4460 belt sander is a 3 inch by 21 inch model, with a belt speed of 900 SFPM, weighing 12 pounds; Rockwell's commercial model, the 4470, draws a half ampere more (7.0 versus 6.5) and weighs just 1 pound more. Add a ¼ pound for either sander with a dust collector. The belt speed of the 4470 is 1300 SFPM. That's a considerable difference considering the small weight difference. The price differential, at this time, is about $20. making the 4470, in my opinion, a better buy for many people.

Using a belt sander is not complicated, but a few points must be kept in mind. First, simply starting the sander and setting it on the work doesn't cut much wood away. It simply walks across the wood. Start the motor, build up speed, and then apply the sander to the work surface, using a firm grip. Don't bear down with bodyweight, though.

Lift the machine as you come off the edge of a piece of work, but make sure that it reaches the edge level or you'll have a rounded edge.

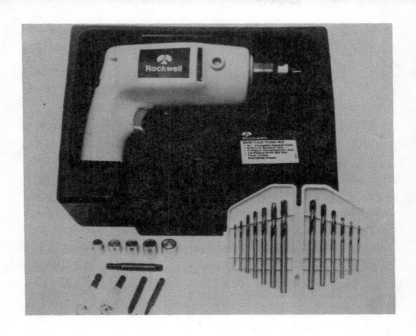

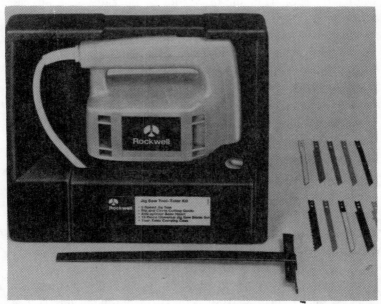

Fig. 2-8. Tool kits, with accessories, are often available at a good saving over single purchases. Make sure you have at least an anticipated use for the extras included (courtesy Rockwell International).

Though you'll seldom need the technique when sanding plywood, placing the sander so the belt runs across the grain will remove material more quickly. The resulting scratches can then be sanded out, either with the belt sander or with a finishing sander.

Sanding edges can be a problem when those edges are fairly narrow. Clamping several pieces together is one way of keeping the sander level more easily. If only one piece is to be sanded, try clamping some scrap material to it to broaden the edge and make the job easier.

Finishing sanders, as we said earlier, are available either with orbital action or straight line action. These are pad sanders and are not meant for removing the heavy amounts of material you can easily take off with a belt sander. Often, when plywood or planed woods of many types are all you'll be using, a pad or finishing sander will be more than sufficient for any job you're likely to do. Prices will start as low as $25 and rise past $100 for commercial duty models, so you'll again need to match your needs to your wallet. The more expensive sanders will have larger pads and draw more amperage. The smaller models will generally take sheets cut from standard sandpaper, while the bigger types will need special sheets to fit. Amperage may be as low as 1.5 or as high as 3.5. Weight range is about three to nine pounds (Fig. 2-8)

Finish sanders, whether orbital or straight line action, are used with the grain of the wood, with as fine a grit sandpaper as possible to do the job. If necessary start with a medium grit to remove material, and then change to fine for the finish (Fig. 2-9).

A couple of improvisations may help when doing different jobs. As an example, fir has a hard/soft grain. The sander comes with a soft felt pad which will cause portions, the harder parts, of the grain to be raised if a soft backing is used. Cut a piece of smooth surface hardboard, about ⅛ inch thick, to size and fit it behind the paper in such cases.

The second aid is an even softer pad. These are most helpful when you are sanding between coats of finish material, and are easily formed from a piece of sponge rubber. For sanding between finish coats, you'll need only a thin piece of back-up material, but if you have to sand irregular shapes such

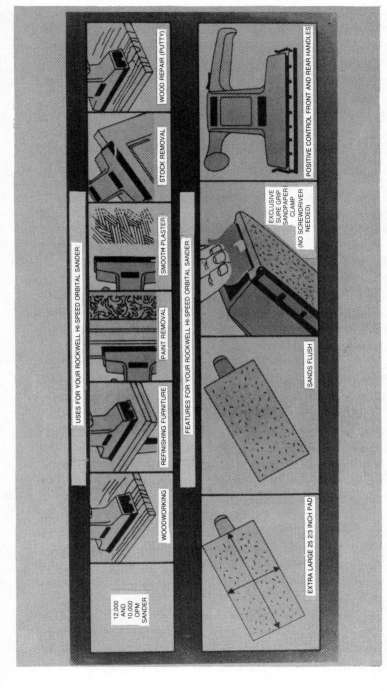

Fig. 2-9. Sanders don't just finish wood. With the correct features, you can do half a dozen or more (courtesy Rockwell International).

49

as concave or convex modelings, you may wish to use a backing as much as 1 inch thick. Make sure you adapt the paper size for these backings so it doesn't pull out of the clips while you're working.

Rockwell makes a speed block sander (#4480—about $65) that is excellent for getting into tight places, and for quickly sanding small surfaces (the pad is 4½ by 4⅛ inches).

ABRASIVES

Using the correct abrasive in your sander is one major step in getting a good job in the least amount of time. Too fine, too coarse or too easily clogged abrasive sheet or belt will mess up the job, require extra time, and, in some cases, even ruin the work totally.

Sizes are of great importance: the grit number used to tell how rough an abrasive is indicates the size of a screen the particles will pass through. A grit size of 12 means that a dozen of the pieces that pass through the screen would, if lined up, cover 1 inch. Grit sizes vary from # 12 to # 600, which is the finest available, and is not much more coarse than finely ground flour.

You should start the job with the finest possible grit that will remove the material in the amounts you need to take it off. Starting too coarse a grit on the work will make it very hard to get out the ridges left by the grits as they cut away at your wood surface. Generally, most plywoods will seldom need a grit coarser than an 80, and even # 100 will do very often.

For the best results, once the first sanding is done, change to smoother grits in two size steps until you reach the finest grit you plan to use. In other words, if you start with a grit of # 100, go to # 150, then to #220, # 280 and so on until you get your fine finish.

Different types of abrasive material are used in the grits, and the material is placed on the sheets or belts in different ways to provide the needed characteristics for any particular job. Aluminum oxide can be bought with paper or cloth backing, and is useful as a dry wood sanding material. For machine work, use the cloth backing for greatest durability. This material is easily found today, as it is about the most popular for wet and dry sanding in the home shop.

Silicon carbide and emery are most useful in wet sanding applications on metals. Garnet paper comes with a paper back, for dry sanding only, and is also good for wood sanding in the home shop. Aluminum oxide will be a better choice in most cases when you use power tools for sanding, but garnet is excellent for hand sanding. Flint paper is cheapest of all, comes with a paper backing and is for dry sanding only. It's not too useful for machine sanding as durability is low, but you might wish to cut sheets and use it on finish sanders where you know the work will clog the paper quickly.

Paper clogging, or, more accurately, the clogging of the grit on the surface of the paper, is controlled to a good extent

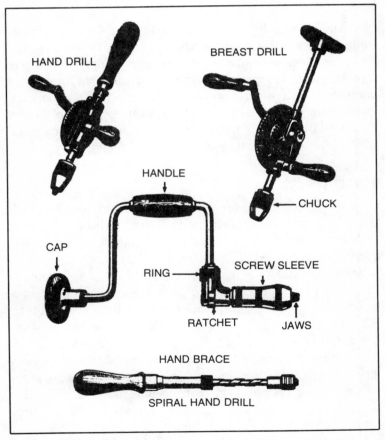

Fig. 2-10. A bit brace and drills.

by the placing of the grit material. Closed coat surfaces make for durable and quick cutting abrasives, but the surface will clog badly when working with certain materials or taking off old coatings on wood or metal. By applying grit to 50 to 70 percent of the backing surface, manufacturers come up with open coat abrasives which do not clog as easily. The open coat abrasives don't cut as quickly as do the closed coat, but they are much more durable on certain jobs. If the wood you're using tends to be gummy or have a lot of pitch, or if you are removing old finish of almost any kind, open coat abrasives are the correct choice.

HAND TOOLS

Non-powered hand tools provide the basis for most shops, no matter the kind of work being done. Power tools are today just about essential in a well equipped shop, but the basic crosscut saw, hammer and screwdrivers still can't be totally done away with if you wish to complete a job. Such tools are often just as easy to use for small jobs as are power tools which may need to be set up, tugged around and lifted (and will often weigh many pounds more than the hand tools).

BORING TOOLS

Boring tools are simply those which are used to drill round holes in wood (for the purposes of this book, as boring tools are used with other materials). Bits, drills and points are used in braces, hand drills and push drills to make the holes. Reamers are used to enlarge or smooth holes, and counter-sinks are used to drill tapered holes allowing the head of a woodscrew to be sunk even with the work surface. A counter bore provides a hole that allows the wood screw to be sunk below the surface (for later dowelling) (Fig. 2-10).

A bit brace, or brace, is a hand tool that allows you to hold bits of various sizes in its chuck. Turning the handle allows you to bore holes, countersink, ream, counterbore, etc. The bit shank is placed in the chuck jaws and the shell of the chuck is rotated until the bit is held tightly. The head of the bit is pressed with either the body or the hand not doing the turning.

The hand drill operates by gears, with you turning a small handle to rotate a large gear against a smaller one which then rotates the chuck holding the bit.

A push drill is operated by your pushing it into the wood. The pushing action forces the chuck to rotate, and this rotates the bit.

Auger bits are for wood only, and are corkscrew shaped, most often with a small "lead" screw to center the auger over the hole being drilled. The corkscrew portion serves to remove wood from the hole as it is drilled, while the cutters do their job. Diameters available range from about ¼ inch up to 1 inch. The standard auger bit is 7 to 10 inches in length, but extensions and longer shanks are available for special purposes (Fig. 2-11).

Countersinks come into use after you have drilled the hole for the fastener (usually a wood screw). Place the countersink in the fastener hole and drill. Check with the head of the screw every so often to make sure you get the correct depth.

Counterbores are also used after the fastener holes are drilled. Some such counterbores have depth gauges, while on

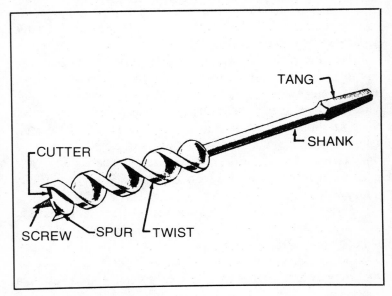

Fig. 2-11. An auger bit.

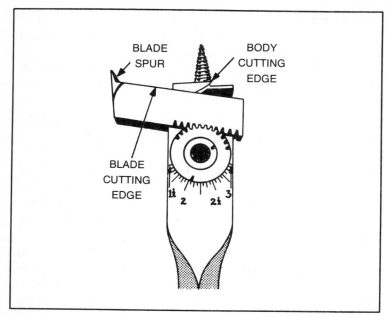

Fig. 2-12. An expansive bit.

others you may have to measure, or make your own depth gauge (I have found that using six or eight wraps of tape at the correct distance on the shank works well when no depth gauge is part of the counterbore).

Expansive bits are used for drilling holes larger than one inch in diameter. They can be used only in hand bit braces, and have a tapered lead screw just as the auger bit does. The cutter, though, is adjustable on a gear (usually with a dial to tell what size hole you will be drilling). You drill a pilot hole first, usually 3/16 of an inch. Set the adjustable cutter. Insert the lead screw in the pilot hole and bore away. You can drill hole sizes from 7/8 to 3 inches in diameter with expansive bits (Fig. 2-12).

Hole saws are most often used with electric drills, but can work with some bit braces. These will drill holes up to about 3 inches in diameter, and no pilot hole is really needed, though accuracy of placement may be helped with one. The lead bit on the hole saw can get awfully hard to see when you're setting a 3 inch cut in place.

HANDSAWS

There are a great many types of handsaws available, and most will prove useful at one time or another in the plywood workshop. Beginning with the crosscut saw, each and every shop should have a good selection of the most often used handsaws, including coping saws, backsaws, compass saws and a keyhole saw. In addition, a miter box is needed (the backsaw is of little use without a miter box).

The cross cut saw is the first saw for any shop or home. Used to cut across the grain of wood, it will also, though not as efficiently, cut with the grain, making it a dual purpose saw. The first cross cut saw added to your shop should be a medium fine toothed model, with, perhaps eight teeth per inch. Later, a coarse saw with about five teeth per inch can be added, as can one even finer with ten teeth per inch (this is actually tooth points per inch). These teeth cut on both forward and rearward strokes. Select a crosscut saw with a blade length of 24 or 26 inches unless you expect to be doing a lot of cutting in confined spaces (Fig. 2-13). (You will find blade lengths as short as 16 inches for that purpose.)

Crosscut saws are used at 45° to the work, and the best results are had when the saw is kept sharp enough so that its own weight will draw it through the wood on the down cut, with you drawing it up for the rearward stroke. Don't force the blade, and if you do push on the down cut, push gently.

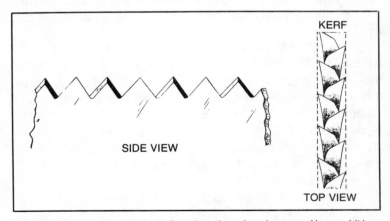

Fig. 2-13. Crosscut saw teeth are finer than those in a ripsaw and have a bit less set.

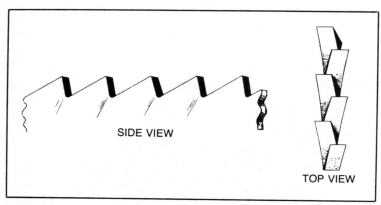

Fig. 2-14. Ripsaw teeth.

Ripsaws are cross cut saws counterparts. They are designed to cut with the grain of the wood, and the teeth cut only during the down, or push, stroke. Seldom used in the plywood emphasizing workshop, the ripsaw is actually a rarity in any tool box not owned by a professional carpenter. They are handy, almost invaluable, at times, but those times are very infrequent for the home worker (Fig. 2-14).

Backsaws are used to cut wood joints in a miter box (or should be used in a miter box for greatest accuracy). Essentially a bucksaw is a crosscut saw with very fine teeth, a rectangular instead of a tapered blade shape, and a rigid back brace. Backsaws are just about essential when making moldings to fit correctly, making cabinets, or cutting picture frames.

If the saw is used with a miter box, it will have a blade from 22 to 30 inches long, and will have 11 or 13 points to the inch. Great accuracy in cutting angles and straight cuts across a board can be had with these saws, providing a very, very smooth and accurate joint, especially if you remember the blade is quite thick and heavy. Because of this thickness, make sure to cut with the teeth just touching the outside of the marked line, or you will not get an accurate length. You will end up with a botched joint.

Miter boxes can vary quite a lot in complexity and cost. A cheap miter box can be bought for about $3, and will serve very well for most people starting out in woodworking. The top of the line models, including backsaw, can go well over $150 in price. Obviously there is a great difference in accuracy, durability and general features with these boxes. Examine your needs carefully, though, before laying out $200 or so for a miter box and backsaw. If you plan to do a lot of cutting of angles, and need super accurate joints, then such a purchase is going to be worthwhile. If you seldom need an angle cut, and then can get along with one that is of only moderate appearance, you'll be wasting a great deal of money by getting a top of the line miter box and backsaw (Fig. 2-15).

No matter how inexpensive your miter box is, though, it must be made of kiln dried rock maple or oak. The box may be only a foot long, with a capacity of possibly 2 inches by 4 inches, or a bit less, and it will have saw blade slots cut at 90° and 45°.

Professional style miter boxes will be made of steel, with a wood platform. The backsaw will fit in a swinging arm arrangement that will pivot at the rear. At the pivot there will be a dial indicating the degrees of angle being cut. The capacity of the cut will usually determine in large part the cost of the

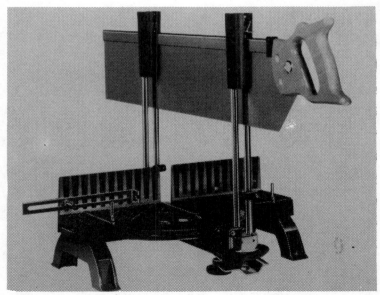

Fig. 2-15. Miter boxes and backsaws are essentials for accurate joints (courtesy Stanley Tools).

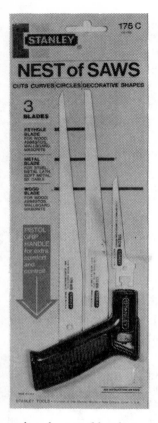

Fig. 2-16. Tight corners are easily handled with a nest of saws (courtesy Stanley Tools).

miter box and backsaw. A 30-inch backsaw will obviously give a greater cut capacity than will a 2 footer, so some more thought is needed about the size of the moldings and other material you might be cutting on the miter box.

Compass saws are used to make straight and curved cutouts in wood. For the plywood workshop, you'll need at least one, and possibly a couple, if you plan to do any work where paneling is to be put up (to make cut outs for electrical boxes, etc.), or to do work where you may need to make cut outs to let down supports, or to place dividers in a room where access to electrical outlets must be maintained. You start with a small hole, bored, and go from there. The compass saw will have a blade 12 to 14 inches long, with eight to ten points per inch. Some are available as a nest of blades, with a single handle. These are relatively inexpensive (the saw itself is a relatively cheap tool to buy), and are probably the best bet for most people (Figs. 2-16 and 2-17).

Compass saws have rather wide cuts, so it is again necessary for you to make the cut with the teeth just touching the marking line, in the scrap area.

Keyhole saws are similar to compass saws, except that the blades are narrower and they come with ten points per inch. You can cut a tighter radius with this saw. Most nested compass saws will have a keyhole saw blade.

Coping saws are those skinny little bowed backsaws that look like undernourished hacksaws. Generally, a coping saw will be about 1 foot long, with a throat opening of 4½ to 7 inches. The blade will be about 6½ inches long, and can be had in widths from 1/6 to ⅛ inch. Points per inch will vary with the material being cut, with availability running from ten to twenty points per inch.

Coping saws allow you to cut inside and outside patterns that would otherwise be impossible. So if you expect to do any fancy work at all, one of these inexpensive tools would be a fine addition to your shop.

Hacksaws are most often thought of in relation to cutting pipe and other metals, as well as plastics and such things. You will seldom find an actual use for one in a plywood workshop, but you may well find a need for one in working with trim of various kinds on projects. Select a good, sturdy frame and get a variety of blades. Eighteen tooth blades are all round models, while the 14 tooth models do rougher work, and the 24 and 32 tooth models do finer work.

Saw care is an overlooked subject in most shops. Too many workers, including the writer, don't take the best care of

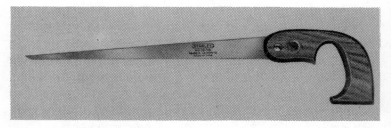

Fig. 2-17. Compass saws handle the less tight internal cuts (courtesy Stanley Tools).

these useful tools at all. I'm better than most only because I worked for an old Polish carpenter many years ago. Charlie had a temper that made a volcano look tame. Mess up a tool and that temper went off.

Never lay a saw down where something may be placed on top of it. This will warp the blade in quick order, making for great problems in getting a straight cut.

Apply a light coat of oil to the blade immediately after each use (I prefer a material known as Tri-Flon, but it is quite expensive—about $40 a gallon—and still a bit hard to find as the company is small and growing. You may well want to stick to one of the regular lubes (the expense is offset by the small amount you need to use, though). The Tri-Flon Company, 3180 Pullman St., Costa Mesa, Calif. 92626 may be able to supply the name of a local distributor for you, but first check with shops selling chainsaws and motorcycles.

For pitch coated or clogged saw blades, soak a rag in kerosene and wipe the blade briskly. You may have to soak the entire blade to get it clean, and even add in a bit of scraping. (One reason I like Tri-Flon as a blade lube is simply because the Teflon particles in it keep down such build-ups).

Leave sharpening, on those saws which can be sharpened, to the pros. It's a tedious hand job, and one easy to botch if you have no experience. Hang hand saws up whenever possible. Watch for nails in the work and pull them before continuing the cut. Keep strokes short enough so that the blade of a crosscut or rip saw won't hit the ground and bend. A few seconds of care can add a great deal to the life of most any hand saw.

HAMMERS

Wood workers hammers cover a bit wider range than most people realize, and, with screwdrivers, they're right up there in the most often misused and mistreated tool category.

Claw hammers are the most familiar type for almost everyone. These hammers are designed to drive pointed fasteners (nails, brads, tacks, staples, etc.) into materials of relatively soft composition. Curved claws and straight claws are available. Each has a purpose. The curved claw is useful for pulling partially driven nails of moderate sizes, while the straight claw (also called a ripping or framing hammer) can be used in rougher work to pull boards apart. The straight claw is more easily jammed between boards for this purpose. Still, no matter how such a hammer is otherwise used, it comes to us constructed primarily for driving nails. Any other use is secondary, and too much board ripping or nail pulling is going to damage the hammer, sooner or later. Usually sooner. Use wrecking bars and cat's claws for those jobs whenever possible, and you won't have to change hammer handles so often (Fig. 2-18).

Hammer handles today come in a great many materials and styles, fiberglass, hickory and solid or tubular steel. All are good, when properly designed and installed, and the basic decision on which material to use should actually be made on which handle feels best to you. I have hammers with all three primary materials (no solid steel), and use them all, though not equally (the 28 ounce framing hammer is the least used for obvious reasons). Hickory handles are the most easily replaced should they break. Steel are the hardest to break, but nearly impossible to replace at home.

Your first hammer should probably be a 16 ounce curved claw model with a smooth face (claw hammers can be had with cross hatched faces, but these should be reserved, as mine are, for framing and other rough carpentry, not for most types of plywood work). From that point, I would go down to a 12 ounce curved claw. If framing is to be done, do it with a 20

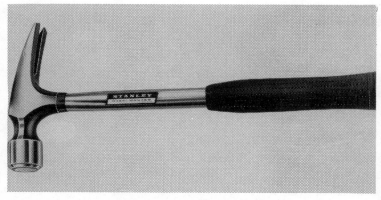

Fig. 2-18. A straight claw hammer (courtesy Stanley Tools).

ounce straight claw, with a smooth face so it can sometimes serve a double purpose. Very few of you will ever need, or wish to use, something on the order of my 28 ounce Craftsman framing hammer. I bought that specifically to work on post and beam framing, where heavy spikes need to be driven quite often. Head weights for claw hammers range from five to 32 ounces. I have never used a five ounce hammer, and don't want to (except for tack hammers), but some of you may wish to get one for cabinet building where small nails, or brads, are used to reinforce glue joints. Twelve or 13 ounces is about the smallest practical general use weight.

Wood mallets are handy in the workshop, for they can be used to drive those tight fitting parts together without marring the wood. In some cases, though, even this is too hard on the material (most wood mallets have beechwood heads, and a good shot with this hardwood is liable to really mess up soft pine). I tend to prefer a piece of soft pine, hit with a claw hammer. For really touchy jobs, I spread an old towel between the work and the soft pine to prevent just about any chance of marring the work surface.

Tack hammers are upholsterers' tools, but some of the plywood work you may be doing could require covering. They can also be used to tack picture frame corners and so forth. Most tack hammers have five ounce heads and 10 inch handles, with one end of the head magnetized to hold tacks ready for use. The true upholsterer's version of the tack hammer has an even smaller face to keep from marring the wood around the fastener.

Hammer care involves proper use, like driving nails or tacks. Pulling nails and ripping things apart are the province of other tools, though in a pinch you can use your hammers for these jobs, and even get away with it, if you use care and a bit of thought.

An occasional wipe of the hammer head with kerosene or other solvent will aid in keeping things clean (there's nothing like a dirty or oily smudge from the hammer head on a nice large piece of light wood). If the hammer face becomes scratched or gummy, a piece of fine emery cloth can be used to clean things up. Wooden handles can be sanded smooth if they get scarred up, and an occasional coat of boiled linseed oil will protect the handle from dampness (the handles are originally lacquered, but I don't care that much for the slickness it imparts, and the linseed oil does at least as good a job.

If the face of the hammer gets nicked or battered—if used properly, it shouldn't—you can dress the smaller nicks with a file. Never use a high speed grinder as this will foul up the heat treating of the metal too easily.

Make sure the handle is tight. If it isn't, pick up another wedge and drive it in.

And that about concludes hammer care, one of the simplest jobs of all, and one that starts by simply using the hammer in question only for those jobs it was designed to do.

SCREWDRIVERS

When working on many plywood projects, a good set of screwdrivers is just about an imperative tool kit addition. The joints held together with screws are a great deal stronger than those held together with nails. And they are often neater.

Screws and screwdrivers come in many styles, though the basic screwdriver is a very, very simple tool, being little more than a wedge with a handle to facilitate turning the screw (Fig. 2-19).

Screwdriver blades come in three basic designs. The most often used in woodworking is the straight slot fitting screwdriver, or conventional model. It is probably the tool you'll use more often than any other, with the possible exception of the hammer, and is also the one more people misuse more than any other, again possibly excepting the hammer. Screwdrivers are used for just about any job, from their intended purpose of tightening or loosening screws to acting as pry bars and can openers. I don't know of a single person who has used tools and never misused a screwdriver. Not one.

For this reason, I keep at least two sets, and usually most of three sets, around the house. One set is for use in the correct manner, while the other two sets get varying degrees of misuse, allowing me, usually, to keep the one set in good condition with little extra effort.

I would suggest that anyone starting a tool kit locate a cheap set of conventional blade screwdrivers first. These can then be set aside for use in opening paint cans (and stirring the contents), punching holes in cans, tightening eye bolts and prying things loose. Now go out and buy a good, complete set of top quality screwdrivers (such a set will have from 20 to 35 pieces), and lock them up where you are the only one to be able to get to them. Make sure the tools are entirely different colors and designs, so no mistakes can be made, and go on about your business.

A conventional screwdriver will have a shaft about 2 to 16 inches long, with blades of varying sizes to fit many different size screws. A screwdriver that properly fits the screw slot will go from edge to edge of the slot. A too thin or too narrow tip will damage the screw, and eventually the screwdriver.

Use the longest possible shanked screwdriver for any particular job. You will have a choice of square shanked screwdrivers, or those with round shanks. The square shanks allow you to apply a wrench and get more torque on the tip for loosening or tightening screws, but they are seldom really needed in woodworking.

Phillips head screwdrivers have tips designed to fit only Phillips head screws. The fluted portions come off at about 30° and the end of the screwdriver will be blunt. Four sizes match available Phillips screws: 1, 2, 3, 4. Blade lengths can vary from 1 inch to about 18 inches. You won't need these too often when woodworking, but it's a good idea to have a set around for other jobs.

Reed and Prince screwdrivers do not fit Phillips screws, and vice versa. Reed and Prince screws have flutes at 45° angles and also have a sharp point at the end. You will almost never need a set of Reed and Prince screwdrivers around the home.

Screw-holding screwdrivers are sometimes needed to start screws in tight spots. There are a variety of screw holding arrangements, and the sizes of the screwdrivers vary to fit the screws needed for the job.

The spiral ratchet screwdriver (Yankee screwdriver is Stanleys' trademark) is a very handy tool for woodworking. You simply push in on the handle and the ratchet action drives the screws. These have jaws which will hold any of a variety of screwdriver heads, both conventional and Phillips.

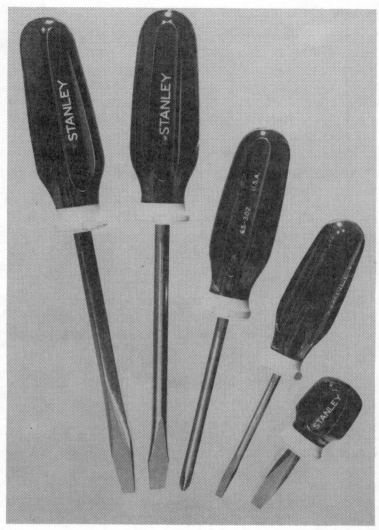

Fig. 2-19. A good set of screwdrivers for the home shop (courtesy Stanley Tools).

  Screwdrivers require little care if used as intended. Wear will eventually tend to round the edges of the blades of your most heavily used types. In such cases, the tips must be reground to size. Use a tool rest when grinding and do the job slowly, so as to be certain of the fit. Keep the screwdriver tip as cool as possible when grinding (dip in water every few seconds).

CLAMPS

Clamps, and vises, are needed to hold pieces together during gluing or other shop operations. They are essential tools in any woodworking shop doing much more than cutting boards to length. Generally, you'll be able to start out with a C clamp, a couple of bar clamps, or a strap clamp, and a hand screw clamp. The first C clamp you buy should probably be the largest, a 12 incher. From there, you can move down through the range to 1 inch clamps, if you ever need them (I have several 1 and 2 inch clamps somewhere, but their use is so slight I haven't seen them for upwards of three years).

C clamps have one fixed jaw and one movable jaw, and are made of malleable metal. The top size available is about 18 inches, but most homes seldom need one over a foot in jaw opening size. Throat size can be shallow or as deep as 16 inches.

For plywood edging use, a special type of C clamp, with a second adjustable jaw in the back arm of the clamp, is very useful. Clamp the C clamp jaw (standard jaw) first, then place the edging material on the wood, and clamp it tight with the edge clamp.

All C clamps will damage soft wood surfaces, so it is best to use a piece of scrap material under both the fixed jaw section and the movable one(s).

Bar clamps can also be called pipe clamps. These are clamp fixtures (the jaws) that attach to sections of pipe of the length needed for a particular job. The end of the pipe is threaded to accept the fixtures. They are screwed on and work is begun. You can save money buying only a single set of bar clamp fixtures, and keeping several threaded pipe lengths around the shop for use on different jobs. Generally, the adjustable portion of these clamps will move only about 2 inches, so, of course, you must have pipe lengths within 2 inches of the final job size.

Hand screws can be used to clamp wood together while you're gluing it, or to clamp several to-be-drilled sections of wood together so the holes will line up. They can also be used when you're trimming edges or sanding. There are many jobs to be done, and these clamps can help do most of them.

Hand screw jaws are made of hardwood, usually rock (sugar) maple, while the screws are of metal. A few can be had with metal jaws, but with those you'll have to use scrap lumber to keep from scratching the work. Jaw lengths of 4 to 18 inches can be found, and openings of 2 to 14 inches are available.

A basic advantage of the hand screw is the jaws can be set at just about any angle needed, as you have two screws, one left hand thread and the other right hand, to work with (Fig. 2-20).

Clamps require little care if treated reasonably well. If your metal clamps are the type that rust, wipe on a light—very light unless you care to leave smudges on wood—coat of lubricant, and keep the threads on all clamps lightly oiled. Coat wood parts of clamps with boiled linseed oil to keep them from drying out.

Vises can make a long job short. Wood vises come in many configurations, from bench attached styles to those

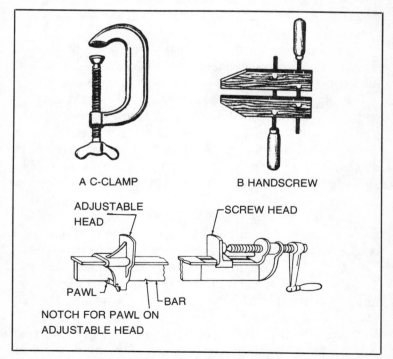

Fig. 2-20. A C-clamp, a handscrew and a pipe or bar clamp.

which can be moved about and clamped to sawhorses and other surfaces. Most often, you'll be using a wood vise of one kind or another in your shop. These tools have replaceable wood faces, and may have wood or metal frames, screws and handles (usually, today, you'll find the basic parts made of metal). Most are mounted on the workbench, and used there. Get as good a wood as you can possibly afford. Over the years, while planing, gluing, drilling, and screwing it will be a lot of help and get a great deal of use (Fig. 2-21).

Other clamps are available, and some can be made up of materials at hand. Strap clamps are available commercially, with heavy nylon straps and tight closing fasteners. You can improvise with nylon or cotton cord. Wrap several turns of the cord around the parts to be clamped, push a stick through the cord and twist until it is as tight as need be. Lock the stick in place (here's an improper, but harmless, use for a screw-driver, by the way) by tying it to the cord so it can't turn.

For small objects, you can use alligator clips, spring type clothespins, rubber bands or tape, if the glue is a quick setting type.

For flat surface gluing, you may simply just want to cover the surface with an old sheet or blanket and load it up with bricks, books, or concrete blocks until the glue sets.

From this point, it becomes a matter of using your imagination. Of course, sometimes the hardware store is a better place to search. Miter joints being glued require a miter clamp, which is a bit difficult to dream up in the home shop (it can be done, as can anything, but the cost of the clamp is reasonable, so it seems to me the work involved in building the improvisation is a waste).

Saw horses are an essential ingredient of any shop where you'll be working with plywood. Many brands of sawhorse brackets are on the market, so I'll not bother to show how to build the non-bracket style. The only angle cut needed with these brackets is the bottom of the leg, and you can often just forget about that, so building them is quite simple. I would, though, do one thing the bracket instructions don't tell you. Use screws rather than nails if you intend to get any heavy duty use from the sawhorses. I've had too many nails pull out of these things when they got kicked around and carried heavy

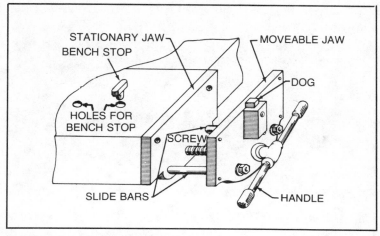

Fig. 2-21. A woodworking bench vise.

loads. So use round head wood screws to fasten the brackets to the wood. Make size adjustments to fit your own working style, shop saw heights and your own height. My sawhorses are some 3 inches higher than those most people care for. The reason is simple. I didn't quit growing soon enough back in my teens. Regarding screw size, 1 ½ inch number fives should do it.

FILES AND RASPS

Files are one of the least important tools in the plywood shop, but they sometimes can play a reasonable part in getting a fit when no other way works too well. Basically, you may want a rasp and a woodworker's file. The rasp is used first, then the woodworker's file to smooth things down. In my opinion, rasps for woodworker's can be easily replaced by Stanley's Surform tools (Figs. 2-22, 2-23, and 2-24).

PLANES

For the plywood workshop, block and trimming planes are of greater importance than are jack planes and spoke shaves. Both the block and trimming planes set at a low angle to the base, so that they can be used to trim small amounts of wood across end grains without grabbing and tearing the wood. The block plane is small, seldom over 7 inches long,

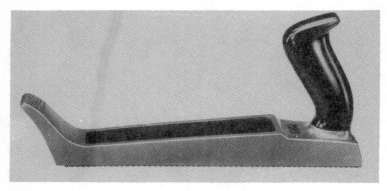

Fig. 2-22. One type of surform (courtesy Stanley Tools).

with a blade angle ranging from 12 to 21°. The trimming plane is even smaller, usually about 3 inches long, with a blade width of 1 inch or so (the block plane blade will be about 1½ inches wide). Block planes have the blade bevel mounted up, that is, towards the base of the plane.

It is useful for trimming doors, drawers and other pieces where an exact fit is necessary (Fig. 2-25).

Care of planes involves little more than preventing rust and making sure the blade stays sharp and nick free. To keep the blade sharp, pick up an oilstone and hone it as often as needed. Hold the blade level at a 30° angle to the oilstone when honing, and keep it steady. If you can't hold it steady, or feel unsure, slip down to the hardware store and buy a sharpening jig that will do that portion of the job for you.

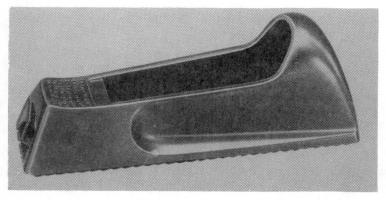

Fig. 2-23. A smaller surform tool for tighter spots (courtesy Stanley Tools).

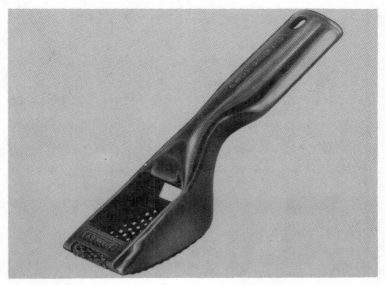

Fig. 2-24. A surform for really tight spots (courtesy Stanley Tools).

The cap iron that fits over the plane is attached just back of the beveled edge of the blade, and on the unbeveled side of the blade. Keep the distance at about 1/16 of an inch for softer woods, and a bit less than that for harder woods.

MEASURING TOOLS

What with the trend towards metrics, measuring tools are getting a bit more complicated (thus more expensive), though in most cases the complication is nothing more than a

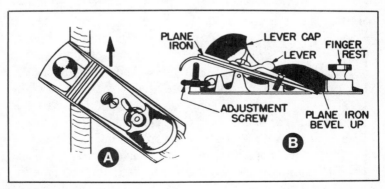

Fig. 2-25. A block plane.

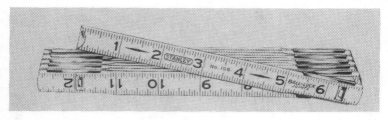

Fig. 2-26. A good folding rule is essential (courtesy Stanley Tools).

duality of marking on the tool. For wood working you could probably get along with nothing more than a folding rule, 8 feet long, and a chalk line. Tape measures and an occasional addition, such as an edge marker, can often speed up the work being done, as can squares of various kinds.

The folding rule is a basic carpenter's tool that can be applied to such a variety of jobs that I can't understand why almost everyone wouldn't wish to have one in the shop or around the home. Available most easily in 6 foot lengths, I feel the harder to find 8 footers are worth looking for. Select a rule with a brass extension in the first stick of the tool so you can more easily make inside measurements. Opening the rule in a window frame usually results in a half fold too much or a half fold too little, so the extension is slid out to make up the difference and get the measurement (Fig. 2-26). The rule should be of hardwood and have clear markings.

Tape measures come in a variety of styles and sizes, ranging from about 6 feet on up past 100 feet. For home work-shop use, the handiest size is likely to be 12 or 16 feet. If you expect to do extensive outside work on projects larger than that, get a 50 foot tape. The tapes found today may be fiberglass or metal. In either case, the tape must be clearly imprinted. Most tape measures have replaceable tapes these days, which can be a handy feature should someone manage to break or cut your tape (as too often happens) (Fig. 2-27).

Try squares and combination squares are tools used for marking the edges of boards at right angles. Most try squares will be available with blades ranging from 6 inches to about 3 feet long, while combination squares usually have a blade about 1 foot long. While the shorter blade in the combination square limits marking on sheets of plywood, the sliding handle is handy for edge marking, and almost all offer a 45° angle marking, too (Fig. 2-28).

Chalk lines are just about essential for working with plywood. Trying to hold a straight edge in position and draw a good mark with a pencil or scribe can be an awkward job on an 8 foot long sheet, but a chalk line allows you to make your measurements, attach the line at one end and move to the

Fig. 2-27. The Powerlock rules by Stanley are the best to be found. My 25-footer has the first 7 feet stiff enough to hold straight out, making one man measurements over that distance simple (courtesy Stanley Tools).

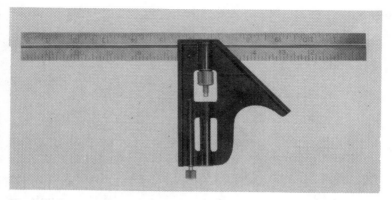

Fig. 2-28. For smaller 90° and 45° cut marking, you can't beat a combination square (courtesy Stanley Tools).

other. Set the line on the mark, snap and there's your cutting mark.

Chalk lines come in two forms, cased and uncased. In general, it pays to get the cased models, for two reasons. First, the chalk mess doesn't get all over the place. Second, the line doesn't get tangled as easily. You simply keep the case full of powdered chalk and are ready to go at a second's notice.

When making a chalk line mark, make sure you lift the line straight up before snapping the mark. Make a single snap from 2 or 3 inches above the workpiece. An off center chalk line snap will cause either a double line as the chalk line comes back to its correct position, or an off center mark.

Scribers are often used for metal work, but I've seen many people using them for wood too. Basically, though, you're better off, in woodwork, using either a chalk line to make a mark, or, for shorter lines, a carpenter's pencil . This is a pencil with a rectangular cross section, not the round style. The point is much less easily broken and is more easily sharpened with a penknife.

Wood marking gauges consist of rods, with markings, a head, a thumbscrew for adjustment and a pin in the rod. Gauges may be of wood or metal, with the metal gauges having more accurate markings (in most cases). These are also called edge marking gauges since their capacity is usually limited to under 1 foot, keeping you pretty close to the edge, especially with plywood.

MISCELLANY

Miscellany for working with plywood includes many tools that in general woodworking are of much greater importance to the final job. Such tools as chisels have great importance in many woodworking applications, but because of the differing grain angles in plywood they receive much less use there.

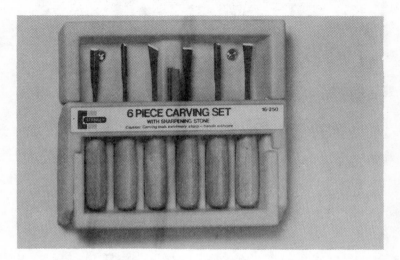

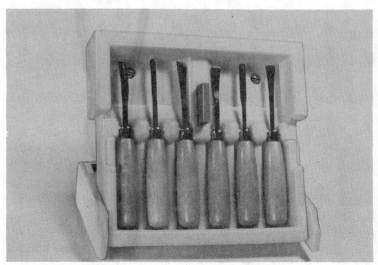

Fig. 2-29. Wood gouges and small chisels are ideal for carving intricate designs (courtesy Stanley Tools).

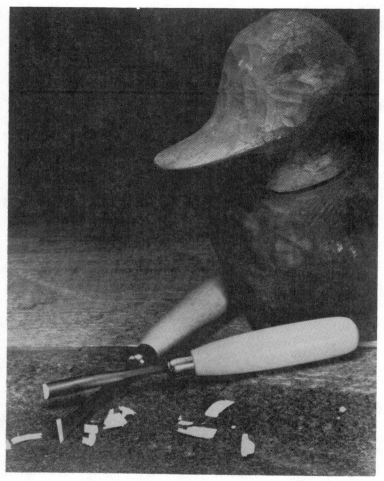

Fig. 2-30. Note the results of wood gouge use (courtesy Stanley Tools).

Often wood chisels are called finishing tools, though how that applies to my collection of framing and rough work chisels I can't imagine. These heavy duty tools are used to make openings for pipe and wiring runs after the framework of a house is up, but the finished look certainly can't be considered very neat or "finished" at all, though no more work is then done on the wood.

These chisels, though, are of little or no interest to the plywood worker. Butt chisels, 7 to 9 inches long, for use in tight spots, are the shortest wood chisels you'll find. Pocket chisels are about 10 inches long and are great for general use around the shop. Mill chisels are very long, up to 16 inches, and will seldom be found in plywood shops.

Two other designations help tell what a chisel is to be used for. Paring chisels are thin-bladed and hand-driven (and are the most useful types with plywood); firmer chisels are thicker bladed and usually hammer driven, taking off much more material in a single pass.

Chisels come in several different constructions, too. My framing chisels are all metal, one piece, with one having a blade 1 inch wide, another 2 inches, and another 3. The paring set goes up to 1 inch, from ⅛ of an inch. These have wooden handles which are never hit. Others will have wooden or molded handles that may be tapped (Fig. 2-29).

Gauges could prove useful in working designs into plywood. They are nothing more than another form of paring chisel, with hollow blades that are bevel ground on the inside or outside, depending on the shape and intended use of the gouge. They do a fine job with curves and odd shapes of most kinds (Fig. 2-30).

An awl is a reasonably cheap tool with a variety of uses. Use it to scribe wood, start holes for small nails or brads, make starter holes in wood for drilling, and so on.

Utility knives of various kinds can often prove handy in the workshop. Electrician's knives fall in this category, as do the small bladed types used basically for cutting shingles, roofing paper and plastic tiles (Figs. 2-31 and 2-32).

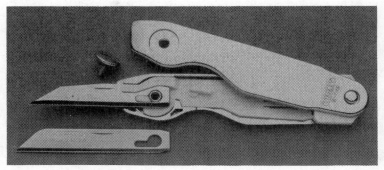

Fig. 2-31. Utility knives are extremely handy (courtesy Stanley Tools).

A nail set is invaluable for two things. First, its primary use is setting small finishing nails below the surface of the work; second, it can be used to drive almost any nail the last fraction of an inch to prevent marring the surface of fine work. Different point diameters are available.

Among the miscellany falls the bench grinder. Bench grinders are needed for many sharpening and polishing jobs in almost every shop; yet many home shops do without one for far too long. These tools allow you to sharpen your own chisels and to regrind the blade tips on conventional screwdrivers, among a multitude of other jobs. Select one that draws from two to three or more amperes and has two wheels, so that one can be a fine grinding wheel and the other a medium or coarse (or one can be a wire wheel, or a buffing wheel). The grinder should have rests attached and should also have shields to keep down flying sparks and abrasive particles, but should still never be used without some sort of eye protection. A water cooling tray is handy but not essential, as you can always stand a tray full of water nearby.

Face and eye protection is an essential safety factor in any shop, of any kind. For work on hot days, a pair of ventilated goggles is handy, but for general use I prefer a face shield with a flip up shield. The reason is simple. About the fifth or sixth time a chunk of ground off metal snaps you on the cheek at a good velocity, you want to stop the nonsense and get overall protection.

Wet and dry vacuum cleaners are available all over the place now. For any shop producing large amounts of sawdust and chips, they are an exceptionally handy supplement to the basic list of shop tools. Generally, these vacuums can be found in capacities ranging from five gallons on up past 10 gallons, dry. Prices may range from as little as $30 to well past $175 for super heavy duty models. Basically, make sure the motor has a draw of at least five amperes, that the hose is at least 2 inches in diameter, and 6 feet or more long, and the unit is UL listed for both wet and dry use. A wheeled dolly is a good idea if you have a shop that's fairly large. Most are also available with an optional (at extra cost as usual) set of 1½ inch hoses and wands for pick up of more ordinary items, too.

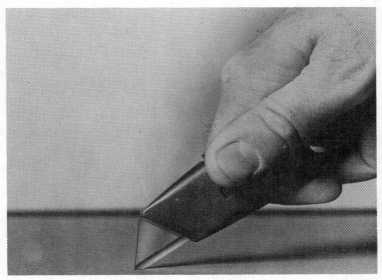
Fig. 2-32. Laminate cutting is often easier with a utility knife than any other way (courtesy Stanley Tools).

This brief look at workshop miscellany doesn't begin to cover all items, from pegboard and the multitude of accessories to make it easy to store small and large items on to wood carving tools of the sort made by X-acto and others. A basic plywood shop can start with nothing more than a crosscut handsaw, a block plane, a claw hammer and a couple of conventional screwdrivers. It is possible to turn out just about anything you could want with those tools, and one or two clamps and some glue and screws. From there, the outfitting of the workshop is up to the worker, and moves rapidly from the handtools, both power and non-power, just described into the more accurate, and more expensive, field of stationary power tools of many kinds (Fig. 2-33).

STATIONARY POWER TOOLS

The stationary power tool category covers a great many of the more complex and accurate tools that become extremely useful when you wish to move into projects requiring great accuracy in joint making. They are also useful in production methods to turn out many similar pieces, as in making, for example, doors for kitchen cabinets.

Basically , these tools include table or bench saws, radial arm saws, jig saws, band saws, drill presses, lathes, jointers and planers, shapers, and belt and disc sanders. The bench grinder could be considered a part also, but we've already taken a quick look at that under miscellany, so it won't be covered again in this section. Nor will I cover lathes, for there is little to be done on plywood with these machines. Drill presses will get only the briefest coverage, as their expense far outweighs their real usefulness in home shops of all but the most sophisticated kind. A good drill press with an 11 inch capacity will cost upwards of $200 most of the time. Find a used one in good shape, and it may be a worthwhile purchase. For those who are interested in wood turning, a good wood lathe, with no motor and no stand, will also run over $200, and probably up into the $350 range for one with a large capacity. Figure in about $125 more for a 1/3 horse motor and the stand.

TABLE SAWS

Table saws improve the work coming from your shop immeasurably. The reasons are fairly simple. With a circular saw, there is a great allowance for human error that cannot be eliminated. Table saws, on the other hand, are designed and built so as to cut out as much chance of human error as possible, while being easier to set up for repeat processes (just think, every cabinet door you cut will be as close as is mechanically possible to every other in size, straightness of cut and squareness of corners). Table saws require less energy to make the cuts. You don't have to move the cord around to keep from cutting it. Nor do you have to hold the weight of a saw that may weigh as much as nine pounds while making sure the work piece doesn't slip in some way.

Table saws are basically the same, no matter the capacity and price. Naturally, the more the saw costs the more features to ease the workload it will have, in addition to greater capacity. The basic table saw consists of a table, with a saw projecting through it, and provisions for a miter gauge and an adjustable rip fence. From this point, quality adds accessories and accuracy.

Fig. 2-33. If your shop has these tools, you can do almost anything (courtesy Rockwell International).

For the home shop, a 9- or 10-inch blade should be more than sufficient. If you wish to go to a 12 inch blade, you'll probably have to go to a contractor model saw. When considering this purchase, don't think only of the, at least, $125 jump in basic saw price; think also of the extra cost for each saw blade over the years. In a hollow ground blade, there is at least a $5 difference in price at this time. For a combination blade the difference is about $6 per blade. The differentials hold true right on through the line of blades.

Basically, with a 10-inch saw of good quality, you will get a cutting depth maximum of a bit over 3 inches, while the 12-inch blade will move that up just over 4 inches. That's at normal setting. At 45°, a 10-inch saw will cut just over 2 inches, while the 12-inch saw will be a bit more than ½ inch over that. If you do a lot of heavy work, it's a worthwhile expenditure, but for most of us, it isn't. A 9-inch saw will see those figures reduced to almost exactly 2 inches, with the 45° cut being a bit over 1½ inches. Such a saw may be as much as $175 cheaper than a top quality 10-inch model, though, and the savings may be useful (Fig. 2-34).

Let's look at one top quality 10-inch table saw, with a price presently under $400 (well under, not $399.99).

This saw, the 10-inch model 34-345, includes a 1 1/5 horse motor, drawing 13 amperes at 115 volts, 60 cycles. Rip capacity with the included rip fence in place is 2 feet, which will take you right up the center of a 4 × 8 plywood panel. The table in front of the blade is 16 inches wide, and this is an important measurement for any table saw. The wider this part is, the more easily you can make accurate cut-offs without having to worry about tipping the workpiece and getting a sloppy cut. The depth of cut is 3 ¼ inches, at 45° 2 ⅛ inches. The table size is 40 by 27 inches. The package includes guide bars, rip fence, miter gauge and extensions. You can get just about the same saw, with a smaller motor, and minus one or two other items (the table is smaller and allows 11 ¾ inches in front of the blade) for about $100 less.

A comparable 12-inch saw, with a four horse motor, 25 inch rip capacity, and 4 ⅛ inch depth of cut (2 13/16 inches at 45°) will run you about $125 more.

The saws described here are Rockwell's, but other makers have similar versions. Things you should look for once you've made the decision to get a saw of a particular size, and in a particular price range, include self-aligning rip fences, with two locks, ball bearings throughout the construction of the unit where bearings are needed, motors with built-in thermal overload protection, a tilting arbor for miter and bevel cutting, and a splitter and anti-kickback attachment, easily reached and operated controls. All controls should be at the front of the tool, the spot where you'll be standing to operate the thing. Make sure extension wings are available for the brand you buy if none are included in the package. Most blade and molding cutter attachments can fit any saw, assuming the arbor sizes are the same and the saw has a detachable plate at the blade to allow larger size accessories to be used.

The owner's manual of your table saw will provide an array of safety procedures for you to follow. My best recommendation is to do so. I have been working with table saws since sometime back around my twelfth birthday and have yet to sustain an injury. No matter how dangerous the tool is, you and everyone can keep from getting hurt on it *if* proper safety methods are followed. Most are downright simple, such as using pusher sticks on small workpieces and staying out of line with possible kickback. New saws have anti-kickback prevention, but I still feel a bit chicken about getting smacked somewhere on my body with a chunk of wood should such protection prove not perfect.

Set the saw up so that it is level and securely in place. Provide clear, and sharp lighting as shadow free as possible. Check all adjustments and bolts for corrections and tightness. Have all electrical connections professionally made, according to the National Electrical Code or your local code, whichever is the most strict. If your workshop tends to be damp, I would also recommend the use of a ground fault circuit interrupter for greater electrical safety.

Your saw will most likely be delivered with a combination saw blade, for both rip and cross cuts. Your first accessory for working with plywood, then, will be a plywood blade of top quality. The combination blade should never be used on

Fig. 2-34. To add precision, add a table saw (courtesy Rockwell International).

plywood, as the teeth are far too large to give even a moderately smooth cut.

Blades should be cleaned regularly and sharpened as soon as they show any signs of going dull (dragging and snatching in the cut, for instance).

For those who wish to use the same blade for most all jobs, consider paying the price of a small tooth carbide tipped blade. This will almost never need sharpening, which helps to offset the almost incredible first cost (right now, carbide tipped blades, 10 inches in diameter, sell for between $50 and $60, compared to about $11 for a standard blade of the same size).

For the smoothest cut possible, no matter the blade type or style or size, feed the work slowly into the saw. The slow feed allows more teeth to hit any given spot on the work, so that the result is a smoother cut. This slow feed is especially important with plywood, as a too fast feed can cause splintering that may be quite bad at the end of the cut. Keep to a steady speed when feeding the work through so that the entire cut is smooth.

Accessories should probably be bought as needed. It is possible to go wild with dado head sets, dado table inserts, molding cutters, sanding discs, extra miter gauges (using two miter gauges when making an angle cut gives a more accurate cut because of the greater support provided with the second gauge) and so on. Get, first, the saw blades you are sure you'll need most often. After that, start to consider such accessories as a dado head if you end up making frequent grooves, a sanding disc set up if you do a lot of end grain sanding, and so on.

Molding cutters are not often used with plywood since they would have to be set at an extremely shallow point to keep from going through the top layer of laminate. Still, they can be a great addition to the table saw if you wish to design your own moldings. They cut designs in just about anything. They serve much the same purpose as does a hand-held router.

RADIAL ARM SAWS

Radial arm saws offer some advantage over a table saw, while, as with all compromises, adding a few disadvantages.

Fig. 2-35. For many jobs, the radial arm saw outperforms the table saw (courtesy Rockwell International).

The radial arm saw is particulary adapted to cutting off, accurately and easily, the ends of long pieces of stock. The table can be extended to support stock of almost any length that will fit in your shop. The arm can be swung, tilted, raised and lowered to provide many different cuts, and there are as many, or more, accessories available as there are for table saws (Fig. 2-35).

If my shop were to have only one saw, I would buy the absolute best radial arm saw I could find in preference to a table saw. The disadvantages, such as shortness of crosscuts as compared to a table saw (most radial arm saws are limited to about 1/16 inch or less crosscut), offer few problems, and the better models will rip at 2 feet, about equal to most table saws with rip guides in place. Once you take the capacities into consideration (a table saw actually has no such limits, with cuts being held to a particular size more because of shop size limits than anything else, since special supports can be easily fabricated to allow for workpiece support) you can work, I feel, more easily with a radial arm saw. This prejudice may stem from the fact that I have over the years gained a great deal more experience with radial arm saws than with bench or table

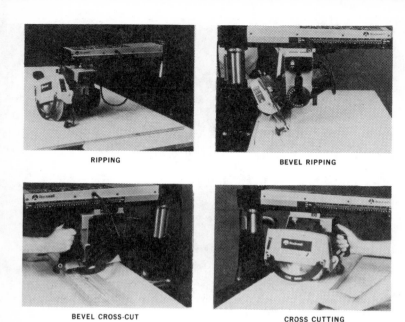

RIPPING

BEVEL RIPPING

BEVEL CROSS-CUT

CROSS CUTTING

Fig. 2-36. A few of the jobs you can do, with great accuracy, with a radial arm saw (courtesy Rockwell International).

saws. It would pay you to consider very carefully all the options open to the one saw shop.

Basically, a radial arm saw has a heavy table with a tubular arm at the rear supporting an overhead arm upon which the saw slides back and forth. The saw/motor unit is pulled toward the operator to make the cut, with the workpiece held against the support at the back of the bench. To make an angle cut, simply swing the arm to the position you wish, tighten the adjusting bolt or screw and make the cut. For a compound miter, the blade and power unit can be tilted on the overhead arm. The saw blade rotates towards the rear of the table, which helps to hold the work in place, and also makes any kickback more likely to go away from you.

For rip cuts, the blade and power unit can be rotated 90°. The one disadvantage of radial arm saw ripping is the need to force the work against the rotation of the blade. This is the sort of thing that leads to kickback. Saws come with anti-kickback guards, and these should be always in place and use when ripping is being done (Fig. 2-36).

As always, capacity and depth of cuts varies with the size of the blade and the cost of the saw. I would not recommend a saw with a blade under 10 inches except for the lightest use (say as a supplement to a table saw). Depth of cut for a 10-inch radial arm saw should be right around 3 inches at 90°, with a cut of over 2 inches at 45°. Don't get a saw that will not rip at least 1 foot in width. You are best off, when working with plywood, to also make sure the rip width is no less than 2 feet. You may have trouble with some big panels (don't forget,

Fig. 2-37. Various models and sizes are available, so match the size of your projected future work to the size of the saw (courtesy Rockwell International).

SHAPING

MOLDING

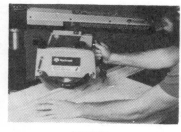
MITERING

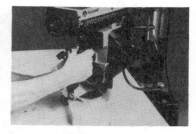
COMPOUND MITER

Fig. 2-38. Here are four more jobs your radial arm saw will do (courtesy Rockwell International).

though, that you can outside rip in a lot of cases—that is, for a piece that needs to be 30 inches wide, you can rip 18 inches off on the inside of the saw blade). Radial arm saws will often have a specified dado width maximum. This should be at least ¾ of an inch for greatest versatility. Twelve-inch blades on these saws will give a cut capacity up around 4 inches, with the 45° capacity about 3 inches or a bit more (Fig. 2-37).

Other features to look for include bevel stops set at the most used positions (0°, 45°, 90°), miter stops at 0° and 45°, both right and left for greatest versatility, a large table (about 40 inches by 24 inches at least), controls up front for ease of handling, ball bearing carriage (overhead arm), a ball bearing motor, and a heavy standard set of arms for rigidity. Expect to pay from from $250 up for a 10-inch saw, and as much as $460 for a 12-inch model (Fig. 2-38).

As with the table saw, blades and accessories should be added as they are needed. Blade types are similar, as are the prices. Most radial arm saws will take small (about 3 inches in diameter) sanding drums as well as disc sander attachments.

Attachments are more easily added and taken off on a radial arm saw than on a table saw since you don't need to change the table insert. Some saws have special adapters so they can also be used with conventional drills (rotation is wrong for most such drills). Others provide drills designed for the "incorrect" rotation. Grinding wheels to sharpen tools can also be used on the radial arm saw, but make absolutely certain the wheel you use is not a low speed type. Most radial arm saws have an arbor speed of over 3,000 rpm (Fig. 2-39).

Naturally, you will take the same number of chances with your safety when using a radial arm saw as you would when using a table saw. None. The owner's manual not only provides set up instructions, but will provide a comprehensive look at safety procedures for this versatile tool.

DRILL PRESSES

Basically, a drill press is meant to form holes, quickly and with great accuracy. It has many other uses, but because I feel the radial arm saw will do 99 percent of those jobs as well,

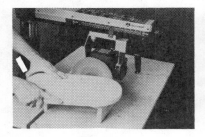

DISC SANDING

DRUM SANDING

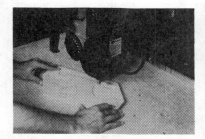

ROUTING

DADOING

Fig. 2-39. Four more radial arm saw jobs (courtesy Rockwell International).

sometimes better, I see little use for a drill press in the home workshop. If you do a lot of work that requires complex hole drilling in a wide variety of styles and shapes, you may be well justified in wanting a home shop drill press. By the same token, if a lot of the work you do requires holes drilled to exactly the same depth, easily and time after time, then you may wish to lay out a couple of hundred bucks for a modest size press. Otherwise, there is seldom a need for one, though like most other tools, there will come a time that you'll wish you had one.

If you do decide to get a drill press, select one that will drill to the center of an 11 or so inch circle, using a half horsepower or larger motor. For the really rich person radial drill presses are available (Rockwell's will drill to the center of a 32-inch circle!) with a head that will swivel on through 360° and tilt, right or left, 90°. Such a press, though is going to cost about $300 by the time you add a motor.

JIGSAWS

Jigsaws are often looked at as the toys of the home workshop, and this is a totally wrong point of view. They are probably the lowest cost home stationary saw, but they are certainly not toys. The rotary movement of the belt from the motor is converted to an up and down blade movement with a very narrow blade. Jigsaws are needed for fine scrollwork and design cutouts in stock up to about 2 inches thick (depending, of course, on the overall size of the saw and capacity of the motor).

If you are inlaying a table top or otherwise using this form of ornamentation on a plywood project, the jigsaw is the ideal tool to make those short radius cuts. The blade is held taut between upper and lower chucks, and the table is usually of the type that can be tilted.

Blade heaviness will increase as stock thickness increases, and different styles are available (the extra heavy, or saber style, blades can be used to make piercing cuts without pre-drilling a starter hole, as they are heavy enough to need to be held in only one chuck). Woodworking blades will range from seven teeth per inch on up to about 20 teeth per inch.

BANDSAWS

Bandsaws also serve to cut curved lines, though the radius of those curves must be quite a lot larger than the radius of curves cut on a jigsaw.

Depth of cut capacity is the basic strong feature of any bandsaw, giving you the capability to stack and cut quite a few duplicate parts for most any job. Generally, a machine suitable for the home shop will have a depth of cut around 6 inches, with a frame to blade distance of about 9 1/2 to possibly 14 inches. Tables will tilt to about 45° for bevel cuts, and motor horsepower should be at least 1/3 with ½ preferred.

Sanding belts can be used to do a good job of finishing irregular shapes, and there is a wide variety of blades to be found for both metal and wood working. Home shop style blades will range from about ⅛ inch wide to ½ inch wide, though there are some new blades on the market coated with tungsten carbide which are hard to classify as to width because they are toothless. While the tungsten carbide toothless blade gives an exceptionally smooth cut in wood, it is primarily for use with metals and plastic, so that cut speed is greatly reduced in wood. Wood cutting blades will have four to six teeth per inch, while all purpose blades, called skip teeth (because every other tooth is left off), come with four to six teeth per inch. Blades are sold with a specific listing for minimum cut radius of ¼ inch, and their ½ inch blade has a cut radius of 5 inches.

If you plan to work with projects that may require a lot of wood bending, be advised that the bandsaw will be just about your best friend for such jobs. While radial arm saws and table

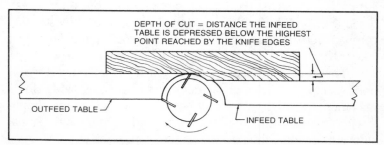

Fig. 2-40. Jointers are needed when fine cabinet work is done.

saws can also be used to kerf wood for bending, I feel the cutting of the kerfs is a bit easier with the bandsaw.

JOINTERS AND SHAPERS

Shop jointers are tools designed to plane away a specific amount of material from the edges of a workpiece so that the fit will be extremely close. Essentially, this is a plane designed to cut out human error to as great a degree as possible, while also reducing the amount of effort needed to do the overall job. The jointer can also make bevel cuts in profusion, and can provide you with rabbets, chamfers, tapers, and tenons of several kinds. It will also surface wood. For plywood, jointers are fed very, very slowly for they work best when cutting with the grain, and on plywood they cannot do just that alone (Fig. 2-40).

Make your cuts on plywood as shallow as possible. Normally, a pass on a jointer/planer should be no deeper than an ⅛ inch in solid stock, so that reducing that down to 1/32 or so will help. Feed the tool slowly and steadily.

Most home shop jointers will have a 6 inch capacity, and use a half horse or smaller motor. Look for positive bevel cut stops at the most widely used settings (again, 45° and 90°). The fence should tilt, and the cutter head should have three knives. Again, look for all ball bearing construction. The table should be no narrower than 4 inches, and at least 2 feet long. Except to pay on the order of $275 and up past $350 for a good quality 4- to 6-inch jointer.

For those who wish to add greater accuracy to the work usually done to shape wood with a router, table saw or other tools, the home shop shaper is a great addition (it's also fairly expensive, though, with most ranging up from $325 these days). Select a shaper that has a no-load speed of at least 6,000 rpm, and look for one that has an even higher speed if possible (the higher the speed, the cleaner the cut, just as in routers).

This tool is something on the order of a luxury for the home shop, but is a great deal of fun to use, and allows maximum creativity in many, many ways. Shapers should never be used with any of their gaurds detached, and manual safety directions should be followed to the letter.

Home Shop Set Up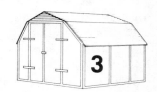

There's no way I can come into your home, measure the appropriate distances, check the wiring and lighting, and make specific recommendations for the set up of your shop, even were I to know how much you can afford, or wish, to spend, and the types of projects you might wish to work on over the years. What I hope to do here is present the basics of one or two shop set ups that will serve as starting points for those who want a well designed and well lit shop to make their work easier.

The best place to start is probably on tool acquisition. We spent a rather long chapter looking at the wide variety of tools available for the home plywood shop, and even then you'll note I admitted to leaving out quite a few. Almost no workshop has them all, and few need even most of the tools to be found on the market.

I would start with a list of hand tools like a sixteen ounce curved claw hammer, an eight or 10 point crosscut handsaw, a set of conventional screwdrivers, several clamps, a ½ inch butt chisel, a backsaw and miter box, and two or three different size nailsets. From there, I would move on to hand power tools, and select a good electric drill and a fair set of drill bits. Also of use would be either a hand drill or a bit brace. Then buy a good quality circular saw, with a 7¼-inch plywood blade. Of course, all of this assumes you have around the house a folding rule or 12-foot tape measure of top quality. Do not ever scrimp on the quality of measuring tools when working with wood or metal or plastic. In the long run, accurate measurements will save you more money than the tools could possibly cost. Next, you may wish to get a router and a selection of router bits.

From this point, it is a matter of filling out the hand tool category as you need, or want or can afford, the varied tools. My priorities will differ from yours and it would be foolish for me to specify exactly what you should buy in any particular order. You may never need a tool I consider essential, while I might not bother to get one you feel is totally essential. I would add, to save measuring time, either a try square or a combination square as soon as possible.

Stationary power tools are a different matter. There are several reasons for taking it very, very easy when you start looking at table or radial arm saws. First, the shop size becomes immeasurably more important, as you can no longer carry the tools to the workpiece. Second, the price of the tools themselves escalates alarmingly. And third, you may end up having to re-wire the entire shop area to handle the large capacity motors and increased lighting needed for safe and accurate shop work

Especially when working with large materials such as plywood sheets, you have to first consider the shop size. If you're using the only available 4×8 corner of your basement, garage or carport, you can immediately put the idea of stationary power tools, for working with plywood, out of your mind. While you might get a sheet of plywood in the shop, you would have no room to maneuver the thing into position for cutting and otherwise working it.

About a basic minimum shop size, for a single stationary power tool shop, then, would provide enough floor space for you to get the 4 × 8 sheet in and be able to feed it to your saw from any direction. That materially means a minimum size of about 10 feet by 12 feet. And that is a tight minimum, very tight. Oddly enough, it is easily possible to go up in shop size only 2 or 3 feet in each direction, and add a second or even third stationary power tool without cramping things much more. This is because you will not be using all the machines at the same time, so that the sheet can overlap any machine not being run while it is trimmed to basic project dimensions. Many stationary power tools can be made less so if mounted on extra heavy duty casters of the locking type, so they can be pushed out of the way when the space is needed for other work.

For a two tool shop, then, consider your minimum floor space to start at about 12 by 14 feet. Obviously, this shape is not essential. As long as you've got 10 feet in width, the length can vary. That 10 feet should allow for those times when you must keep your 4 × 8 sheet intact, but need to plane or shape one edge for a correct fit somewhere. If the shop machines can be arranged so this procedure is not likely to ever come up, it is possible to narrow things down to about 7 feet. This allows a bit more comfortable working space on the 4 foot side of the sheet, but an 8-foot wide shop would be far better. Extend the woodworking machinery along one wall, with a shop this narrow. If shop width goes to 12 feet, you can place machinery along both walls and be assured of sufficient working space to use standard size panels in between. If you have even more space, you're really in luck, for the machines can be pulled from the wall and placed in positions where working is easier. Clean up is not a job of shoving around hundreds and hundreds of pounds of recalcitrant metal.

My idea for a workshop varies with my desires of the moment, but never shrinks under about 16 feet square or a bit larger. Tool supplies would stagger a Rockefeller, if bought all at once. Some necessities are awls (2), bevels (sliding squares) (2), bits (a complete set of Stanley's double twists, plus a set of Power Bore, plus an expansive bit set, plus a bit gauge, plus a bit extension), a bit brace-Stanley's 100 Plus, Chisels: two complete sets, Stanley's 40C and 60C, web clamp, bar clamp, Screw-Sinks (complete set of these countersink-counterbore tools), Doweling jig, hand drill, drill points for the hand drill, yankee push drill and bit points for the push drill.

I'd also include 13, 16 and 20 ounce curved claw hammers, 20 and 28 ounce framing hammers, a five ounce tack hammer, seven ounce upholsterer's hammer, half hatchet, utility knives (six—they disappear too easily), electrician's knives (again, six because of problems with disappearing), levels (one 2 foot and one 4 foot), a miter box and backsaw, with a 7 inch capacity, four corner clamps, nail sets, five from 1/32 to 5/32 of an inch, block planes, one 21° one 12°, tape measures: one 12 foot, one 50 foot, blades ¾ inch wide, folding rules: several six and eight footers, and marking gauges.

Saws include hand saws, rip saw, five or six teeth per inch; crosscut saws, one eight teeth per inch; coping saw, with a couple dozen blades, at least; compass saw; hack saws, two with a wide variety of blades.

Here are other items:

- Screwdrivers: full set of conventional, full set of Phillips, top quality. Half a dozen or more conventional, moderate quality.
- Combination squares: Stanley's EM (English and metric markings—you can't fight it, metric will win sooner or later).
- Try square: again, marked for English and metric.
- Suforms: all eight kinds. Plus drums for power tools.
- Woodworker's vise. Three.
- Chalk line.
- Carpenter's pencils (12 at least).
- Double insulated commercial duty ⅜ inch electric drill.
- Various accessories, from a complete set of twist drills, to a masonry drill set, to several wire wheels, to sockets, to countersinks, to rotary files, to hole saws.
- Any top quality 7¼-inch circular saw, with a complete set of blades, tripled.
- Rockwell's #4392 Tiger saw (saber style), with a total selection of blades.
- Three or 4-inch belt sander, with dust collector.
- Finishing sander.
- Rockwell's #4480 block sander.
- Abrasive sheets and belts in profusion.
- One to 1½ horse router, with about 12 bits.
- Bench grinder.

- Ten gallon wet and dry vacuum.
- Ten-inch table saw, with adjustable dado set, molding cutter heads, extra miter gauge, and all appropriate table inserts.
- Twelve inch-radial arm saw, again with dado head set, cutterhead knives, sanding drums, sanding disc, and other needed accessories.
- Bandsaw with at least 13 inch frame to blade capacity, and 6 inch or more depth of cut, plus miter gauge, sanding belts, and rip fence.
- Six inch jointer, with an extra set of knives.
- Wood shaper, plus a complete set of shaper knives.

There are one or two other small and not so small items that would be added. Probably the most important of the group would be a European woodworking bench, which is rather easily built in the home workshop (considering the ridiculous over $200 price of most of these, there's no other sensible way). You also need several pegboard set ups to hold tools, nails, screws, etc. These are expensive if bought as a unit. The pegboard, though, is cheap, and the fittings add only a few dollars, relatively speaking, to the cost of the workshop. Brookstone offers small jars of plastic which are ideal for brads, small nails and screws. But their tool holders are not very efficient. You will get better use from the more generally available metal types, and you can even form your own with two pairs of pliers (best if one is a locking type such as Vise Grip) and some coat hangers.

As we will see later, there are other materials needed when finishing time comes: very fine sandpapers (abrasives of other types, really), different grades of steel wool, and some stone grinding powders (pumice). An array of different size and shape brushes for applying everything from stains to lacquers and paints will prove handy before you're at the end of your first project.

The assortment of nails, glues, screws, hinges, tapes and other fasteners you will wish to keep on hand will vary widely depending on the type of projects you wish to do, and your methods of working. You'll note I didn't cover clamps heavily. I would probably keep a few C clamps, and a pipe clamp or three on hand, but I prefer to work on jobs where glue is used in conjunction with screws, which cuts way down on the need for clamps. If you do a lot of light nailing and then glue, you will need a greater variety of clamps. If you do almost no gluing, few clamps, if any, will be needed, though they still are extremely handy for holding parts together to make sure holes are drilled in alignment.

Basically, what it amounts to is that my ideal shop is very unlikely to be yours. But we all need our dreams, and that's mine.

For general woodworking, I would add a few tools, most notably a lathe with at least a 36-inch bed capacity and distance of ten inches or more over the bed.

SHOP LIGHTING

Shop lighting seldom receives quite as much emphasis as it deserves. For that matter, home lighting really doesn't get all that much attention beyond us sticking a few lamps where they seem to be needed most. Shop lights are more important because they can add to, or subtract from, safety, as well as cut down on eyestrain.

High intensity lamps, with flexible necks, can be attached to each tool, so that the light shines directly on the work. In many cases, even with good overall lighting, such lights are a great deal of help (consider the case of a radial arm saw which may well throw a shadow from even the best overhead lights, and that shadow may, probably will, be in a position to obscure both the cut and the markings on the workpiece).

Fluorescent overhead fixtures and wall fixtures are usually best for most shops. The light tends to be less glaring than that from most incandescent lamps simply because it is usually spread over a wider area at its source. Fluorescent lights, too, do not add to a possible heat problem when projects are carried out in mid-summer, as intensive incandescent light may.

The fixtures are relatively inexpensive and can be had in about as many forms as there are applications. In most cases, a shop with some 200 or so square feet will need one central fixture, plus a fixture over each workbench and each tool. Track lighting (incandescent) can be installed so that lights can be moved from one place to another. Fixtures over work-benches and tools don't need the capacity of the central fix-ture, as they are supplementary and should be placed to cut shadows, with the central fixture supplying primary lighting.

While a shop that is too brightly lit is better than one that's too dim, such lighting can also cause eyestrain and is a waste of money. It is best to install the central fixture first (the installa-tion placement will vary with the shape and size of the shop, as will the size of the fixture), then check to see where the shadows fall. In most cases, with fluorescent lights, you'll find that 20 watt fixtures will provide excellent supplementary lighting, with the central fixture on. If you plan to use the over-the-tool lighting by itself, then make the fixtures a bit more powerful, and supplement them with high tension lights to cut down on shadow areas.

I haven't seen the latest studios on the subject, but fluorescent lights draw a lot of electricity when started. Then they draw a great deal less than do incandescent lights, so it is generally wiser to turn them on and leave them on if you plan to be in and out of the shop (the last study I saw said that it pays to leave fluorescent lights on for up to four hours without re-starting, as that saves power costs).

Of course, all lights should be installed according to code specifications. In many areas now, you cannot do your own wiring for any job, unless it is inspected before being put in use. Generally, this is a good idea, especially if you are not an experienced electrician. For this reason, details on wiring a shop will be gone over fairly quickly in this book.

SHOP WIRING

The correct wiring of circuits in your shop is a critical factor in your safety and enjoyment. There's nothing quite like a table saw blade losing speed as an upstairs air conditioner kicks in. The cut is messed up and the blade may be harmed. Neither the motor on the saw nor the motor on the air con-ditioner react well to the treatment. There is a good chance of a blown fuse, popped circuit breaker, or more serious wiring trouble.

Workshop circuits should be independent of those used for general house electrical needs. If necessary, a new entry box of the correct capacity should be installed to carry the circuits. Many stationary power tools draw heavy amperage (some as much as 13 amperes on a 115-volt circuit), so that no tool should be on a circuit designed to carry only 15 amperes. Twenty is a minimum. Of course, 230-volt circuits, if needed, will carry more amperage (the minimum is 30 amperes per circuit). Since you will seldom, if ever, use all your power tools at one time, a single circuit will usually suffice for them. It probably would be best, with more than two tools, to separate the circuits. Keep a two tool per circuit limit and make sure those tools are ones that will not be run at the same time, no matter what (any time you kick in a second 13 ampere draw on a 20 ampere circuit, you're going to blow a circuit breaker). Lighting circuits should be separate from tool circuits, and need be only 15 amperes in most cases.

If you have small children around the house, the circuit breakers for your power tools should be located well above their reach. In fact, it would be best to locate a lockable breaker box and shut everything down after use, pop the breakers, and lock the box. It may be a pain to do each evening, but such a course can prevent tragedy.

The code calls for receptacles in a home at what amounts to 12 foot intervals (no wall space is to be more than 6 feet from a receptacle). When wiring a shop, I would specify to the electrician, or for myself, that no wall space be more than 3 feet from a receptacle. I would then mark the receptacles as to capacity, so that the likelihood of drawing down too much current would be reduced. In other words, color the face plates of 15 ampere circuits white, the 20 amp circuits yellow, blue or some other color. In no case should you ever place a stationary power tool far enough away from a receptacle to require any kind of an extension cord.

The added cost of such prolific wiring is easily set aside in favor of greater safety and convenience. Cords draped all over a workshop floor are a major danger in several ways. They provide fine things to trip over, and can wear quickly since most of us will have our workshops in the basement where the floor is of abrasive concrete.

Place receptacles at an easily reachable height along the wall. No lower than eighteen inches, probably, and as high as 3 feet where a great deal of change is likely. Of course receptacles for a workbench should be placed at bench level, or a bit higher. Most wall switches are set at 4½ feet from the floor, to the center of the switch.

If your workshop is in the basement, wiring should be available at about the lowest cost of any you'll find. The beams or floor joists are exposed, and the wiring can be run on the walls, exposed, as long as the correct type of wire is used and some protection is provided where needed.

I've already mentioned ground fault circuit interrupters (GFI), so it is probably a good idea to look at just what they can do for us. In one way, the GFI is a circuit breaker, and can be used as such in some installations. They are available as replacements for circuit breakers in your entrance box, as receptacles for wall sockets, and in portable form to plug into and protect only a single outlet. The GFI cuts off electrical flow when it measures a ground fault passing electricity back at a rate approaching one-tenth of the amount likely to be fatal to a healthy adult. The code now requires their installation in all new bathroom construction. I would add workshops and kitchens and laundry rooms as extremely important spots for the use of GFIs.

You probably should use the breaker box installation, with a GFI for each circuit to be used for everything other than lighting. Cost is about $30 to $40 each, compared to possibly three or four bucks for a standard circuit breaker. If installation saves a single life, or bad injury, the cost becomes meaningless.

SHOP FLOORS, WALLS

With most plywood shops being set up in the basement or garage, we find floors generally made of concrete. Concrete is a substance giving great wear and strength, but not very attractive, and prone to dusting itself, while holding dust from woodworking operations. You have a wide choice of materials for floor finishing today, from epoxy paints that last very well to a variety of tiles in many designs and colors. The choice is yours, but a few things are best kept in mind.

Certain colors and designs make lost screws and such a bit easier to find. Select a fairly light color, and if you must have a design, make the pattern a fairly large one of a color unlikely to match steel or brass screws that may be dropped. If you are painting concrete, get paint that provides an anti-skid surface. Slick floors are a totally bad idea in a workshop of just about any kind. Most tiles suitable for below grade use will not have such a slippery surface, but it pays to check anyway.

I discovered items we used for comfort were also safety features when I was working as an aviation electrician many years ago. The shop had thick rubber mats in front of each workbench for protection against grounding. The rest of the floor was concrete and a few hours of standing on that made the legs ache badly. Moving over and working off the fairly hard rubber kept the aches down quite a lot. Even if you're not worried about leg aches, a rubber mat in front of any bench where electrical tools may be used is a good safety feature (as you may note, I believe in safety back-ups; even with GFIs, I use mats).

There are so many materials and ways to finish walls today as to almost require a book simply to cover the different types of paneling (you could use plywood paneling and make your shop walls one of your first projects, if you want). Or you can simply paint the walls. Ceilings offer the same wide range of finish materials. In both cases, I would select paint or paneling in a light color to reflect light, but keep a semi-gloss or flat finish to cut down on glare.

For basements, if there is room, a slightly dropped ceiling can keep down some of the noise that might otherwise reach upstairs.

Plywood Working

Shop techniques for working with plywood differ in some respects from working with other woods, and in some respects differ not at all. Sometimes the differences make things easier, sometimes a bit harder, but in general it works out to the easy side if a bit of care is taken.

The first chapter pretty extensively covered the types of plywood available, so you will have some idea of just how to match the wood to the project. Certainly you won't select a C-D underlayment grade to build a desk, but you also don't need an A-D or A-B grade to go under your new bathroom tiles. Cost and appearance variables, then, are of great importance to the final looks and durability of your job. If you're building a garden shed, don't select a plywood with interior glue types, no matter how great the salesman at your lumberyard tells you it is for outdoor use. It could do well, but probably won't. The few extra dollars spent on exterior glue plywood will be returned, in the long run, by the durability and appearance of the finished project.

LAYING OUT PLYWOOD

You're starting with a large sheet, and the immediate temptation is to slice it in half, crosswise or lengthwise, to make the material a bit easier to handle, especially if you happen to be working with plywood ¾ of an inch thick. Don't. I've succumbed to this temptation a few times, and it invariably ends up wasting material for me. Lay out the entire job, first, and then cut the panel into smaller pieces as needed.

Probably the simplest and most material saving way to lay out a plywood project is to make butcher paper templates of the various pieces. These templates can then be arranged on the face of the plywood (on the back if you're cutting with a circular saw) until you have the optimum layout, the layout that gives the least possible waste material between pieces. In other words, you take your standard plans and make sort of a dressmaker's pattern from them. Then apply the pattern to the wood, sketch around the paper laid on the wood, check the measurements, curve radii (if any), and make sure you have allowed enough distance between pieces for the saw cut (kerf line). Not allowing for that kerf is the cause of many measurement and fit problems later on in the project. Make sure there is plenty of distance (if you're not sure how much to allow, and it will vary from saw to saw, simply run a short cut into a piece of scrap lumber and measure the cut width).

Whenever possible, lay out the work so that the fact grain runs the long way on the piece being cut, assuming the plans don't say otherwise.

Start by making the first cut so as to reduce the size of the panel for easier handling. If different cuts must be made (bevels, etc.), make all cuts with one saw setting. This will mean that any mating surfaces are made with the same saw setting (on power saws) and will match more closely when fitting time arrives.

If you are making your cuts with a hand saw, use a cross cut saw with at least ten points to the inch. Lay the plywood with its good face up, support it firmly and start the work. Keep the saw at a low angle (Fig. 4-1) to reduce splitting of the back side of the panel. For furniture use, where the back side is going to be visible partially or wholly, place a piece of scrap material under the panel and cut that along with the panel (great for the arm muscles). Make sure the saw is sharp, too, as this provides a much smoother cut.

If you're using a table saw or a radial arm saw, the good face of the plywood is also placed up, as with the handsaw. Use

Fig. 4-1. Properly used, a handsaw will do any job, or almost any job, a power saw can do

either a very sharp combination blade, or, preferably, a fine tooth plywood blade with almost no set to the teeth. On a table saw, the blade should just barely protrude above the face of the plywood (Fig. 4-2) (don't take the guard off the blade, as that is for demonstration purposes only).

For large panels when no one is around to help, you will want to build a roller to hold one end. You can make a full sized roller, or simply a small one to clamp to one of your sawhorses. Use furniture casters of the ball type for rollers.

Again, with power saws, make sure the blade is very sharp if you want a smooth cut.

Portable circular saws require a slightly different method. The wood, as noted earlier, is marked on the back, and the good side is turned down for cutting. Support the panel solidly with saw horses. Use a plywood or very sharp combination blade to make the cuts.

Many people recommend tacking a strip of scrap lumber to the top of the sawhorses so that the cutting won't damage

Fig. 4-2. A table or radial arm or circular saw will add to accuracy and speed your work

the sawhorse. I don't care for this, for a very simple reason. Sooner or later that saw blade is going to hit one of the nails used to take the scrap lumber to the sawhorse. Then you've got a sharpening job coming up if you're lucky. If you're not, you're out a blade. I simply set the circular saw blade for a depth that just makes it through the plywood (as with the table saw), and then go ahead and slice ¼ inch or so into the sawhorse. I find that doing so eventually weakens the sawhorse, so that possibly once every year I need to replace the top piece of 2 x 4. The 2 x 4, though, is still cheaper than a blade or a sharpening job.

When using a saber saw to cut curves and other odd shapes, place the front of the saw platform on the plywood. Then tilt the saw downward into the wood to pierce the panel. Thus you need drill no pilot hole. Use the finest saber saw blade you can, consistent with actually making the cut at all, so that the cut will be as smooth as possible.

If a sharp saw blade is used, your edges should seldom need to be planed for smoothness. Occasionally you'll find that cut markings were a hair off, not enough to require another cut, but enough to keep from getting a good fit. When planing, work from both ends toward the middle so you won't rip out the center plies of the sheet. Use a plane with a low angle (the block plane) blade that is very sharp (Fig. 4-3).

According to the American Plywood Association, overlaid plywood is exterior type plywood with a permanent resin face protection, in either medium or high density. Generally, this plywood is worked as are other types, but there are a couple of exceptions. In every case, cutting and drilling of overlaid plywood requires that the blade of the tool enter the *face* of the plywood, never the back. For portable circular saws, use scrap wood as a back up on top of the plywood to hold down chipping. Make sure you use a hollow ground blade that has recently been sharpened. For gluing operations, overlaid plywood must have the surface lightly roughened by sanding.

JOINTS

Butt joints such as those shown in Figure 4-4 are the simplest of all joints to make. When you use plywood ¾ of an

Fig. 4-3. Specialty tools aid edge finishing

Fig. 4-4. Strong butt joint corners are reinforced when lighter wood is used

inch thick, no extra support should be needed. For thinner materials a reinforcing block, or nailer strip, is needed to make a strong joint. Whether you use ¾ inch or thinner stock, or use a nailing block or not, glue is needed to provide the maximum joint strength (screws will also give a stronger joint, combined with glue, than will nails).

Framing the inside, as shown in Figure 4-5, will make the overall construction with thinner plywood possible, while still giving great strength. Use glue or nails (or screws).

Rabbet joints, such as the one in Figure 4-6, are neater and stronger than butt joints. They make a near ideal joint for drawers, chests and cupboards. Miter joints are probably the least easily noticed of all exterior joints if done properly, but they require care and some experience in cutting angles, gluing and clamping.

Dado joints are rapidly made with power saws, and are exceptionally useful for inserting shelves (Fig. 4-7). The dado

Fig. 4-5. Further reinforcement may be desirable

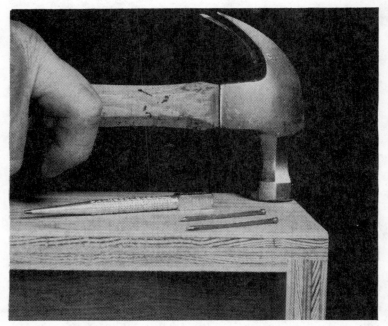

Fig. 4-6. Finishing nails are used, and then the nails are set below the surface

Fig. 4-7. Shelves fit into grooves cut with a router or a dado blade on a power saw

joint can be cut with a single pass if a dado head is used, or in multiple passes with a standard blade.

FASTENING

Plywood can be fastened with material used to fasten other woods, though some special needs are evident. Generally, for strongest construction, all nails should be used with glue. You should, when working near the edge of any piece of wood that will be visible, pre-drill holes so that there will be no splitting. Actually, pre-drilling preserves strength even in non-visible work.

Nail size is determined pretty much by the thickness of the plywood being used. For ¾-inch plywood use six penny casing nails or eight penny finishing nails. For ⅝-inch plywood, the same sizes are used. When the plywood drops to ½ inch thickness, the nails go to four penny casing, six penny finishing. Three-eighths inch plywood requires three penny and four penny nails, while ¼-inch plywood will use ¾ or 1 inch brads, or three penny finishing nails (Fig. 4-8). One inch blue lath nails can also be used for ¼-inch, when used as a backing with no objection to visible nailheads.

When pre-drilling for nails, use a drill bit that is just slightly smaller in diameter than the nail shank (Fig. 4-9).

Usually when working with plywood on smaller jobs, the nails will be spaced no more than 6 inches apart (Fig. 4-10). If the plywood used is very thin, and in an application where it might buckle in use, the nails should be spaced more closely.

Fig. 4-8. Nail sizes vary with wood sizes

Fig. 4-9. Predrilling prevents wood splitting even in plywoods

Use nails and glues together whenever possible if you need a strong joint.

Flat-head wood screws, used with glue, provide just about the strongest joint possible in plywood (or most any other woodwork). Again, the thickness of the plywood determines the basic screw size for the work, but all sizes provided in Table 4-1 are minimums. If the size of the job permits you to, it is best to use slightly larger screws whenever possible.

Table 4-1. Use this table in selecting proper screw sizes.

Plywood Thickness	Screw Length	Screw Size	Drill Size for Shank
¾ inch	1 ½ inch	#8	11/64 inch
⅝	1 ¼	#8	11/64
½ inch	1 ¼ inch	#6	9/64 inch
⅜	1	#6	9/64
¼	1	#4	7/64

Figure 4-11 shows the relationship of the various thicknesses of plywood to the nail sizes.

Screws, and nails, are countersunk to just below the surface of the plywood (a nailset is used for doing the job with nails, of course). Wood filler is then used to fill the holes. Bring

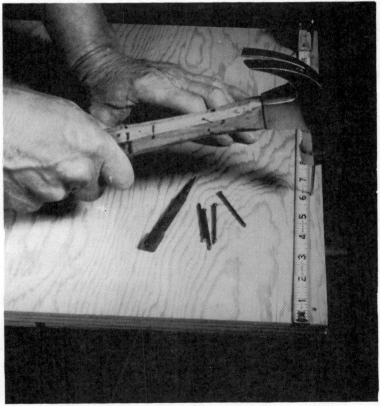

Fig. 4-10. Nails must be properly spaced

Fig. 4-11. Screw sizes also vary with wood thickness

the filler up slightly higher than the surrounding wood, and sand down to the correct level (Fig. 4-12).

If you have difficulty driving screws in wood, assuming holes are drilled and the screwdriver is the correct size, then get a bit of liquid soap and lubricate the threads of the screws. Beeswax can also be used.

When gluing plywood the American Plywood Association recommends three basic types of modern glues, though there are others useful in special applications.

Urea resin glue comes as a powder, is mixed with water and must be used within four hours. The color is light, and the glue provides a strong joint if the parts fit tightly. This is a general woodworking glue, and will stand some exposure to dampness as it is moisture resistant. Joints fit tightly, and solid, tight clamping is essential. Drying time is about 16 hours. Use at 70° or warmer, only.

Liquid resin (white) glue comes ready to use, and is not affected by application in cool temperatures. It is quick setting and strong, but not quite as strong as urea resin glue. Uses include indoor furniture and cabinetwork. The glue of choice for small jobs where a good fit or tight clamping isn't possible. Any glue that squeezes out on to surfaces to receive a stain must be thoroughly cleaned for the stain to take. Setting time is about an hour and a half, and clamping is best. The preferred temperature is 60° or above, though it can be used in cooler temperatures.

Resorcinol waterproof glue comes as a powder, plus a liquid for mixing just before each use. It is dark colored and exceptionally strong. Completely waterproof, it is the glue of choice for uses with exterior grade plywoods, and in any work that is going to receive prolonged exposure to dampness. Resorcinol glue is expensive, a bit of trouble to mix, and can cause problems with stains because of its dark color. A tight fit and solid clamping are essential. The glue must be used within eight hours of mixing, and can only be used when the temperature is 70° or above. Drying time is 16 hours.

Contact cements are used to apply laminates and edge strips to plywood, and are not useful for structural joints.

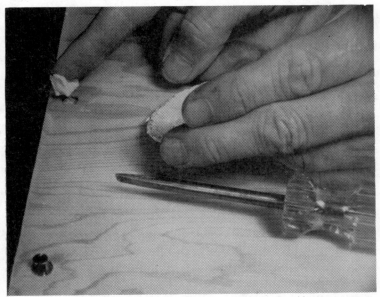

Fig. 4-12. Screw heads are countersunk and the holes are fitted for best appearance

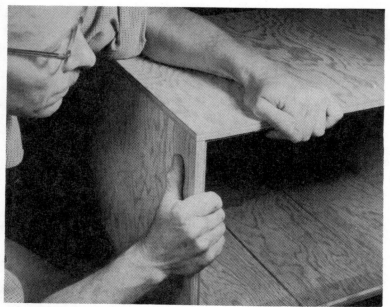

Fig. 4-13. Assembly requires care

Wall panel adhesives are used to apply decorative paneling or facings, though a few nails per panel are usually used to keep the panel from pulling away from the wall because of warping.

Casein glues are exceptionally slow setting, require clamping, and are only useful when the slow setting time is needed for you to assemble complicated structures.

The first step in any gluing job is to check the fit of the joint (Fig. 4-13). Check for contact all along the joint for greatest strength.

Glue is applied with a brush or a stick (glue tends to ruin brushes in a rush, so I prefer the stick method). Give end grain a preliminary coat, as it absorbs glue quickly and will need two coats in most cases. Give the first coat five minutes or so to soak in before applying the second coat. Be careful with your application if you plan to stain or varnish the piece, as most glues will mess up such a finish if they're allowed to slop over on the surface of the work (Fig. 4-14).

Assemble the work, and clamp tightly (Fig. 4-15). Nails or screws will often serve in lieu of clamps. Use scrap wood

Fig. 4-14. Glue is applied to add strength

Fig. 4-15. Most glue types require clamping

Fig. 4-16. Drawer bottoms are nailed on

under the jaws of the clamps to prevent marring the surface to be finished. Quickly wipe off any excess glue that squeezes out of joints. Sand the area as soon as the excess glue spot dries. Once the piece is clamped, test the corners for squareness. If all is well, allow the glue to set and dry.

ASSEMBLY

Plan your assembly procedure before starting the gluing if the project is at all complicated. You will usually find that a complex project will go together much more easily if it is first put together in various sub-assemblies. Of course, anything put together this way must be precisely cut, and each sub-assembly must be square and true, or the sub-assemblies will never line up into a final assembly.

DRAWERS

Drawers always seem to be the nemesis of the beginning woodworker, though the actual construction, especially using

118

butt joints, is quite simple and straightforward, whether you use hand or power tools.

Remember to nail and glue (or use screws and glue) all butt joints (Fig. 4-16), and use a reasonably heavy piece of plywood for the bottom of the drawer. You should have no problems. Large drawers need ½ inch plywood bottoms, while smaller drawers can get by with ⅜ inch material.

For reinforcement of some kinds of drawers, you may wish to nail and glue a strip of wood along the bottom of the front panel, as shown in Figure 4-17, so that ¼ inch plywood can be used on the bottom (if the size of the drawer is much larger than that shown, go to ⅜ inch plywood anyway).

If power tools are used to make the drawers, you'll most likely move away from the simple butt joint. Dadoes along the edges allow you to increase strength by inserting the bottoms edges right into the sides. Then insert the sides into backs and fronts. When nailed and glued, this makes an extremely strong joint (Fig. 4-18).

Fig. 4-17. Bumper strips are nailed and glued on

Fig. 4-18. Drawer fronts and backs are routed or dadoed to fit and provide a stronger joint

Drawer guides can be made two ways with dado heads. A nailer strip along the side of the cabinet will fit into the dadoed groove plowed into the side of the drawer, as shown in Fig. 4-19, while another style allows you to plow the groove in the cabinet and place the guide strip on the drawer. Such guide strips should, at the very least, be nailed and glued. But I would, as usual, prefer to use screws and glue for greatest durability (Fig. 4-20).

Before installing drawers in a finished cabinet, you will wish to coat both guides and grooves with beeswax or paraffin for smoothest operation. This can also help during assembly checks, but make sure you don't get the wax in the areas to be glued.

Probably the simplest of all drawers to assemble, this unit has a bottom made of ⅜ or ½-inch plywood that extends beyond its sides to form a lip (Fig. 4-21).

To keep your tool needs to non-power types, pieces of ⅜ inch plywood are glued to the inner surfaces of each side of the cabinet. Leave a space just wide enough to take the lip you've left on your drawer (Fig. 4-22).

If you have power tools available, the cabinet will be lighter and simpler to make, using exactly the same drawer design. The bottom of the drawer is now cut ⅜ inch wider than the drawer, on both sides (Fig. 4-23). Next, dado slots to fit the ½ inch plywood bottom in the ¾ inch plywood sides of the cabinet (Fig. 4-24), and you have a simple, sturdy and attractive cabinet when done.

Fig. 4-19. Dadoing and a nailed and glued guide strip provide good drawer guides

Fig. 4-20. A nailed and glued strip can be placed on the side of the drawer and used for a guide strip, with a dadoed cut in the cabinet side

Sliding cabinet doors sometimes seem like very complex work, especially if you desire a particularly tight fit. The secret is a simple one. Rabbet the top and bottom edges of each door, doing the back of the door to slide in front and the front of the door to slide in back (Fig. 4-25). This cuts way down on any dust passage, and will provide fractionally greater cabinet interior size when you're tight for space. For ⅜ inch plywood doors rabbeted to half their original thickness, plow the two grooves on the top and bottom of the cabinet half an inch apart. The doors will just about touch with this measurement. Seal all door edges, and paint both sides of the doors so that one side can't absorb more moisture than the other and thus cause warping.

For removable sliding doors, the bottom grooves are dadoed 3/16 of an inch deep while the tops are cut in ⅜ of an

Fig. 4-21. Drawer ends may also be nailed and glued on

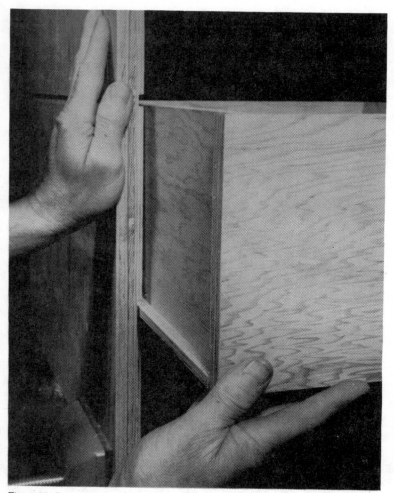
Fig. 4-22. Drawer bottoms can extend over the sides and may be used as guide strips

inch (Fig. 4-26). The doors are installed by pushing them up into the excess space in the top groove and then letting them drop down in the bottom groove. If you don't wish to dado for this type of door, three or four companies make metal or fiber tracks that can be screwed in place to accept the doors.

Again, sliding doors, as most other things, can be made without dadoing, thus cutting out the need for power tools. You can either use the already described commercial tracks,

Fig. 4-23. Butt joints all around, but the drawer will be sturdy because of the use of nail and glues, as well as heavier wood

Fig. 4-24. Fit must be good, neither too tight nor too loose

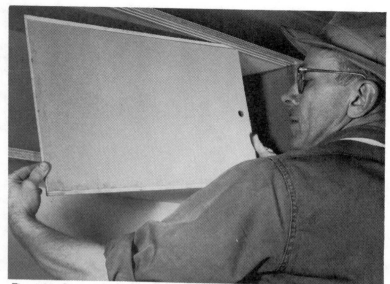

Fig. 4-25. Cabinet doors fit in grooves

Fig. 4-26. Double doors fit in double grooves

or make your own of quarter round molding, or strips of plywood (Fig. 4-27).

While dadoing is about the neatest and strongest way to install a shelf in any cabinet, you may either not wish to use the power tools necessary or have a dado head. In such cases, or in cases where you wish to make the shelves adjustable, plug-in shelf supports are used. The holes, sized to the particular brand of support you buy, are blind drilled into the

Fig. 4-27. The grooves can be built of small strips instead of being routed or dadoed

Fig. 4-28. Adjustable shelves are easily installed using commercial hangers set in drilled holes

plywood sides of the cabinet, going about ⅜ inch deep (Fig. 4-28). You will also find slotted strips on the market which can simply be screwed to the sides of the cabinet to provide adjustable shelf supports.

CABINET BACKS

The more or less standard method for fitting cabinet backs calls for rabbeting the sides of the cabinet, at the rear, to

128

the depth of the material used for the back if a flush back is desired. You may rabbet deeper than the backing board if the unit may have to set against walls that are not flush or plumb. The lip left by rabbeting to the extra depth can then be trimmed to fit the out of plumb wall (Fig. 4-29).

To simplify matters for those using only hand tools, quarter round molding is nailed, and glued, to the cabinet for the back to rest against (Fig. 4-30).

Several other back installation methods are possible. In one the back is set flush with the outside edges of the cabinet, nailed and glued. If the stock used is heavy enough, the back can also be set ½ inch or more inside the edges of the cabinet. I don't really see a great advantage to this type of back design unless your measurements are a bit off and you come up short on material (Fig. 4-31).

Cabinet backs that have been installed without rabbeting can be beveled with a small block plane to make them a bit less visible. The backing material should be at least ⅜ inch thick for this procedure, and the strokes of the plane should be very

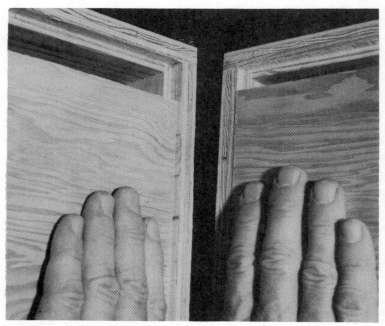

Fig. 4-29. Two different back designs

Fig. 4-30. Mitered joints cut out the need for covering edges

light. Again, as always, plane from the edges in to the center whenever possible (it won't always be, and isn't as essential here as you should be cutting only into the outside ply) (Fig. 4-32).

As Fig. 4-33 shows, cabinet backs are nailed into the rabbet, with the nails driven at a slight angle to the outside edge of the cabinet. Use four penny finish nails and a bit of care to keep from driving the nails through the sides of the cabinet.

If you find yourself committed to a job that requires much nailing of backs (possibly a job on the order of making one's own kitchen cabinets), you could well find it a good idea to get all cabinets assembled to the point where the backs are ready to go on. Cut to size all the backs and then go out and rent a heavy duty stapler/nailer as shown in Fig. 4-34. This speeds up the work quite a lot.

EDGES

Plywood edging is a major point of concern when you start building projects that are to have a furniture look. That raw edge, showing all the ply materials, is quite ugly unless something is done to cover it. A lot of people avoid plywood work because of these edges, but it simply isn't necessary to spend a lot of time worrying about them. Several methods for covering the edges of plywood are available. You can, for really fancy work, cut a V groove in the edge and install a strip of matching or contrasting wood (for greatest neatness here,

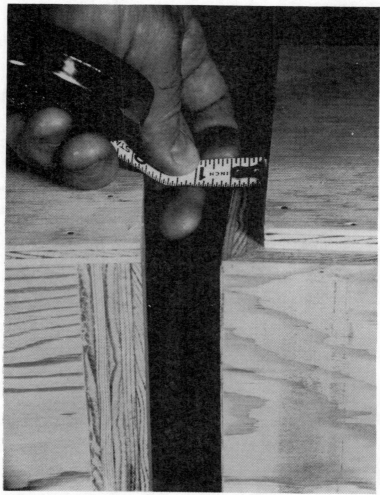

Fig. 4-31. An outset back provides a bit more interior room than does an inset, but use care in nailing if you work the style on the left

Fig. 4-32. Edge trimming is a delicate job on plywood, and must be done with a small plane

great care is needed both in cutting the groove and cutting the strip of wood). Easier than this is a selection of one of the easily found strips of edge banding of real wood now available everywhere. These are backed with pressure sensitive adhesive. Cut to fit, peel off the backing and press in place. That's it.

End grain on plywood to be painted is filled with a wood putty type edge filler which may come either powdered for

Fig. 4-33. Edge nailing must also be done with care

Fig. 4-34. Hammer-driven staples can also be used

Fig. 4-35. Edge filler is used to hide edge plies

home mixing or ready to use. The edge filler is allowed to dry, sanded smooth and painted. In cases where there will be little or no flex of the end part of the plywood, you can even use spackling compound, but make sure the end grain will not be exposed to moisture if you do (Fig. 4-35).

For plywood that is laminated for use as table or counter tops, the same material may be applied to the edges, using the identical contact cement used for the surface laminate. Usually this material is available in strips for edges as well as sheets for the top, so you can avoid all but the smallest amount of cutting and trimming (Fig. 4-36).

HARDWARE

Figure 4-37 shows a few of the types of drawer hardware that you will find available today. The variety is far too wide to cover here, but you can select hardware for just about any design.

Fig. 4-36. Preglued edging strips are also available for hiding edge plies

Fig. 4-37. The variety of finish hardware is extremely wide

Fig. 4-38. Drawer pulls and door pulls also come in a wide range of styles

If you're building sliding doors for cabinets, the easiest sort of pull for them is a cup that is simply pressed, in a force fit, into a round hole. Sliding doors generally don't offer the clearance needed for round pulls shown at the top of Fig. 4-38. The wooden pulls shown can be easily fabricated in just a few seconds.

For a simple drawer pull for either single or stacked drawers, just cut a notch in the front center of the drawer, finish the edges and you're ready to go (Fig. 4-39).

Catches come in as wide a variety, or close to it, as drawer pulls and handles. The type being installed in Fig. 4-40 is a touch type, while a magnetic catch is shown at top left, a roller spring at top center and a spring cabinet style at the right. Other types are on the bench.

For a rustic look, you can use surface mount hinges that require little more than careful measurement to be attractive. No mortising is needed, and the job goes quite rapidly, even with a large number of hinges to install (Fig. 4-41). These are

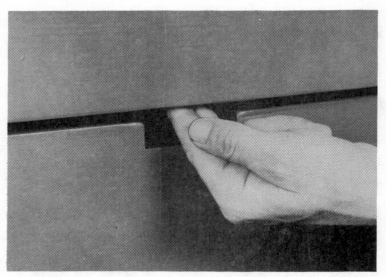

Fig. 4-39. In some cases, a simple cutout works as well

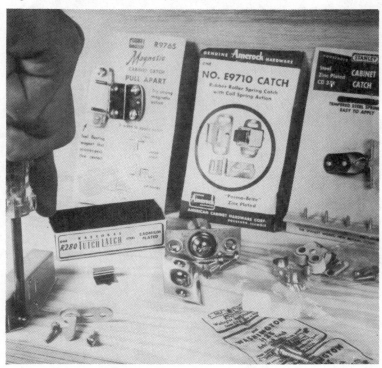

Fig. 4-40. Latch hardware is just as varied

137

Fig. 4-41. Installation of surface hinges is the easiest

also available in some not so rustic designs, but they don't look as good to me.

Overlapping doors (with rabbeted lips) can easily use what are known as semi-concealed hinges. These hinges are also easily installed without mortising. The set shown has a ½ inch inset for doors of ¾-inch plywood rabbeted to leave a quarter inch lip (Fig. 4-42).

For modern styles, concealed pin hinges are often needed. In this case, the hinge is designed so that only minor mortising is needed. Once the hinge is in place and the door is closed, only the pivot can be seen from the front of the cabinet (Fig. 4-43).

Another semi-concealed style hinge is the loose-pin style shown in Fig. 4-44. Once the door is closed, only the barrel of the hinge will show. These work very well for flush plywood doors since the screws go right into the flat grain of the wood and, thus, hold strongly.

Sliding door installation is simplified by the use of metal brackets that fasten to the top of each door. These brackets

Fig. 4-42. Semi-hidden hinges are not much harder to install

simply screw in, and the nylon wheel then rides on a double-lipped track (single lipped for single doors) (Fig. 4-45). The bottom of the door is kept in line with a T guide (Fig. 4-46). If you don't have the power tools to make the dado shown, form the slot with two strips of ¼-inch quarter round molding.

Hardware for sliding, or rolling, doors used in many places today is available for either top or bottom mounting (that is, the rollers may be mounted top or bottom). All three of the installations shown use top mounting, which is smoother in use than bottom mounted rollers (Fig. 4-47).

PANELING

Interior plywood paneling is one the quickest methods of completely changing the looks of a room, group of rooms, or of finishing a previously unfinished area such as a basement or attic. It is also one of the most attractive if care is used in selecting and installing the materials. Add to this the fact that a good quality plywood paneling job is one type of decorating

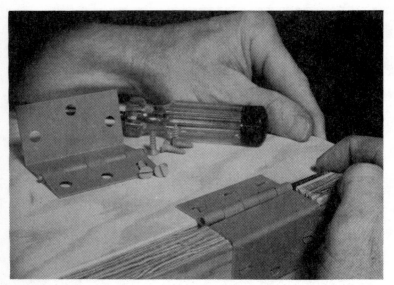

Fig. 4-43. Other types may require mortising

that doesn't have to be redone every three or four years as paint does, or every six to eight years as wallpaper, and it is easy to see why paneling is popular all over the country. The durability, though, is another reason for making sure of the attractiveness of your paneling. If you come to hate the design or color in a couple of years, you will still have to live with it until you either move or rip it down and replace the walls. And good plywood panels are not exceptionally cheap, so tearing down a wall for no reason other than a dislike of its color or pattern is not an economical way to go. Take plenty of time to make up your mind before starting the job and you'll be much more sure of enjoying the results for the next decade or two. Many of the new plastic finishes over real wood require little more than a wipe with a damp, soapy cloth to clean. They also seal out air borne grit, grime and grease that would otherwise tend to darken and discolor a paneled wall, so that even more life is added to the product.

If you want to be sure of liking the panel design, I would suggest you start out by simply paneling a single wall as a kind of accent wall, before carrying on with the entire room/ basement or whatever.

Panel installation has been made so easy as to be almost ridiculous today, though care is still needed for the best, longest lasting job. You can apply paneling directly over new or old studs, directly over old walls in many cases, and over masonry walls, if properly furred out. It can be installed horizontally or vertically, and you can find narrower panels to install in a herringbone or chevron design if you so wish.

For new walls, directly over studs, 4 x 8 sheets will have their edges fall over the center of vertical studs (in vertical

Fig. 4-44. Final hinge installation must be done with care to be certain the door fits properly

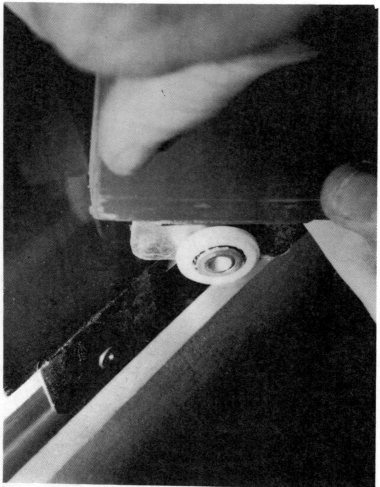

Fig. 4-45. One type of sliding door hardware

installations) whether your house is built in 16-inch center framing or 2 foot on center framing (some newer homes are using 2 x 6s spaced 24 inches on center in order to allow for greater insulation depth). The standard 8 foot panel length will usually strike a good fit right at the top and bottom plates of the framing. If the plates do fall under the panel ends, you will have to install 2 x 4 nailing cats which do. Horizontal installation will almost always require the installation of cross blocking (see top part of Fig. 4-48 for the nailing cat or block installation). Every unsupported edge must be blocked. If you are making a vertical installation with ¼ inch or thinner paneling, it is best to install nailing cats at the 4 foot mark, or to use ⅜-inch gypsum board behind the paneling.

If you're working over old walls, start by locating the studs. Usually, this is easily done by checking to see at an outside corner (the outside of the house, but inside the room) if the nailer stud is in place. If it is, and the house has been built within about 30 or 35 years, you can almost bet there will be a stud every 16 inches along the wall. Since the old wall will be covered, you can test by driving a nail part way in to locate the studs for sure. Older homes could be on 2 foot centers, or just about anything, depending on the design and age. In cases where you cannot locate studs to fall under the edges of the plywood paneling, you will need to furr the wall out so that the 1 x 2 furring strips support the edges (run these strips both horizontally and vertically).

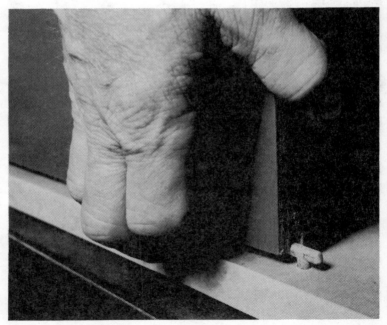

Fig. 4-46. Bottom grooves and rods keep the floor from flapping

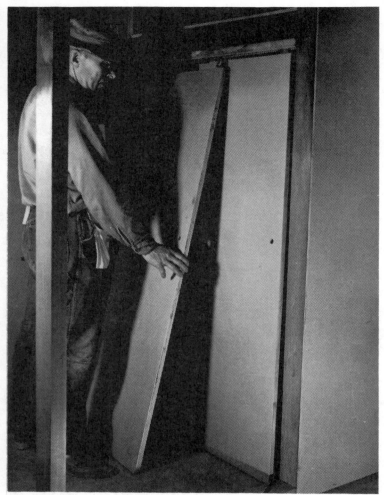

Fig. 4-47. The doors are then set in place

Masonry walls have to be furred out for you to install paneling, but the job is easily done using either concrete nails or construction adhesive, if the walls show no signs of excessive dampness. If excessive dampness is present, you'll need to find a way to bring this under control before installing the paneling, as moisture will quickly ruin both the furring and the paneling (see the bottom drawing in Fig. 4-48 for the process of furring and paneling a masonry wall).

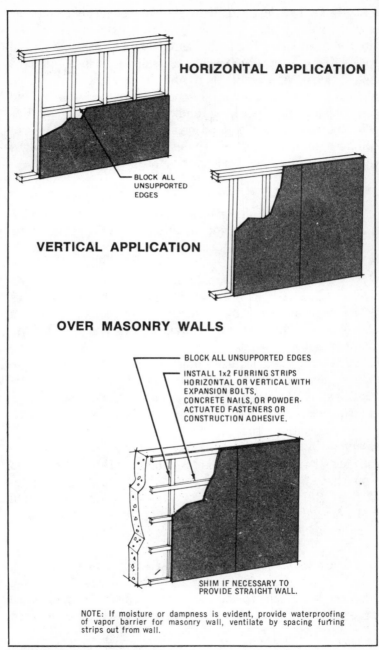

HORIZONTAL APPLICATION

BLOCK ALL UNSUPPORTED EDGES

VERTICAL APPLICATION

OVER MASONRY WALLS

BLOCK ALL UNSUPPORTED EDGES

INSTALL 1x2 FURRING STRIPS HORIZONTAL OR VERTICAL WITH EXPANSION BOLTS, CONCRETE NAILS, OR POWDER-ACTUATED FASTENERS OR CONSTRUCTION ADHESIVE.

SHIM IF NECESSARY TO PROVIDE STRAIGHT WALL.

NOTE: If moisture or dampness is evident, provide waterproofing of vapor barrier for masonry wall, ventilate by spacing furring strips out from wall.

Fig. 4-48. Methods of applying plywood

Today, paneling can be installed more quickly using only one or two (actually, three or four are best) nails per panel, along with adhesive, if the studs are clean and dry (or if the old wall is in good shape). For old walls in poor shape, you have two choices. Number one is to furr the wall and shim where needed to get wall plumb. Number two is to rip off the old paneling, plaster or wallboard and work with the studding. For adhesive use, select a good quality panel adhesive or use contact cement, but make sure the wall or furring or framing is clean, dry and free of wallpaper before starting.

EXTERIOR SIDING

Plywood is available in many designs and finishes to make it an almost ideal siding and sheathing material on new and remodeling construction jobs.

I was surprised to find that some people still seem to view plywood siding and sheathing as a second choice material, one that isn't as strong as board siding and one that is much less desirable in appearance and durability. This came out in a conversation with a friend shortly after I had handed him the hammer and sat down to rest after putting siding on a building extension for him. We used board siding, for a very simple reason. The wood used was custom cut at very lost cost at a local sawmill (the actual cost was nil, as he traded two logs for each one cut into lumber, which is a handy way to do things if you have enough timber on your property and can locate a mill willing to work on such a basis). He remarked on how quickly the siding had gone up, and I mentioned the fact that plywood would have had the job completed in about one-third the time. Or less. Regardless, he didn't like the idea until I explained that correctly installed plywood siding, even without sheathing under it, is stronger than board siding in almost every instance.

The reasons are almost obvious, if a little thought is given to how plywood is made. The grain of the various plies runs in different directions providing greater strength. The panels are larger, and are, thus, more rigid when properly nailed in place (Fig. 4-49).

As for appearance, I won't argue with anyone about that. That is a matter of personal taste, and what I like is not at all

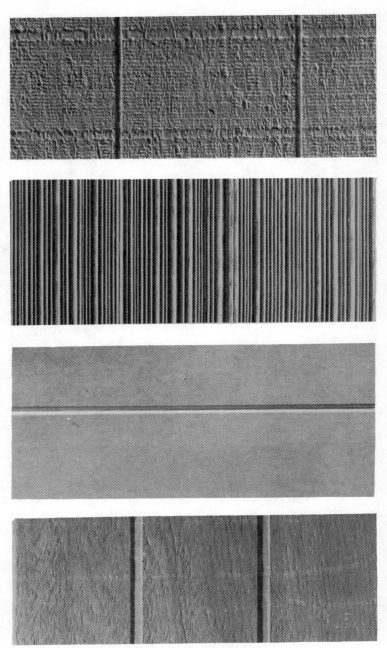

Figs. 4-50 through 4-53. Different finish siding styles

Fig. 4-49. Plywood siding goes up more quickly than do single boards

what someone else may like. And shouldn't be. Still, plywood is available in so many surface designs and forms that it is kind of hard to imagine that some type can't be found to please just about anyone. (Figs. 4-50 through 4-53 show just four of the dozens of surfaces available.)

Exterior plywood panel installation may be for sheathing or as finish boards. In some cases, the finish board siding that plywood provides can go up without sheathing over the studs (in most cases, I would at least use some form of insulating board as a sheathing to cut down heat loss through the studs and add to overall wall insulation density). In cases where no sheathing is used, the paneling must be at least ⅝ of an inch thick for structural integrity.

Vertically applied plywood sheathing or siding is nailed with six penny nails for ⅜ inch or less material, and eight penny nails for ½ or thicker panels. Nail spacing at the edges is 6 inches, while interior nailing is done every foot along the intermediate framing members. Horizontally applied exterior plywood is not as rigid as vertically applied, and requires nailing cats between studs for proper support.

Roof sheathing is laid with the face grain of the plywood perpendicular to the rafters, with end joints falling over the center of the rafters, and staggered at least one rafter (16 or 24 inches depending on the on-center framing distance of the roof). For best quality, use a minimum of ⅜-inch plywood for 16 inch on center distances, and ½ inch for 2 feet on center. Nailing is the same as for wall sheathing (Fig. 4-54). Plywood is often used as subflooring in new home construction today. Special tongue and groove types, meant for gluing and nailing,

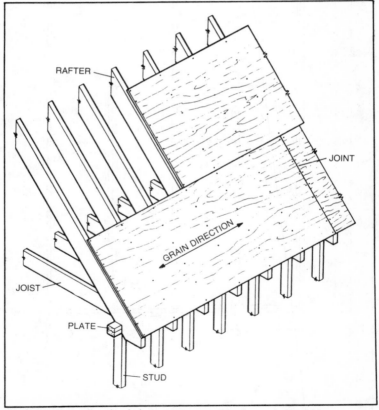

Fig. 4-54. Grain direction is important even with plywood sheathing.

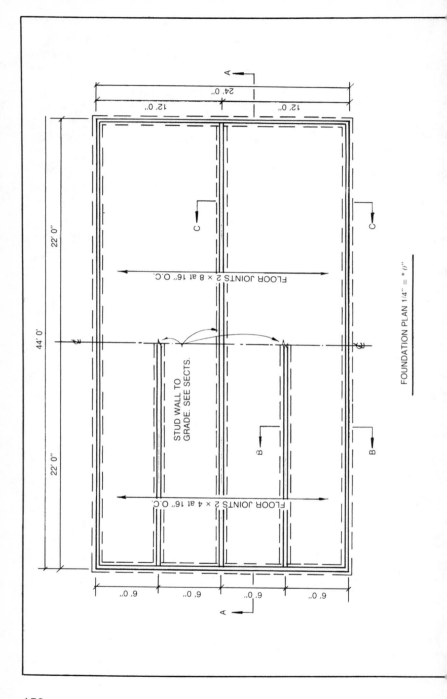

FOUNDATION PLAN 1/4" = 1'0"

150

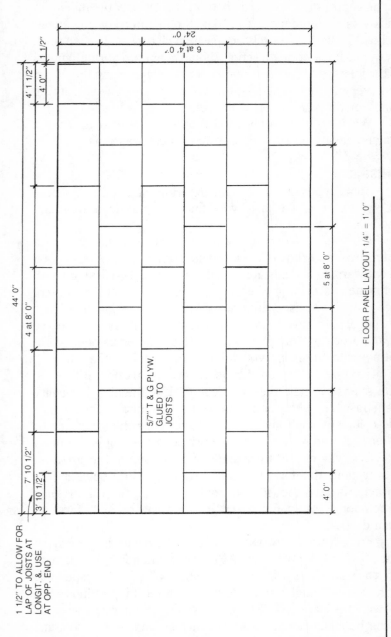

Fig. 4-55. Careful layout plans save plywood when doing roofing, flooring or siding

are readily found. Again, the joints are staggered according to the on center distance of the floor joists. Usually the minimum thickness recommended for 16 inch on center spacing is half inch, while 24 inch on center spacing will require ⅝-inch thick plywood. Face grain direction should again run at right angles to the joists, and nailing is done every 6 inches along the edges and every 10 inches along intermediate joists. The use of ring shank or threaded nails, eight penny size, is best.

When installing a plywood subfloor, it is best to make a drawing laying out the job in order to cut waste as much as possible (Fig. 4-55).

FINISHES

Some types of plywood for exterior use need no finish at all, while others take basic wood finish preparations, tools and finishes.

Exterior plywood should be stored in a cool, dry place if unfinished, and should be placed so that air circulation is good to cut warping and possible mold formation. The first job with unfinished exterior grades is edge sealing. A liberal coating of a good quality house paint primer will seal edges just fine, but if the panel is to have a final stain finish, then it is best to use a clear water repellent preservative that is listed as being compatible with the finish you will use to complete the job.

Textured plywood sidings generally look best if finished with stains to retain their rustic look. Use the highest quality stain possible, whether oil base or latex emulsion. Such stains add color but don't lay on a film to obscure the striations or other textured portions of the surface. Brushing is the most effective way of putting these stains on, giving the greatest penetration, though a long nap roller will do a quicker job. Spraying is not a good idea in most cases, as penetration tends to be poor unless you go over the job with a brush before the stain dries.

For exterior plywood surfaces to be painted, the American Plywood Association (APA) recommends a top quality latex acrylic house paint, after the use of alkyd or latex primer. Make sure, though when you use a primer it is formulated to go with the paint you'll be using since unmatched materials cause bubbling of the surface, cracking and other problems rather quickly (Fig. 4-56).

EXTERIOR APPLICATIONS

	TYPE OF FINISH	RECOMMENDED FOR	APPLICATION
PAINT	Acrylic Latex	Medium Density Overlaid, sanded, or 303 textured plywood.	Apply recommended non-staining primer plus two finish coats.
	Oil—Alkyd	Medium Density Overlaid only.	Apply with zinc-free primer, using two or three coats (including primer).
STAIN	Semi-transparent or penetrating stain	Unsanded plywood (303 textured plywood).	One or two-coat systems as recommended by the manufacturer.
	Opaque or highly pigmented stain	Unsanded plywood (303 textured plywood).	One or two-coat systems as recommended by the manufacturer.

Recent government restrictions on the use of lead and mercury compounds in finishes have resulted in some uncertainty regarding the performance of new paints and stains. In many cases, long-term performance information on the substitutes for lead and mercury is lacking, and results of tests in progress will not be available for some time. American Plywood Association finishing recommendations are based on experience with formulations made prior to the current restrictions. Consult supplier for interim recommendations.

Fig. 4-56. Paint and stain chart

Interior plywood panels that are to be finished can be painted with virtually any type of good quality interior paint, after application of a suitable primer. Select the paint to suit conditions, using semi-gloss or gloss paints where high washability is needed, and flat paints for general applications.

Natural finishes can be applied to either smooth or textured surface interior plywood. Generally, the APA recommends that two coats be applied for best sealing qualities.

Stains and sealers should be matched if you plan to change the color of your paneling. In some cases, the stain and sealer will be a single solution, with a small amount of stain used to tint the sealer which is then brushed on. When the panel has dried, give it a light sanding—very light—and brush on a coat of clear finish (for APA recommendations on the actual products to use, drop them a line—The American Plywood Association, 1119 A St., Tacoma, Wash. 98401 (Fig. 4-57).

FURNITURE FINISHING

In all probablity, a lot of the projects you will make from plywood will be in the form of furniture of one kind or another. The special finishing techniques for all kinds of furniture would require a special book, and there are several good ones on the market, but we'll take a look here at some of the special tools and techniques needed to provide you with one of several kinds of finish.

As the project begins, you will want to consider the wood texture and appearance, including color and grain design. A rough textured wood will require an inordinate amount of work if you desire a smooth finish, while a poor color or grain will mean a need for a paint finish. If you wish to stain or leave natural and varnish, then select for attractive grain, smooth texture and a pleasing color (unless stain is to be used).

Finishes for wood come in many varieties, and can easily confuse even those of us who are used to them.

Varnish may be either natural or synthetic (why the older varnishes are more natural than the urethane resins popular today I don't know—both are chemical types). Varnishes are reasonably easy to apply, give good durability (superb with most of the urethane types), and available in dull (satin),

INTERIOR APPLICATIONS

TYPE OF FINISH*		RECOMMENDED FOR	APPLICATIONS
PAINT	Oil—flat paint, semi-gloss or gloss enamel	Medium Density Overlaid, regular plywood, striated, embossed.	Apply over stain-resistant primer recommended by manufacturer of topcoat.
	Latex emulsion	Regular and textured plywood, Medium Density Overlaid.	Apply over stain-resistant primer recommended by manufacturer of topcoat.
	Textured paints	Regular plywood, Medium Density Overlaid, Texture 1-11.	Use stain-resistant primer recommended by manufacturer of topcoat.
STAINS, SEALERS		Regular plywood, textured.	Apply stains with companion sealer or over sealer separately applied. Follow with satin varnish or lacquer for increased durability. Where sealer alone is desired, use two coats.

*Use only lead-free finishes

Fig. 4-57. Paint chart for interior applications

semi-satin and high gloss forms. The carrying vehicle evaporates leaving a coating of resins on the surface of the wood. Modern varnishes provide a dust free finish in one to four hours, can be handled in about eight hours and can be sanded and a second coat applied in about 24 hours. Varnishes tend to intensify wood tones, thus bringing out, or accentuating, the grain and giving the wood a warmer appearance.

Varnish goes on easily, and a good quality varnish will "level" well. Still, most people end up with imperfect surface effects for the reason that varnish is, or seems to be, a magnet for small dust motes. Even the newer styles are relatively slow to dry dust free (a lot of dust can fly around in a couple of hours). Make sure the finishing area is dust free. If you're working on a concrete floor, it is a good idea, if the concrete is unfinished, to dampen the floor slightly to hold down dusting.

Shellac does away with the slow drying of varnish, is lower in price and even easier to use. Shellac, though, does not resist water and water marks nearly as well as varnish. It comes in two colors, white and orange, though the shellac seems to show up little differently when finally applied to wood. Shellac does not offer the durability of varnishes in most situations, though with proper precautions in use it will last and be attractive for a long while. Recoating time is cut to an hour, so you can easily understand why dust is less of a problem.

Lacquers for wood will use cellulose nitrate or acrylic or vinyl resins in combination with other materials, providing good durability under most conditions. For most of us, it is best to brush on lacquers which don't set up quite as quickly as do the spray on types (those set up just about instantly, and, if brushed on, will have a really messy appearance). Dust marks are seldom a problem because even the brush on types dry with great rapidity. Lacquer offers real ease in building up coat after coat. These are basically the same materials used by auto painters who will sometimes, in custom shops, use half a dozen gallons of lacquer to give 50 or more coats, and a superbly deep finish, to a special car.

Probably the most popular finish for furniture today is the penetrating resin finish. It has an ease of use most old-timers couldn't even dream about, and provides an extremely tough and long lasting finish. It also provides a warmth and color that is available in no other way. Basically, penetrating resin finishes have a carrier which penetrates the wood, carrying the plastic resin into the wood's pores where the carrier evaporates. The resin dries and the wood ends up with essentially a tough plastic coating, without having a plastic coated appearance.

It's easy to see why the stuff is so popular. You just soak a rag in the finish and flow it on the work. Keep the work wet for half an hour to an hour, and use plenty of rags to wipe off any excess liquid on the surface. Second coats (a good idea if the wood is as porous as, say oak or mahogany) should be done within three hours or so, before the first application has completely dried. Wipe off the second coat just as completely as you did the first coat. That's it. Once the drying is done, you have a finished project with a hard, durable surface.

The resin, once dry, resists water, alcohol and most household chemicals quite well. Resins are also resistant to heat, don't abrade easily and are difficult to scratch.

No matter the type of finish you select, remember that the final finish cannot possibly be any smoother than the wood under it. Surface preparation is of great importance to the final appearance and feel of your project.

Once assembly is completed, check the surfaces to be finished. If the wood is already quite smooth, you can start sanding with a fine grit paper (possibly a very fine), but if the wood is a bit rough, start with a 120 grit (still listed as fine). Once the surface has been well done with 120 grit paper, move to a 280 for the finish sanding. Use a sanding block on flat surfaces, and make sure you give each section and every inch of each section the same amount of sanding. It won't even hurt to count the strokes in each spot. The sanding affects not only the final smoothness of the job, but also the way the wood will take the finish or stain.

Now dampen the work surface as evenly as possible. This causes the wood fibers to swell and raises whiskers, which are then sanded off with extra fine sandpaper, or very fine steel wool. Make certain, though, that the wood is completely dry before you do this last sanding.

At this point you may find the wood throwing up a sort of surface fuzz no matter how much sanding you do. If it does, you now need a sanding sealer which will set these fibers up and stiffen them so they can be sanded off. Use care with sanding sealer, though, as it will keep stains and penetrating resins from getting as deeply into the wood grain as they will do without the sealers being used.

Joinery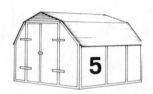

5

We've already covered several types of joinery back in the last chapter, but because making joints and actually joining the pieces of wood is the most basic woodworking skill for almost any kind of work, more attention is needed to types of joints and methods of joinery.

Butt, lap and miter joints are the simplest of all and are very frequently used in all types of woodworking (Figs. 5-1, 5-2, 5-3 and 5-4). More complex joints start with the rabbet (Fig. 5-5) and move on to dado and gain joints (Fig. 5-6), and into mortise and tenon and slip tenon joints (Fig. 5-7). Dovetail joints are considered the craftsman's drawer joints (Figs. 5-8 and 5-9). Edge joints, from the plain butt to dowelled, tongue and groove and spline (Fig. 5-10) can be used to make boards in a size greater than is generally available if you don't wish to, or can't use, plywood. On top of this, the various joints can be combined, as in Fig. 5-11, showing a variety of combination joints.

A basic rule of good joint making is a simple one. Always cut on the waste side of the material, no matter the kind of saw being used, or the type of joint being made. Cutting right on the line will take away excess material and produce a loose joint every time.

Fig. 5-1. 90° butt joints.

Half-lap joints usually are used to join members of the same thickness. Measure off the desired lap distance from the end of each member (from the needed point in cross half-lap) and square a line all the way around the material to be removed on both pieces. Score a line at half the thickness of the member, again on both pieces. Make your cuts setting the saw so that it will just reach the scribed mark halfway through the members. Make these cuts, and then make the cut along the scribed line at the mid-point of the members. These joints can

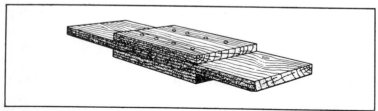

Fig. 5-2. An end butt joint with fish plates.

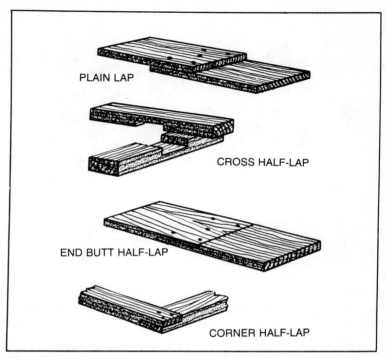

Fig. 5-3. Lap joints.

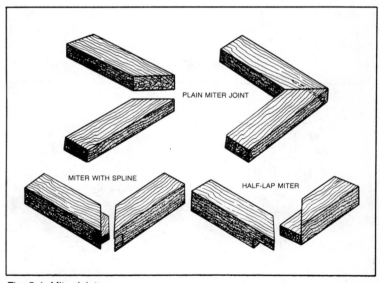

Fig. 5-4. Miter joints.

Fig. 5-5. Rabbet joints.

easily be made with either hand or power saws. A chisel can be used to clean up any material interfering with the close fit of the joints.

Miter joints are most often made in miter boxes, with backsaws, unless you are using a table or radial arm saw. The accuracy of miters cut with circular saws and freehand with hand saws leaves a lot to be desired.

Miter joints are most often used where two pieces of wood meet at 90°, but this is not an essential. Miters are one half the total angle; with a 90° meeting, the end of each piece of wood would be cut at 45°, while a 120° meeting would need a 60° miter. Wood miter boxes allow only squaring and end mitering to 45°, but professional style miter boxes offer an almost unlimited range of cuts, as do table and radial arm saws.

DADO JOINT

GAIN JOINT

Fig. 5-6. Dado and gain joints.

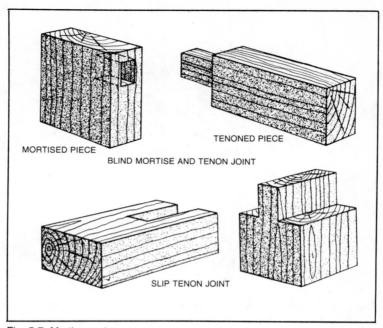

Fig. 5-7. Mortise and tenon joints.

Grooved joints are those which provide a three-sided recess running along the grain of the wood, while dadoes run across the grain. These may or may not extend all the way across the piece of wood. Rabbets are two sided recesses along the edge(s) of a piece of wood.

Grooves and dadoes are cut with dado heads most easily, though a table or radial arm (or circular) saw can be used with a

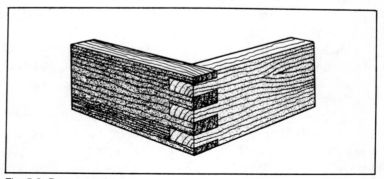

Fig. 5-8. Box corner joint.

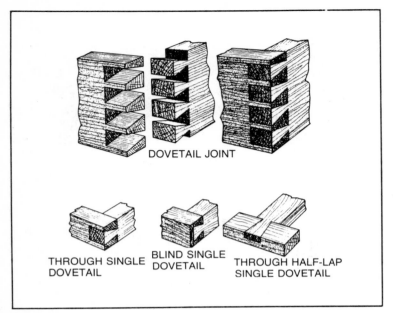

DOVETAIL JOINT

THROUGH SINGLE DOVETAIL

BLIND SINGLE DOVETAIL

THROUGH HALF-LAP SINGLE DOVETAIL

Fig. 5-9. Dovetail joints.

standard blade. First, lay out the groove or dado on the end or edge wood. Set the saw blade to the desired depth, and set the fence (or other guide) so that the first cut will run just on the waste side of your layout line. Make a little, light cut first and then examine the piece to see that the depth and placement of this first cut is correct. Finish the first cut if all is well, and move the saw blade over the width of the kerf and make another cut. Continue making cuts until you've grooved or dadoed to the width needed.

Dado heads do the same job in a single pass (up to the limits of the particular head being used).

Rabbeting with a circular saw requires you to make the shoulder (the portion at the top of the board) cut first, and then bring in the cheek cut from the side of the board. Measure depth carefully for both cuts once you've laid out the rabbet.

Dado heads again make the job easier, as only a single pass is needed. Simply set the dado head for the depth (down the narrow side of the board), set for the correct rabbet height by adjusting the amount of blade showing above the table, and pass the board, edge first, over the dado head.

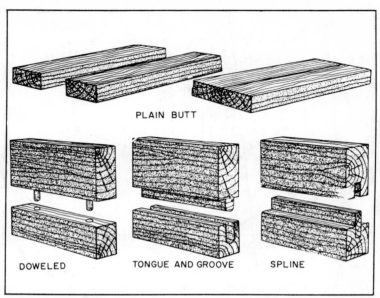

Fig. 5-10. Edge joints.

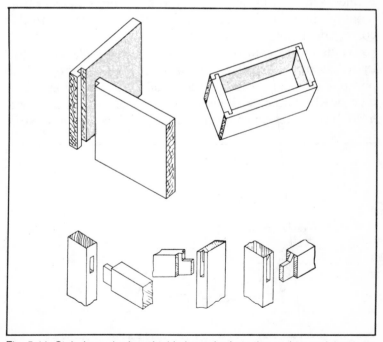

Fig. 5-11. Stub, haunched, and table-haunched mortise and tenon joints.

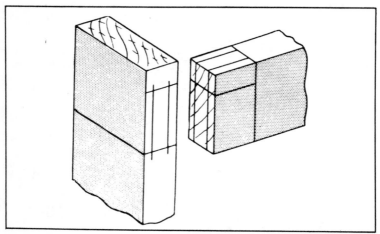

Fig. 5-12. Layout of stub mortise-and-tenon joint.

Mortise and tenon joints are strong and used in many ways for furniture and cabinet making. Mortising gauges provide the best way to make these joints. The faces of the members must be plainly marked, with the tenon member (the tenon is the portion inserted in the mortise) marked to the correct depth and size (usually specified in the project, but if you're designing your own, tenons are usually 1/2 to 1/3 the thickness of the mortise member). Tenons are the easiest portions of these joints and are made just as if they were four-sided rabbets, with either the circular saw or the dado head. If you don't have a mortise chisel machine, the mortise is

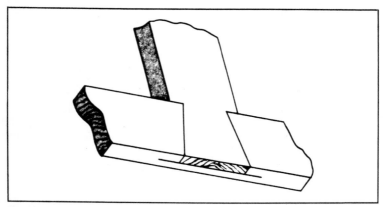

Fig. 5-13. Dovetail half-lap joint.

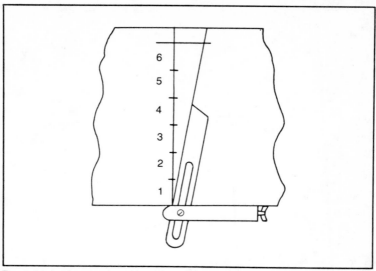

Fig. 5-14. Laying out the 10° angle for the dovetail joint.

chiseled out by hand (you can also cut them with saber saws). Mortise and tenon joints are normally fastened by gluing, though in many cases a hole is drilled through both portions and a peg is also driven in (Fig. 5-12).

Dovetail joints are just about the strongest woodworking joint possible. They are exceptionally useful for drawers and other furniture parts that receive a lot of banging around stress (Fig. 5-13).

The simplest way to make this joint is to use your router, with a dovetail jig (Fig. 5-14). Otherwise, the amount of layout work, cutting and chiseling is likely to drive you nuts if you're making more than a single drawer. In fact, because the dovetail jigs for use with routers come with great instructions and are simple to use, I will give no details of hand making dovetails here. I've done it. Once. That was totally and forever enough to last me. After all the time was spent on doing a neat, tight job, I then went to a router and cut much neater and tighter dovetails in less than 1/20 the time needed for hand work. It just isn't worth it.

Projects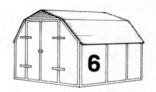

This chapter contains instructions for building 21 projects, ranging from a greenhouse to a new room for your home. The latter project may require you to enlist the services of a professional carpenter. Many of the items, though, can be built easily and fairly quickly. There are plenty of diagrams and illustrations to assist you.

Teco's gambrel roof design utility barn for suburban yards is not that difficult to construct. You'll need a few items not considered part of plywood working (Fig. 6-1). But all angles and rafter lengths are called off at the outset, so the really complex work has been done for you.

Carefully follow the frame cutting instructions in Fig. 6-2. Lay out the frame, using Fig. 6-3. Attach frames to sills with Teco framing angle on each side. Follow Figs. 6-4, 6-5 and 6-6 when making the roof and attaching purlins. Figures 6-7, 6-8 and 6-9 cover rear elevation, door details and front elevation, respectively.

With different coverings the barn becomes a greenhouse, and, if it stays a barn, you can select from exterior paneling in rustic or contemporary styles (Fig. 6-10). The barn may also be used for a lawn shed, potting shed, storage shed, playhouse and workshop.

Interior height to the peak is 6'8", enough for all but Wilt Chamberlain and width is 8 feet, an easily worked unit. The roof framing is done at 30-inch intervals, with the basic barn length being 96 inches, though you can extend it to fit your needs by simply continuing to carry out wall and roof framing. I would suggest, if you extend, that you stick with some multiple of 4 feet so that you can use as many full sheets of material as possible.

BILL OF MATERIALS			
QUAN.	DESCRIPTION	QUAN.	DESCRIPTION
28	2' × 4" 8 FT. LONG	40	TECO C-7 PL'TS
9	4 ' × 8' × 1/2" PLYW'D.	30	TECO JOIST H'G'R.
2	1" × 4" 6 FT. LONG	12	TECO ANGLES
1 ROLL	ROOFING FELT	30	TECO A-5 PL'T'S.
1 GAL	ROOF. CEMENT	3	3 BUTT HINGES
1 GAL	BARN-RED PAINT	1	HASP & LOCK
5 #	6 d COM. NAILS		90# CONC. MIX
2#	12 d COM. NAILS	10 BG.	OR
2#	1/2" ROOF. NAILS	4	6" × 8" ×8' RAIL TIE

Fig. 6-1. Here are materials needed to build the barn storage shed (courtesy Teco Products and Testing Corporation, Washington, D.C. 20015).

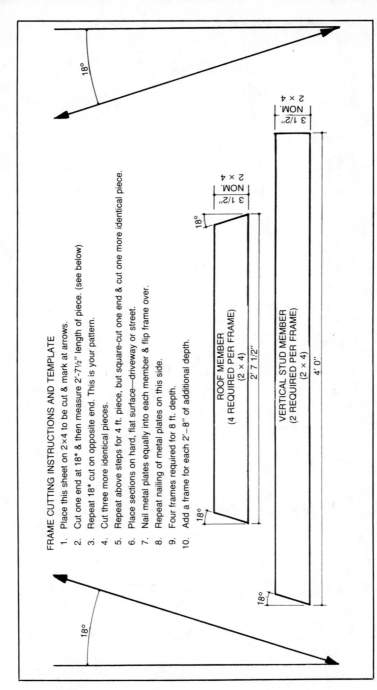

FRAME CUTTING INSTRUCTIONS AND TEMPLATE

1. Place this sheet on 2×4 to be cut & mark at arrows.
2. Cut one end at 18* & then measure 2'-7½" length of piece. (see below)
3. Repeat 18* cut on opposite end. This is your pattern.
4. Cut three more identical pieces.
5. Repeat above steps for 4 ft. piece, but square-cut one end & cut one more identical piece.
6. Place sections on hard, flat surface—driveway or street.
7. Nail metal plates equally into each member & flip frame over.
8. Repeat nailing of metal plates on this side.
9. Four frames required for 8 ft. depth.
10. Add a frame for each 2'–8" of additional depth.

ROOF MEMBER
(4 REQUIRED PER FRAME)
(2 × 4)

18°   18°

2' 7 1/2"

NOM.
3 1/2"
2 × 4

VERTICAL STUD MEMBER
(2 REQUIRED PER FRAME)
(2 × 4)

18°   18°

4' 0"

NOM.
3 1/2"
2 × 4

18°   18°

Fig. 6-2. Follow these frame cutting instructions (courtesy Teco).

171

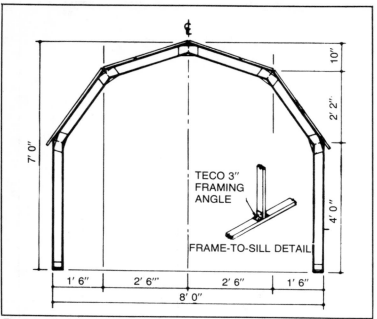

Fig. 6-3. Attach frames to sills with a Teco framing angle on each side (courtesy Teco).

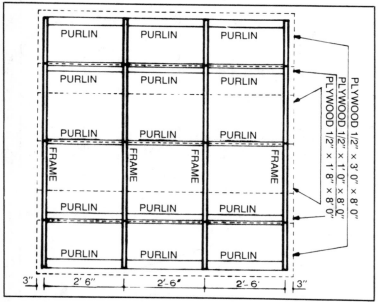

Fig. 6-4. The roof framing plan (courtesy Teco).

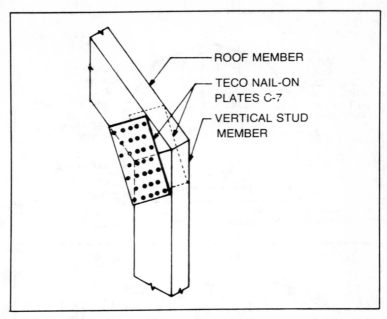

Fig. 6-5. The frame joint detail (courtesy Teco).

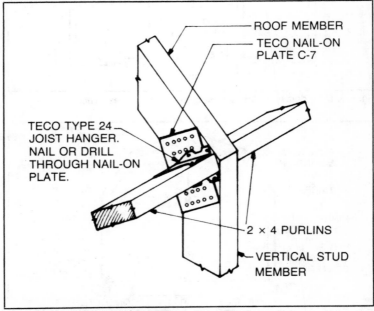

Fig. 6-6. A purlin attachment detail (courtesy Teco).

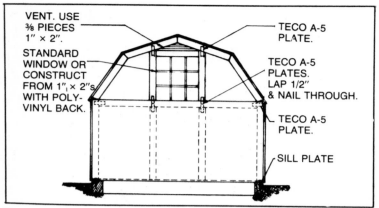

Fig. 6-7. Shown is a rear elevation diagram (courtesy Teco).

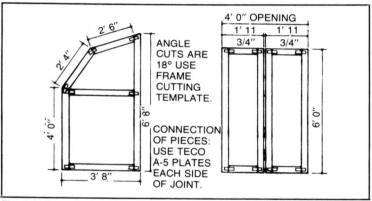

Fig. 6-8. Door details for the barn storage shed (courtesy Teco).

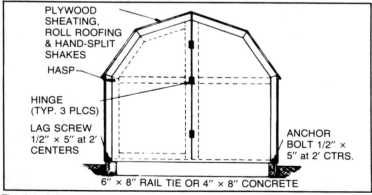

Fig. 6-9. A front elevation guide (courtesy Teco).

174

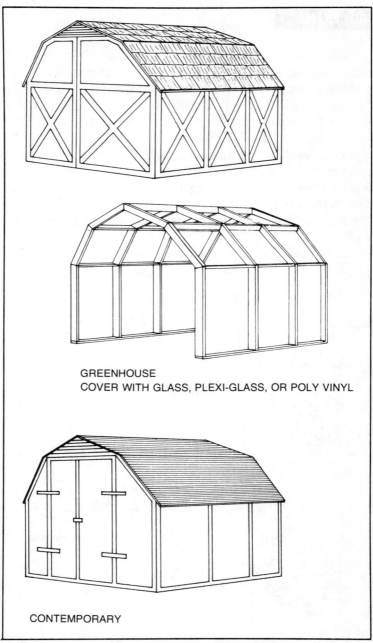

GREENHOUSE
COVER WITH GLASS, PLEXI-GLASS, OR POLY VINYL

CONTEMPORARY

Fig. 6-10. These designs are reasonable and attractive alternatives (courtesy Teco).

175

This project is highly variable, with a wide number of uses. Basically a cold frame, it can easily be adapted for use as a window box, organic hotbed, seed incubator, worm farm, vegetable and flower starter, a lean to greenhouse against the side of your house or an electrically heated hotbed (Fig. 6-11).

Using Teco framing anchors allows for use of adaptability. First, decide on the size, then build the bottom frame, and add the corner and center framing as needed. Framing of covers is made simple by using Teco Rite Angles, but you can also do the job by selecting old window sashes, making sure you measure them before building the bottom frame (Fig. 6-12).

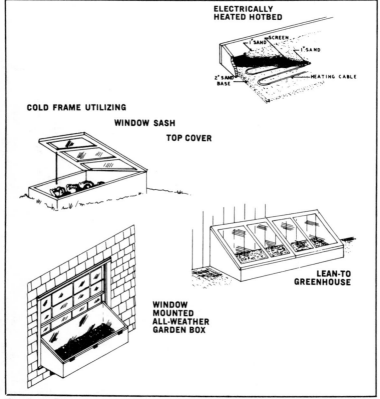

Fig. 6-11. This cold frame has many uses (courtesy Teco).

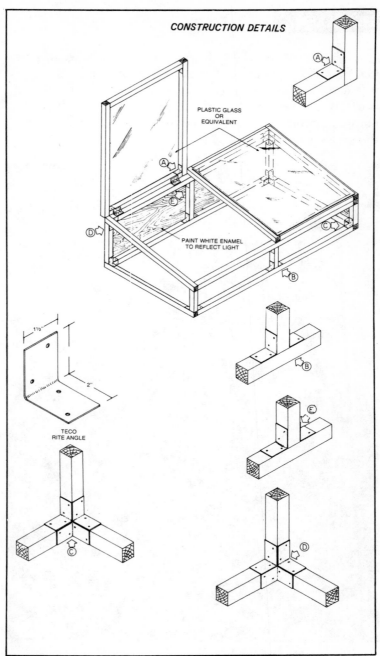

CONSTRUCTION DETAILS

PLASTIC GLASS OR EQUIVALENT

PAINT WHITE ENAMEL TO REFLECT LIGHT

1½"

2"

TECO RITE ANGLE

Fig. 6-12. Here are construction details for the cold frame (courtesy Teco).

The American Plywood Association provides this detailed and interesting greenhouse plan, with variations in sizes included. The use of greenhouses is increasing all over the country, for reasons ranging from a winter-long wish for non-plastic tomatoes to a desire to have fresh-cut flowers in the house year round (Fig. 6-13).

Fig. 6-13. Store plants in this greenhouse

A reasonably skilled home handyman can build the greenhouse in a couple of weekends. The basic materials are APA grade-trademarked plywood, lumber framing, and plastic sheet (Fig. 6-14). You may use either the 8' × 12' plan or the 8' × 8' plan (Figs. 6-15 and 6-16). Use the plywood panels as shown in Figs. 6-17 through 6-23. Figures 6-24 through 6-34 detail proper construction techniques.

Recommended playwood: 303® textured plywood siding with desired surface texture, APA grade-trademarked.

A-C or C-C Exterior plywood, APA grade-trademarked for shelves.

PLYWOOD

Quantity	Description
5 panels	3/8 in. × 4 ft × 8 ft Exterior plywood siding
2 panels	1/2 in. × 4 ft × 8 ft A-C or C-C Exterior plywood

OTHER MATERIALS

Quantity	Description
80 lin. ft	10, 3/8 in. × 6 in. × 8 ft basket weave-type fencing
228 lin. ft	2 × 4 lumber for framing
24 lin. ft	1 × 2 lumber stiffening for shelves
30 lin. ft	1 × 4 lumber for door casing
68 lin. ft	2 × 2 lumber for door framing
12 lin. ft	1 × 2 lumber for door insert framing
15 lin. ft	1 × 2 lumber for door stop framing
As required	Plastic for seasonal use: 6 to 10 mil polyethylene. One continuous piece 12 ft wide × 17 ft long. Two pieces 8 ft × 8 ft for doors and ends.
Optional	For more permanent installation use corrugated fiberglass panels applied horizontally on the roof and down to the sides—applied with corrugations running vertically on the ends and doors.
2 pieces	Aproximate size: 36 × 42 in. sections of screening
6	Door hinges (3 per door) 3-1/2″ butt hinges
4	Vent hinges (2 per vent) 1-1/2″ butt hinges
10	2 in. galvanized carriage bolts
40	1 in. round-head machine screws (washers not necessary)
As required	1 in. construction nails
As required	Caulk, sealant or flashing material to fill any joints, etc.
As required or desired	Finishing materials—stain or paint, wood preservative (see Building Hints)

NOTE: In areas of heavy snow, do not allow buildup on the roof.

Fig. 6-14. You'll need these materials to build the greenhouse

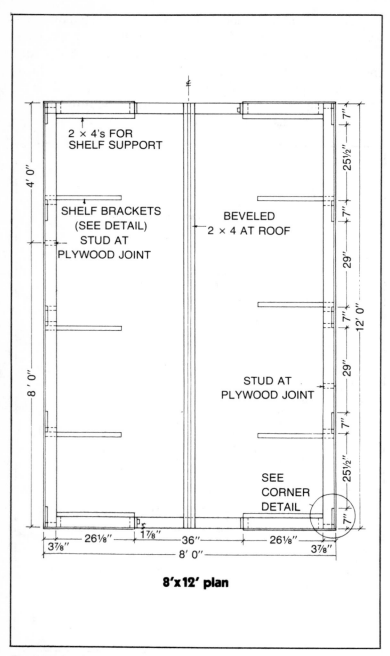

Fig. 6-15. An 8' × 12' greenhouse plan

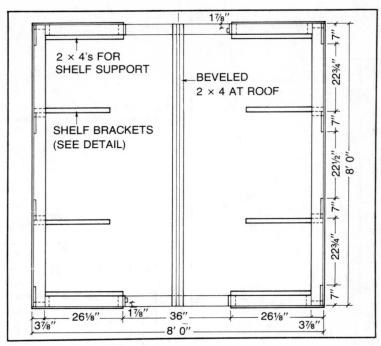

Fig. 6-16. An alternate 8' × 8' plan

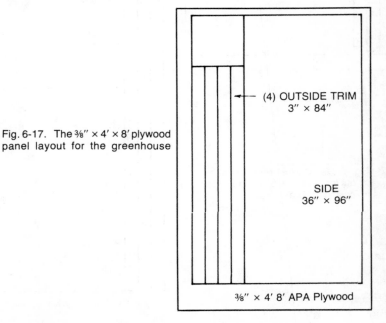

Fig. 6-17. The ⅜" × 4' × 8' plywood panel layout for the greenhouse

(4) OUTSIDE TRIM
3" × 84"

SIDE
36" × 96"

⅜" × 4' 8' APA Plywood

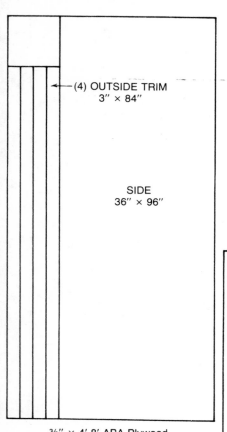

(4) OUTSIDE TRIM
3″ × 84″

SIDE
36″ × 96″

⅜″ × 4′ 8′ APA Plywood

Fig. 6-18. The ⅜″ × 4′ × 8′ plywood panel layout for the greenhouse

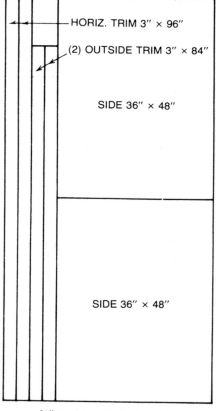

HORIZ. TRIM 3″ × 96″

(2) OUTSIDE TRIM 3″ × 84″

SIDE 36″ × 48″

SIDE 36″ × 48″

⅜″ × 4′ × 8′ APA Plywood

Fig. 6-19. Another required panel layout for ⅜″ × 4′ × 8′ plywood used in making the greenhouse

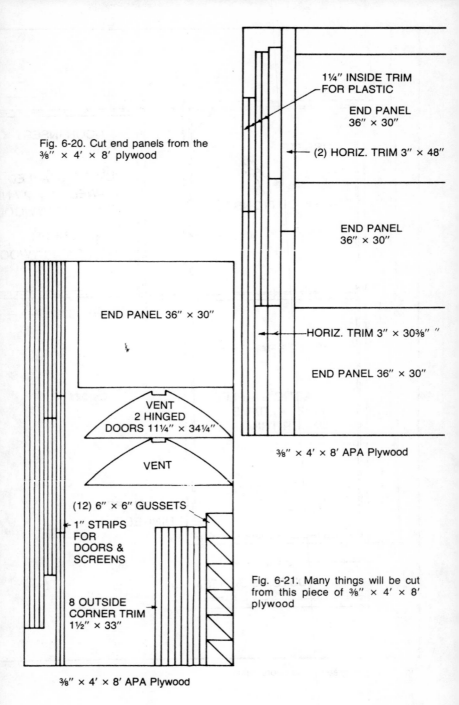

Fig. 6-20. Cut end panels from the ⅜″ × 4′ × 8′ plywood

1¼″ INSIDE TRIM FOR PLASTIC

END PANEL 36″ × 30″

(2) HORIZ. TRIM 3″ × 48″

END PANEL 36″ × 30″

HORIZ. TRIM 3″ × 30⅜″ ″

END PANEL 36″ × 30″

⅜″ × 4′ × 8′ APA Plywood

END PANEL 36″ × 30″

VENT
2 HINGED
DOORS 11¼″ × 34¼″

VENT

(12) 6″ × 6″ GUSSETS

1″ STRIPS
FOR
DOORS &
SCREENS

8 OUTSIDE
CORNER TRIM
1½″ × 33″

Fig. 6-21. Many things will be cut from this piece of ⅜″ × 4′ × 8′ plywood

⅜″ × 4′ × 8′ APA Plywood

183

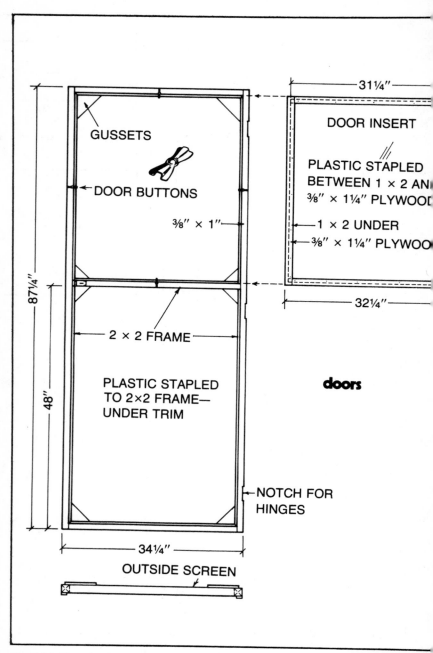

Fig. 6-24. The greenhouse doors detail.

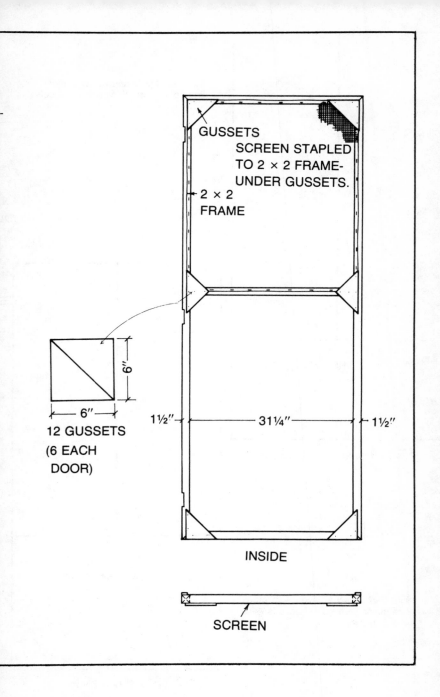

GUSSETS

SCREEN STAPLED TO 2 × 2 FRAME- UNDER GUSSETS.

2 × 2 FRAME

6″

6″

12 GUSSETS (6 EACH DOOR)

1½″ — 31¼″ — 1½″

INSIDE

SCREEN

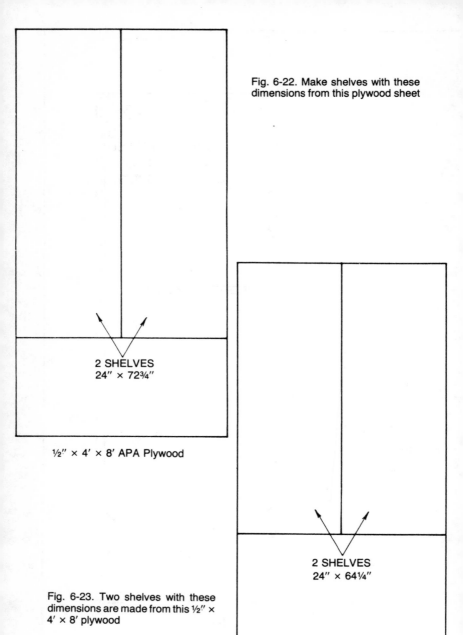

Fig. 6-22. Make shelves with these dimensions from this plywood sheet

2 SHELVES
24″ × 72¾″

½″ × 4′ × 8′ APA Plywood

2 SHELVES
24″ × 64¼″

Fig. 6-23. Two shelves with these dimensions are made from this ½″ × 4′ × 8′ plywood

½″ × 8′ APA Plywood

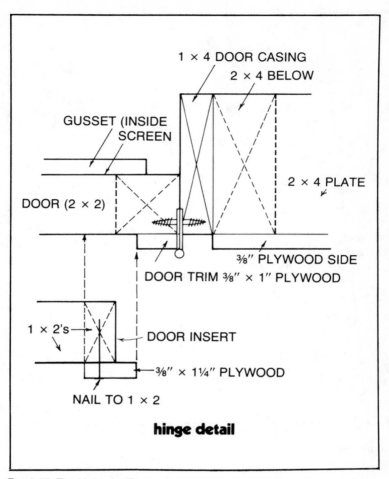

Fig. 6-25. The hinge detail

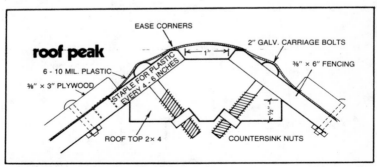

Fig. 6-26. The greenhouse roof peak

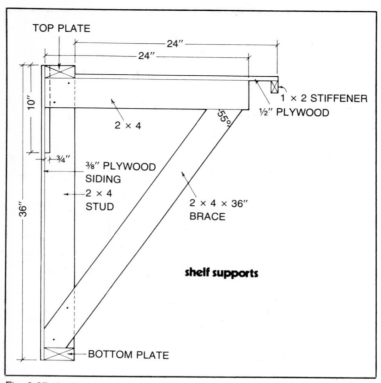

Fig. 6-27. Shelf supports are made in this manner

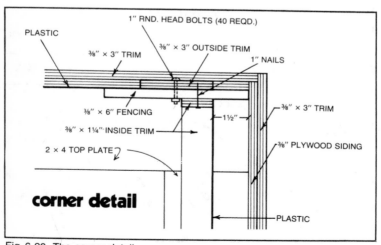

Fig. 6-28. The corner detail

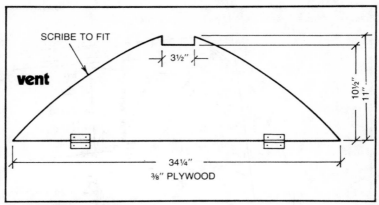

Fig. 6-29. The greenhouse vent

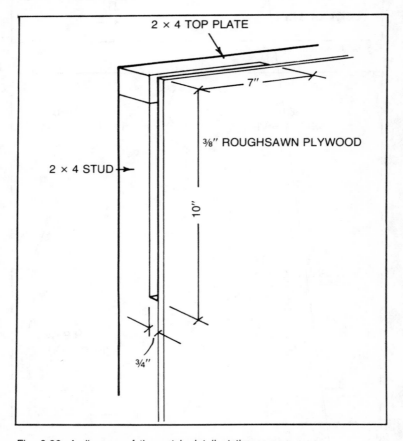

Fig. 6-30. A diagram of the notch detail at the corner

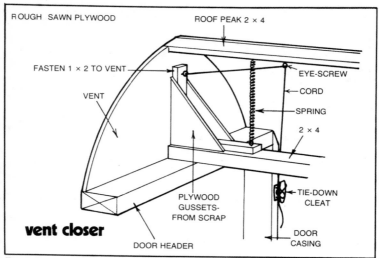

Fig. 6-31. Another vent detail

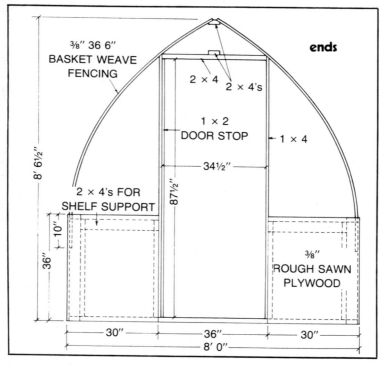

Fig. 6-32. Make sure that dimensions are correct

190

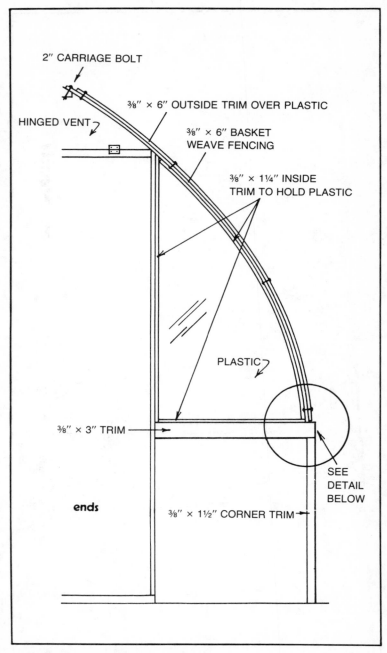

Fig. 6-33. Fasten the ends in this manner

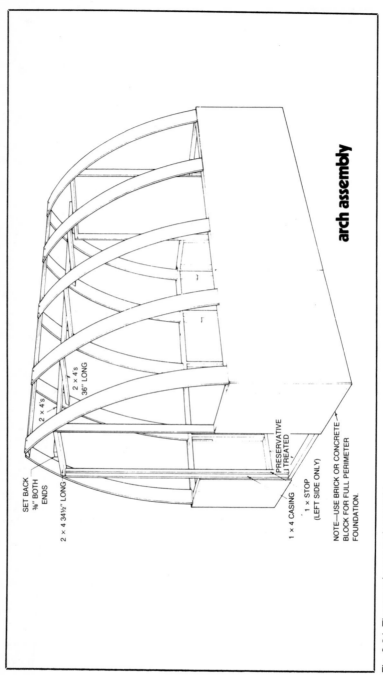

SET BACK
³⁄₈" BOTH
ENDS

2 × 4s

2 × 4s
36" LONG

2 × 4 34½" LONG

PRESERVATIVE
TREATED

1 × 4 CASING

1 × STOP
(LEFT SIDE ONLY)

NOTE—USE BRICK OR CONCRETE
BLOCK FOR FULL PERIMETER
FOUNDATION.

arch assembly

Fig. 6-34. The greenhouse arch assembly.

You've got all those tools for yard care and for working the greenhouse you built last month. Where can you store them? The American Plywood Association has your solution. This 8' × 8" garden storage building is simple to build (Fig. 6-35). It should fit in well with any style home.

Refer to Fig. 6-36 for materials. Use Fig. 6-37 when cutting pieces for the shed. Figure 6-38 illustrates a plan view and floor framing. Figure 6-39 shows the roof and roof framing. Figure 6-40 details the back, front and ends. And Fig. 6-41 diagrams the door, ramp, shelves, counter and rafters.

Cut 2 × 4 floor framing members so that floor framing, when assembled, will measure exactly 6' × 8" in width and length, outside to outside. Use 16d common nails and assemble on any reasonably level surface. Set 4 × 4 treated skids in place and check to see that they are level. Toe-nail the floor framing to skids through floor joists. Cut the plywood floor panels to size and nail to all supports with 8d galvanized box nails 12" off center. Cut the studs and top and bottom plates. Tilt walls into place and fasten with 8d nails through the bottom plate into the outside floor framing under the plywood. Check with a carpenter's level to be sure framing is plumb. Nail through studs to fasten framing at each corner.

Apply plywood siding with 6d cement-coated or galvanized nails, spacing nails 6" apart along panel edges and 12" apart into other studs. Cut 2 × 2 rafters to fit ridge and fascia boards. Notch the rafters to fit over plates and toe-nail with 8d nails into plate and ridge board. Cut the fascia board to length and nail it to the ends of rafters. Fasten roof sheathing with 6d common nails to the framing at 6" spacing at panel edges and 12" spacing elsewhere. Apply 1 × 2 fascia and then install built-up or 90-lb. roll roofing over the plywood.

Construct the door by fastening cut-to-length 1 × 6 stock lumber frame with 6d finish nails and glue to plywood siding previously cut to door size. Nail and glue 1 × 6 lumber and ⅜" plywood to 1 × 6 frame on the door to form fronts on shelves. Apply hinges and hang the door. Install a key-lock with hold-open latch. Cut and assemble plywood shelves and counter

Fig. 6-35. This shed stores everything from a lawnmower to flower pots

MATERIALS LIST

Recommended plywood:

303® textured plywood siding, and A-C Exterior APA® grade-trademarked plywood

PLYWOOD

Quantity	Description
4 panels	3/8 in. x 4 ft x 8 ft A-C plywood for roof sheathing
2 panels	3/4 in. x 4 ft x 8 ft A-C plywood for floor and counter
9 panels	5/8 in. textured plywood siding for door, walls, siding, and ramp

OTHER MATERIALS

Quantity	Description
184 lin. ft	2x2 lumber for wall studs, counter framing, top and bottom plates (based on 8 ft lengths)
3 pieces	2x2 lumber 12 ft long for roof framing
7 pieces	2x2 lumber 10 ft long for roof rafters
2 pieces	4x4 lumber 8 ft long for skids (if two 6 ft lengths are available, use those)
152 lin. ft	1x2 lumber for fascias, and battens at 2 ft spacing
8 lin. ft	1x4 lumber for shelf fronts
5 pieces	1x6 lumber 8 ft long for door shelves and framing (if 6 ft lengths are available, use those)
3	3-1/2 in. x 3-1/2 in. fast-pin zinc-coated hinges for door
1	Key lock and latch
1-1/3 squares	Asphalt or cedar shingles or cedar shakes or built-up or 90-lb roofing as selected
As required	8d common nails for roof, wall, and door framing
As required	5d, 6d, and 8d galvanized or cement-coated nails for siding and floor
As required	Paint or stain for finishing

Fig. 6-36. Use these materials to make the garden storage shed

CUTTING DIAGRAM—APA EXTERIOR PLYWOOD

ENDS
(MAKE 2)

3/4"

1 1/2"

7'—0"

7'—5 1/2"

— 3'—3/8" —

3/8" PLYWOOD

ENDS
(MAKD 2)

— 3"—3/8" —

3/8" PLYWOOD

BACK

2'—0" — 2'—0"

1/2"

1 1/2"

3/4"

7'—0"

4'—0"

3/8" PLYWOOD

BACK

1"

7'—0"

4'—0"

3/8" PLYWOOD

Fig. 6-37. Cutting diagrams for the shed

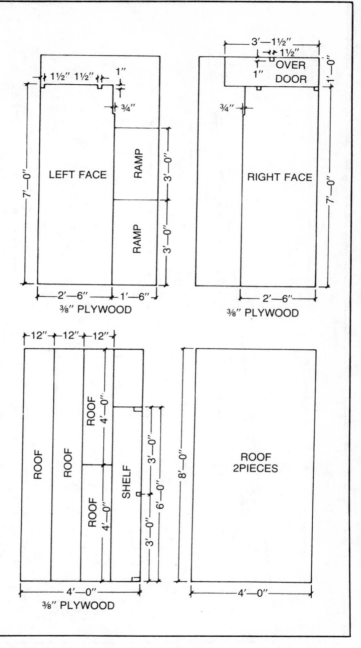

Fig. 6-37. Cutting diagrams for the shed Continued.

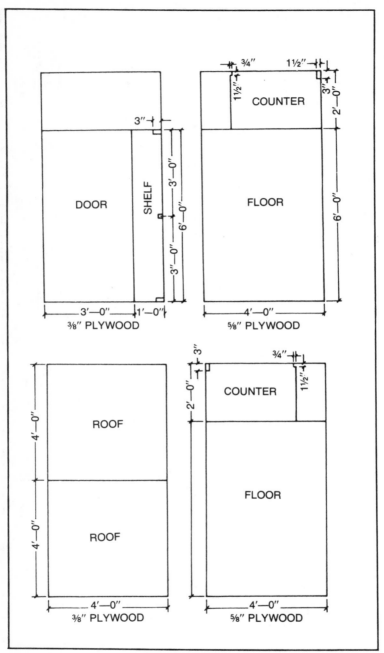

Fig. 6-37. Cutting diagrams for the shed Continued.

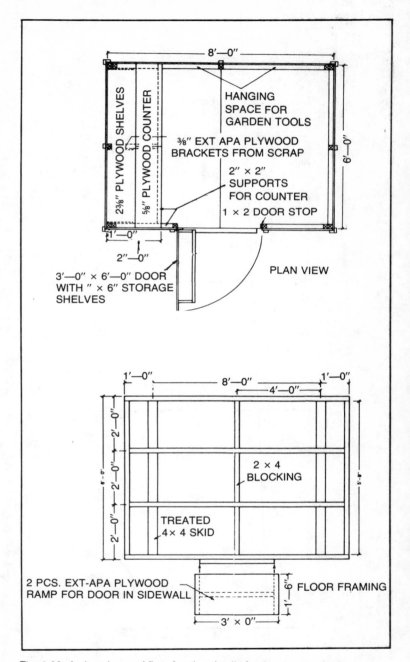

Fig. 6-38. A plan view and floor framing details for the storage shed

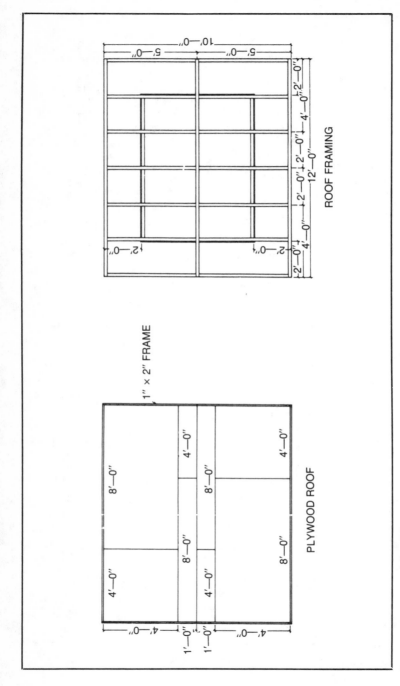

Fig. 6-39. Here are roof dimensions

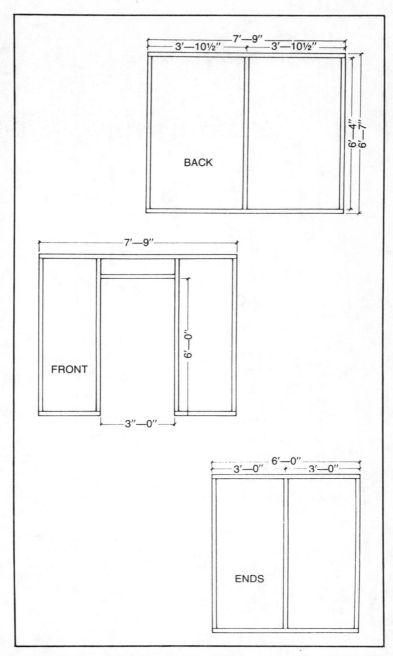

Fig. 6-40. Plans for the shed's back, front and ends

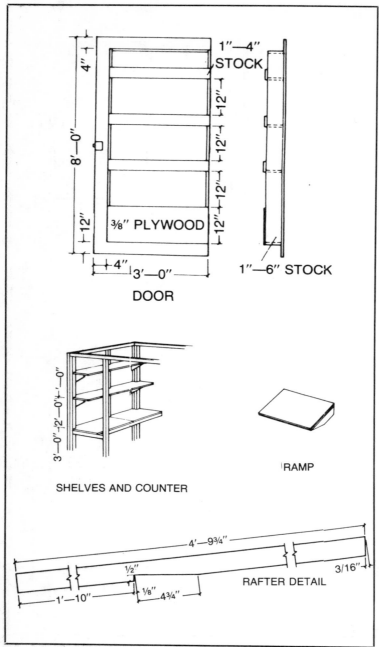

Fig. 6-41. Diagrams of the shed's rafters, shelves and counter, door and ramp

along with plywood brackets and 2×4 supports. Install with 8d common nails or wood screws. Cut and assemble plywood for the ramp to door opening. Use a quality exterior house paint or stain on your new structure.

Are you tired of people peering over your shoulder as you try to grill a hamburger? Teco provides the answer with their louvered fence and deckplans (Figs. 6-42, 6-43 and 6-44). Various portions lend themselves to the use of plywood, from seats to fencing, while I would suggest that you consider using treated wood posts instead of concrete post anchors where building codes allow. Wolmanized copper arsenate treated posts have been tested in the ground in many areas for over 35 years and have yet to show signs of deterioration. In starting a project of this size, move carefully from these general plans to a complete set of your own drawings (on graph paper), and make a check of building codes locally, as well as seeing if a building permit is required.

Elevate the deck and anchor posts as shown in Figs. 6-45 and 6-46. Make the joist-to-beam connection as shown in Fig. 6-47. Attach railings as illustrated in Fig. 6-48. Refer to Figs. 6-49 and Figs. 6-50 when building the stairs. If you want deck accessories, consult Figs. 6-51, 6-52 and 6-53.

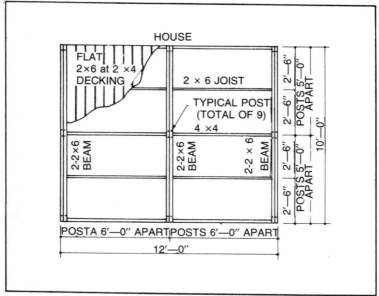

Fig. 6-42. The wood deck plan (courtesy Teco).

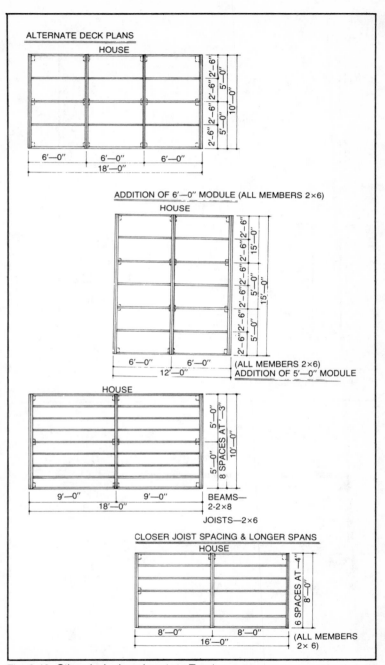

Fig. 6-43. Other deck plans (courtesy Teco).

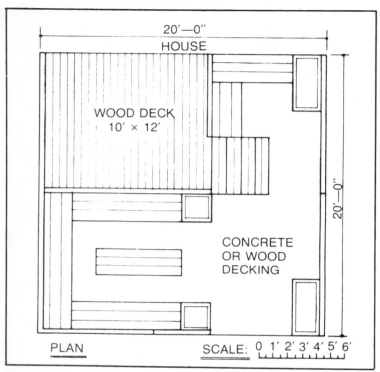

Fig. 6-44. A wood decking diagram (courtesy Teco).

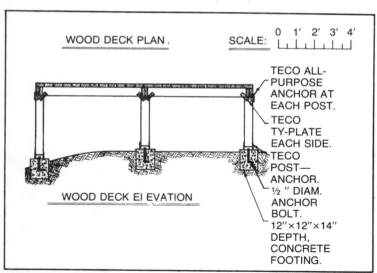

Fig. 6-45. The wood deck elevation guide (courtesy Teco).

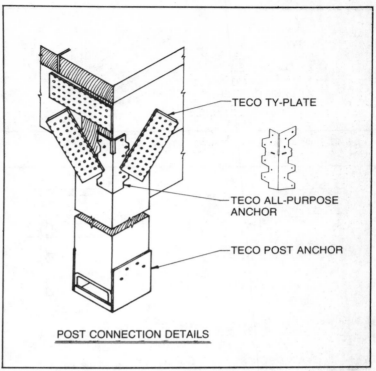

Fig. 6-46. Post connection details (courtesy Teco).

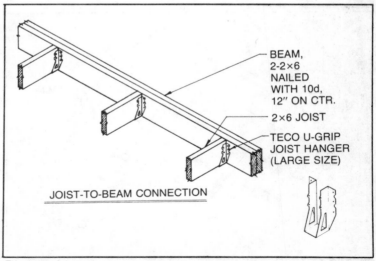

Fig. 6-47. Joist-to-beam connection hints (courtesy Teco).

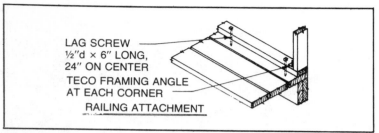

Fig. 6-48. Railing attachment tips (courtesy Teco).

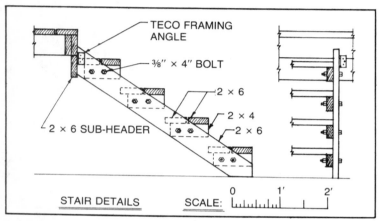

Fig. 6-49. The stair plan (courtesy Teco).

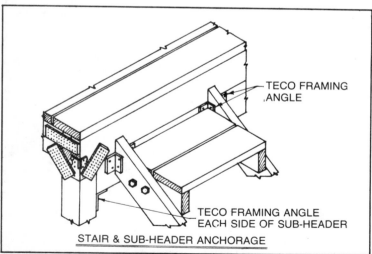

Fig. 6-50. Stairs must be firmly in place (courtesy Teco).

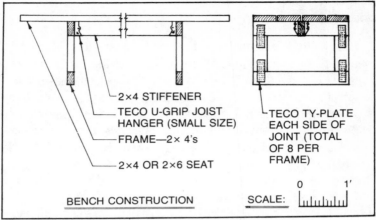

Fig. 6-51. Bench building instructions (courtesy Teco).

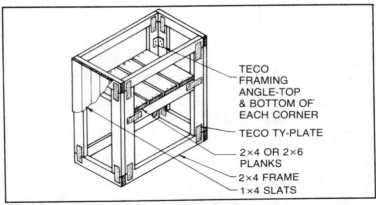

Fig. 6-52. The louvered fence and rail details (courtesy Teco).

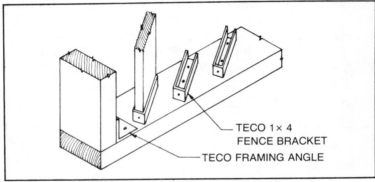

Fig. 6-53. The planter box detail (courtesy Teco).

Probably the simplest of the included projects, this bird house design is suitable for many of the smaller birds, and is complete enough that all you really need to do is cut, assemble and finish. Most parts can be made from lumber scraps picked up at any lumberyard. I would make one further suggestion. When cutting the entrance hole, if it is larger than the house wren size (⅞"), I would use a hole saw instead of a drill.

From ⅜" plywood, cut two pieces 7-15/16" × 7-15/16". These pieces are the front and back, parts F and F-1 (see Figs. 6-54 and 6-55). Drill entrance holes to accommodate the type of bird desired. For bewick wrens, Carolina wrens and chickadees, make the hole 1⅛" in diameter. For the white-breasted nuthatch, drill the hole 1-¼" in diameter. Make the hole 1-½" in diameter for bluebirds and swallows. From ⅜" plywood cut two pieces 7-15/16" × 7-15/16". These will be parts B and B-1, the bottom sides. Cut from ⅜" plywood, 1 top 10-½" × 7-15/16", part T-1. From ¾" wood scrap cut four pieces 6-3/16" × ¾ × ¾" wood strips, or purchase ¾" × ¾" material and cut into lengths.

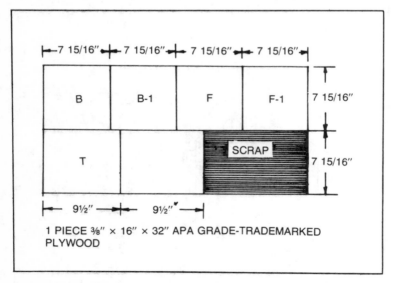

Fig. 6-54. The bird house cutting diagram

CUTTING

1. From 3/8" plywood, cut 2 pieces 7-15/16" x 7-15/16". These pieces are the front and back. Parts F and F-1. See cutting diagram.

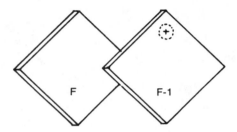

2. Drill entrance hole to accommodate type of bird desired:

House Wren	7/8" dia.
Bewick Wren Carolina Wren Chickadee	1-1/8" dia.
Tufted Titmouse White Breasted Nuthatch	1-1/4" dia.
Bluebird Swallow	1-1/2" dia.

3. From 3/8" plywood cut 2 pieces 7-15/16" x 7-15/16". These will be parts B and B-1 (the bottom sides).

4. Cut from 3/8" plywood, 1 top 9-1/2" x 7-15/16", part T-1.

5. Cut from 3/8" plywood, 1 top 10-1/2" x 7-15/16", part T-1.

6. From 3/4" wood scrap cut 4 pieces 6-3/16" x 3/4" x 3/4" wood strips, or purchase 3/4" x 3/4" material and cut into lengths.

Fig. 6-55. The bird house's front and back

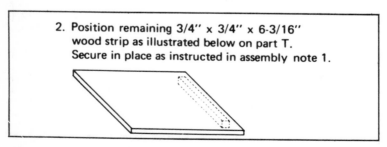

ASSEMBLY

1. Fasten 3/4" x 3/4" x 6-3/16" wood strips to parts B and B-1.
   Note: Set flush with the edge as illustrated below.

⅝" 1⅛" ⅝" 1⅛"

B-1

B

⅝" 1⅛"

Nail and glue wood strips and let glue set up. (Use 1" box nails, galvanized if possible, and white glue).

Fig. 6-56. Fasten wood strips are shown

Fasten ¾" × ¾" × 6-3/16" wood strips to parts B and B-1. Set flush with the edge (Fig. 6-56). Nail and glue wood strips and let the glue set up. Position the remaining ¾" × ¾" × 6-3/16" wood strip as shown on part T (Fig. 6-57). Nail/ glue part B-1 to part B (Fig. 6-58). Next fasten front and back parts F and F-1 to parts B and B-1 with ¾" wood screws (Fig. 6-59). Now fasten top T in place (Fig. 6-60). Fasten top piece T-1 with glue and nails, nailing through T-1 into ¾" × ¾" wood strips attached to top T and bottom B-1 (Fig. 6-61).

2. Position remaining 3/4" x 3/4" x 6-3/16" wood strip as illustrated below on part T.
   Secure in place as instructed in assembly note 1.

Fig. 6-57. Position this wood strip as shown

212

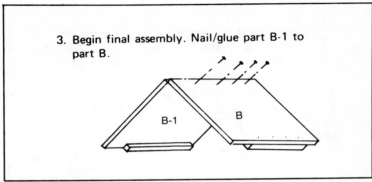

Fig. 6-58. Nail/glue parts B-1 to part B

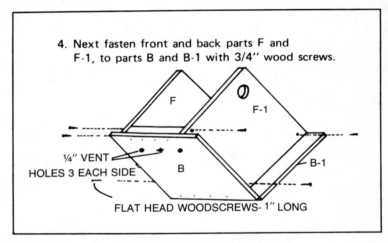

Fig. 6-59. Use wood screws to attach these bird house parts

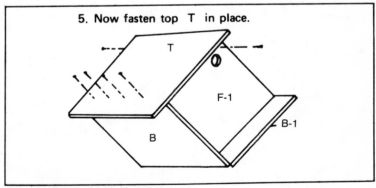

Fig. 6-60. Fasten the bird house top

6. Fasten top piece T-1 with glue and nails, nailing through T-1 into 3/4" x 3/4" wood strips attached to top T and bottom B-1.

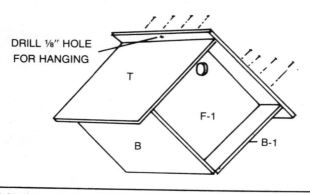

DRILL ⅛" HOLE
FOR HANGING

T

F-1

B

B-1

Fig. 6-61. Assemble the bird house parts in this manner

I really like this one, and will spend a large part of my weekend working some up for my basement. If you are a book nut, the need for new shelves is constant and a real pain, for commercially built wood shelves are extremely costly. This design is quickly built and need not be attached to a wall, a feature that will be extremely handy in my case (Fig. 6-62).

Refer to Fig. 6-63 for materials. Side and front views are depicted in Figs. 6-64 and 6-65. Draw parts on plywood. Draw on the best side of the panel if you'll be using a handsaw or table or radial saw. For portable power saws, draw on the back side of the panel. Cut out parts (Fig. 6-66). Cut upright supports 6' long and shelf supports 18" long. Glue-nail plywood gussets to shelf supports, then to upright supports

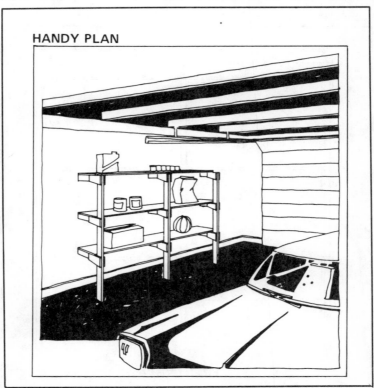

Fig. 6-62. These shelves provide lots of storage space

MATERIALS LIST

Recommended plywood:
A-C Exterior or A-D Interior APA grade-trademarked plywood

PLYWOOD

Quantity	Description
1 panel	3/4 in. x 4 ft x 8 ft plywood

OTHER MATERIALS

Quantity	Description
44 lin. ft	2 x 4 lumber for supports
1 lb (approx)	6d common nails
As required	White glue for glue-nail assembly of supports

Fig. 6-63. Materials for building the shelves

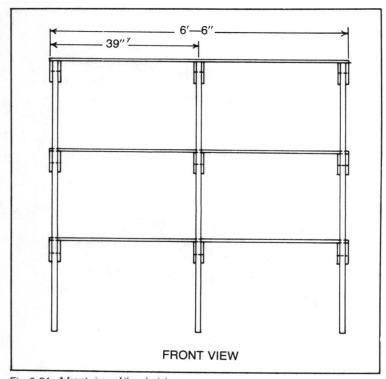

FRONT VIEW

Fig. 6-64. A front view of the shelving

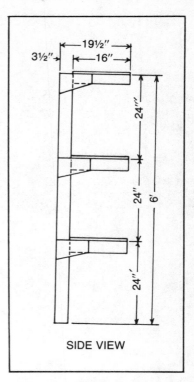

Fig. 6-65. A side view of the shelving

SIDE VIEW

(Fig. 6-67). To glue-nail, apply glue to supports and then nail the plywood in place. Install the shelves. You can either glue-nail them to the supports or use 1-½" or 2" flathead wood screws instead.

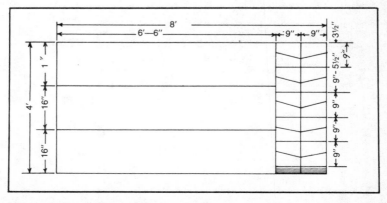

Fig. 6-66. The cutting diagram for the shelves

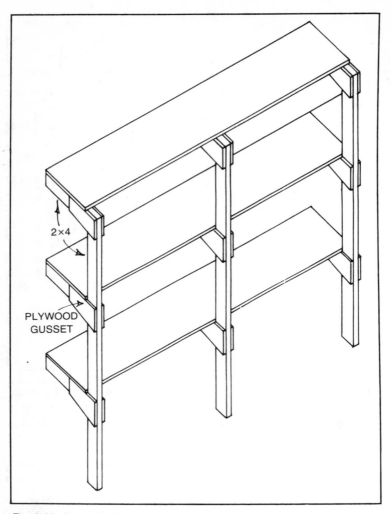

Fig. 6-67. Assemble the shelves in this manner

Dogs may be man's best friends, but anyone who has ever had trash and garbage strewn all over the yard will complain a lot about the evils of hounds. This trash can bin design is built with no more than a handsaw, hammer and a screwdriver (Fig. 6-68). It will discourage even the hungriest canine. Figures 6-69 and 6-70 give materials and plywood parts.

If you're building the bin into an existing fence, adapt dimensions as necessary. If you prefer to build the bin as a separate unit, plan to omit notches at the top rear corners of the side panels, and build a rear perimeter frame of 2 × 4s. For hand or power sawing with radial or table saw, draw parts on the plywood's best side. For a portable power saw or sabre saw, draw on the panel's back side. Cut out the parts and

Fig. 6-68. Keep dogs from making a mess with your trash

```
MATERIALS LIST
Recommended plywood:
Any 303® textured plywood siding or A-C Exterior APA® grade-trademarked
plywood

PLYWOOD
Quantity                          Description
1 panel        ¾ in. (A-C Exterior) or ⅝ in. (303 siding) × 4 ft × 8 ft plywood

OTHER MATERIALS
Quantity Description                              Description
4 lin. ft      2 × 4 lumber for back framing if building into an existing fence
OR
11 lin. ft     2 × 4 lumber for back framing if building freestanding
4 lin. ft      2 × 2 blocking for base
1 pair         Rust-proof hinges (galvanized, brass, bronze, or prime-coated
               steel) to fit ¾ in. plywood lid
As required    8d nonstaining common nails for assembling frame, and 6d
               nonstaining finish nails for glue-nail assembly (see Building Hints)
As required    Water proof glue for glue-nail assembly
As required    Wood dough or filler for filling countersunk nail holes (in
               sanded plywood only), and any small gaps in plywood cut edges
As required    Fine sandpaper for smoothing plywood cut edges and filler.
               Coarse sandpaper for truing parts if necessary
As required    Primer and paint for finishing sanded plywood. Sealer and
               semitransparent or opaque stain for finishing textured plywood siding
As required    Bricks for base
```

Fig. 6-69. Materials required to build the trash can bin

check them for fit (Fig. 6-71). True up joining edges with a block faced with coarse sandpaper. Figures 6-72 and 6-73 show front elevation and a section view, respectively.

Fasten the plywood bottom to rear 2 × 4 and glue and nail 2 × 2 plywood blocking along side edges of the bottom. Line up side panels square and flush with bottom panel and glue and nail in place. Also, glue and nail sides to side framing if the unit is freestanding. Glue and nail on the three front louvers. Glue

Code	No. Req'd.	Size	Part Identification
A	2	24"x33-5/8"	Side
B	3	11" x 24"	Front louver Pieces
C	1	21"x22-1/2"	Bottom
D	1	19" x 24"	Lid
E	1	4-1/2"x24"	Hinge Support

Fig. 6-70. You'll need these plywood parts

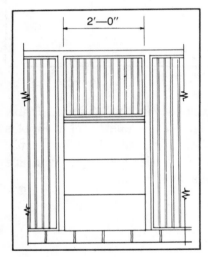

Fig. 6-71. Cutting diagrams for the trash can bin

A	A
B	B
B	D
C	
	E

4'-0" × 8'-0" APA Plywood

2'—0"

Fig. 6-72. Front elevation of the trash can bin

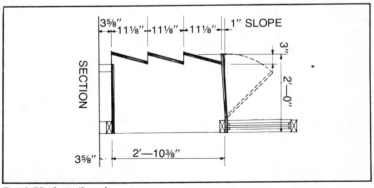

SECTION

3⅝"
11⅛" 11⅛" 11⅛" 1" SLOPE
3"
2'—0"
2'—10⅜"
3⅝"

Fig. 6-73. A section view

221

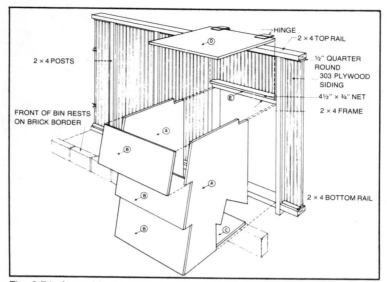

Fig. 6-74. Assemble the trash can bin pieces as shown

and nail the hinge support panel to the 2 × 4 framing. Install hinges and attach the lid (Fig. 6-74). Countersink nail holes and fill if the plywood is smooth surfaced. Also fill any small gaps in cut plywood edges. Sand filler and edges with fine sandpaper, then prime or seal and finish.

How many of us have gotten the charcoal almost to the ready-to-cook stage and then watched rain clouds slide over to dampen our efforts? Just about everyone who has ever cooked out, I would imagine. This 8′ × 12′ patio shelter will end your worries on that score (Fig. 6-75). It can be completed in two weekends. Figure 6-76 lists needed materials. Figures 6-77 and 6-78 offer plan and side views.

If the roof does not have an overhang, you may nail a 2 × 6 ledger to the house and use joist hangers (Fig. 6-79). Otherwise remove fascia from save edge over the patio to determine roof joist placement. Using chalk line or string, lay out shelter on the existing patio, lining up the edge of a joist with the edge of each 4 × 4 support post. Install post anchors, either chipping away and replacing existing concrete, or using a concrete pier block placed beneath the surface or brick or sand patio or wood deck. Build composite beam and install on

Fig. 6-75. Even with rainy weather, the cookout can keep going with this easily built patio shelter

223

```
MATERIALS LIST

Recommended plywood:
For the roof: C-D Interior with exterior glue or C-C Exterior, APA grade-trademarked
For the wings: Any pattern 303 textured plywood siding, APA grade-trademarked

PLYWOOD
Quantity          Description
3 panels          ⅝ in. × 4 ft × 8 ft roof sheathing plywood
4 panels          ⅝ in. × 4 ft × 8 ft T 1-11 or 303 Siding

OTHER MATERIALS LS
Quantity          Description
1                 2 × 6, 12 ft long for shelter fascia
                          OR
8                 2 × 6, 10 ft long for joists (scab installation)
                          OR
                  8 ft long for joists (hanger installation)
                  SEE NOTES ON CONSTRUCTION
1                 2 × 8, 12 ft long for composite beam
2                 2 × 4, 12 ft long for composite beam
5                 2 × 4, 8 ft long for wing caps
3                 2 × 2, 8 ft long for wing inner framing
2                 4 × 4, 8 ft long for posts
2                 Post anchors for 4 × 4's
4                 Post anchors for 2 × 4's
96 sq ft          Roofing material
28 ft             Aluminum drip edge
As required       8d, 10d, and 16d galvanized nails for framing and beam construction
As required       6d nonstaining finish nails for installing plywood siding
As required       Stain, either semitransparent or heavy-bodied opaque, for finishing
```

Fig. 6-76. Materials for building the patio shelter

posts in post anchors. Tie a beam to the posts with 16d nails
(Fig. 6-80). Brace upright temporarily until roof joists are in
place. Build wings (Fig. 6-81). Nail a 2 × 2 along the center line
of the 2 × 4 top cap. Nail plywood siding to the 2 × 2. Nail
another 2 × 2 between the bottom edges of the plywood. Nail
2 × 2 blocks to 4 × 4 posts and end caps.

Slide plywood "sandwich" over nailing blocks on the post
and secure. Insert 2 × 4 end cap into post anchor and fit nailing
blocks into the "sandwich." Secure plywood to end cap. Install
roof sheathing, spacing 8d galvanized nails apart. Install fascia,
2 × 6 roofing, and drip edge. Replace house fascia with
existing material cut to fit and toenail to joists. Finish the
shelter with top quality materials.

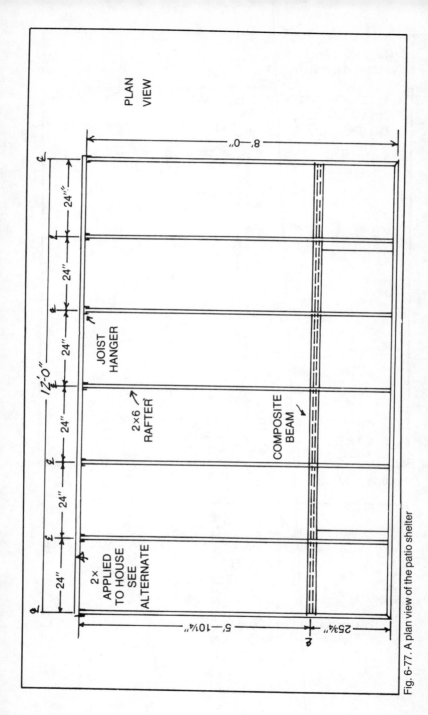

PLAN VIEW

8'-0"

12'-0"

24" 24" 24" 24" 24" 24"

JOIST HANGER

2×6 RAFTER

COMPOSITE BEAM

2× APPLIED TO HOUSE SEE ALTERNATE

5'-10¼"

25¾"

Fig. 6-77. A plan view of the patio shelter

225

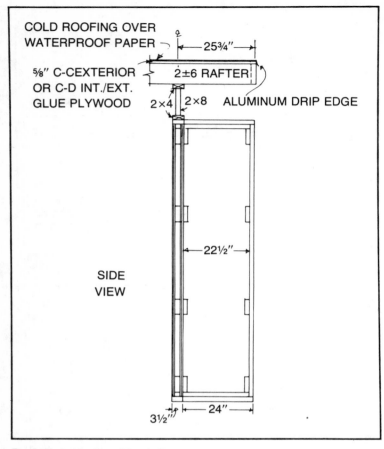

COLD ROOFING OVER
WATERPROOF PAPER

25¾"

⅝" C-CEXTERIOR
OR C-D INT./EXT.
GLUE PLYWOOD

2±6 RAFTER

2×4 | 2×8 ALUMINUM DRIP EDGE

22½"

SIDE
VIEW

3½" 24"

Fig. 6-78. A side view of the shelter

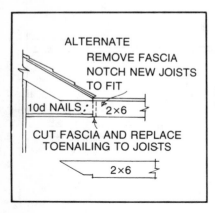

ALTERNATE
REMOVE FASCIA
NOTCH NEW JOISTS
TO FIT

10d NAILS ∴ 2×6

CUT FASCIA AND REPLACE
TOENAILING TO JOISTS

2×6

Fig. 6-79. An alternate method of
construction

226

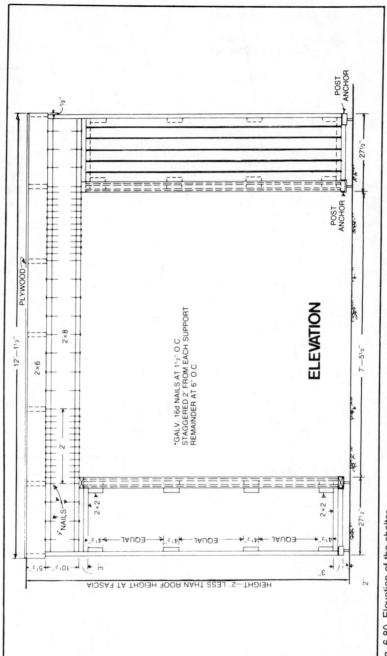

ELEVATION

Fig. 6-80. Elevation of the shelter

227

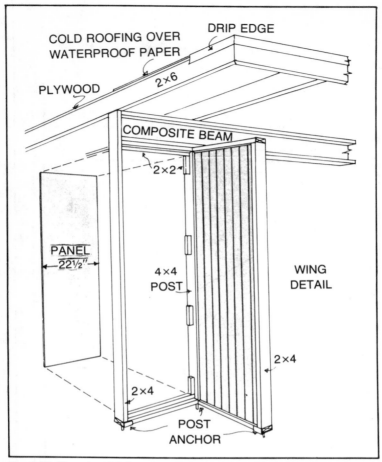

COLD ROOFING OVER
WATERPROOF PAPER

DRIP EDGE

PLYWOOD

2×6

COMPOSITE BEAM

2×2

PANEL
22½"

4×4
POST

WING
DETAIL

2×4

2×4

POST
ANCHOR

Fig. 6-81. The wing detail

228

Stanley calls this the "anything" chest. Who can argue? The interior size is 34½″ × 16½″, enough to hold numerous items. Included are plans for an interior bottle rack and for a tray which would add to the ease of turning this chest into a tool box or tack box. Figure 6-82 covers materials needed for making the chest, tray, bottle rack and whale mascot. Study Figs. 6-83 and 6-84. The chest is a simple rectangular box made of four pieces of 1″ × 12″ stock jointed with butt joints

MATERIALS YOU'LL NEED:

For the basic chest:
1. 10′ of 1″ × 12″ pine
2. 10′ of 2″ or 2½″ molding
3. 14′ of 1⅜″ corner molding
4. 10′ of 5/4″ × pine
5. 14′ of 1″ × 1″ stock
6. 1 piece ½″ plywood 16½″ × 34½″ for bottom of chest
7. 1 piece ½″ plywood 19″ × 37″ for chest lid
8. 1 piece 1/10″ acrylic plastic (Plexiglas) 19″ × 37″
9. Two chest hinges (Stanley No. 838)
10. Rope for handles or metal handles
11. 12 No. 8 flathead wood screws ¼″ long
12. Box of 1″ long brads
13. 1 pound 6d finishing nails
14. Wood glue
15. Spackle or plastic wood
16. Sandpaper

Materials for tray:
1. 10′ of ½″ × 3″ pine
2. One piece acrylic plastic
(Plexiglas) 1/10″ thick 16½″ × 19″ for bottom (or ⅜″ plywood)

Materials for bottle rack:
1. 8″ of 1″ × 4″ pine
2. 10′ of ¼″ diameter wood dowel

Materials for whale mascot:
1. 12″ long piece of 1″ × 4″ pine

If you want to go first class, use clear pine for the 1″ × 12″ stock on the basic chest. But if you are going to paint the chest, save about 60% by using No. 2 pine. Just be sure to pick out the piece yourself so you'll know that the board is straight and all knots are firm.

Fig. 6-82. Materials needed for the "anything chest"

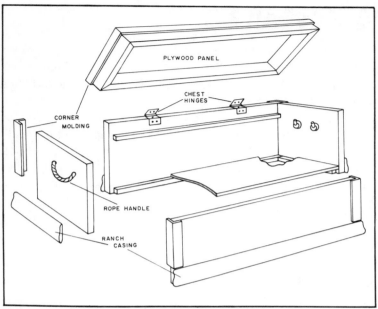

Fig. 6-83. Parts of the chest (courtesy Stanley Tools).

which are eventually concealed with corner molder. The bottom of the chest is supported by 1″ × 1″ rails and there is another set of rails higher up on the side pieces to support the tray. The frame of the lid is made of 5/4″ × 3″ stock so that when it is closed, the top edges of the corner molding will be covered. A sheet of ½″ plywood is nailed to the frame of the lid to provide a solid base for the plastic lid cover.

Out of the piece of 1″ × 12″ stock, cut the two end pieces 16½″ long and two side pieces 36″ long. Double-check your measurements. Cut four pieces of the 1″ × 1″ stock 34½″ long. Nail and glue a strip along the bottom of each of the side pieces so they will be flush at the bottom and ¾″ from each end. Nail the other set of 1″ × 1″ strips to the sides 4″ down from the top edge as supports for the tray. Cut a piece of ½″ plywood for the chest's bottom. Assemble with glue and 6d nails one end piece and the two side pieces. Slip the plywood bottom into place and secure it to the rails with 6d nails. Add the other end piece.

The next move is to add the 2″ or 2½″ molding and this takes miter cuts. Tack a strip of molding into place and then

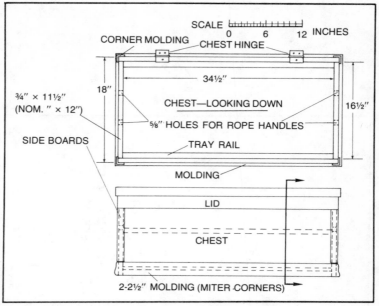

Fig. 6-84. A diagram of the chest (courtesy Stanley Tools).

mark the exact location of the cut. Use your miter box and back saw for these cuts. Fasten the strips of molding in place with 6d nails. Use a miter clamp to hold the pieces together while nailing. Tack the corner molding in place with 1″ brads.

Figure 6-85 gives you the lid in its relationship to the chest. Figure 6-86 shows the detail of the lid looking up and looking down at it, as well as a section detail. Figure 6-87 shows the hinge detail. It helps if you think of the lid as a picture frame. The basic frame is made out of the 5/4″ × 3″

Fig. 6-85. A section view of the chest (courtesy Stanley Tools).

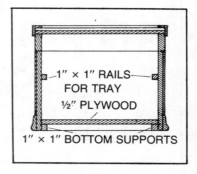

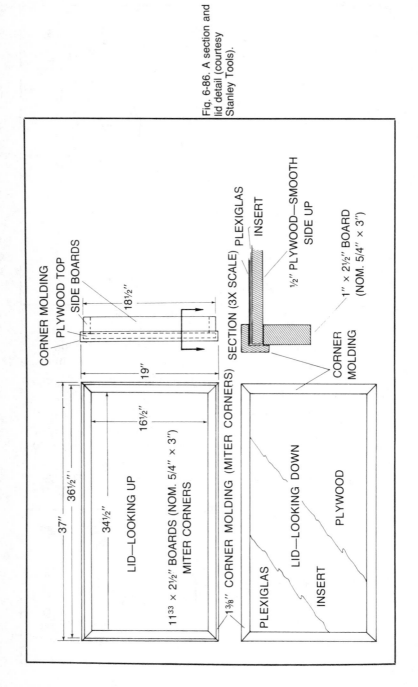

Fig. 6-86. A section and lid detail (courtesy Stanley Tools).

CORNER MOLDING
PLYWOOD TOP
SIDE BOARDS

18½"

SECTION (3X SCALE) PLEXIGLAS

INSERT

½" PLYWOOD—SMOOTH SIDE UP

1" × 2½" BOARD (NOM. 5/4" × 3")

CORNER MOLDING

19"

16½"

37"

36½"

34½"

LID—LOOKING UP

11³³ × 2½" BOARDS (NOM. 5/4" × 3") MITER CORNERS

1⅜" CORNER MOLDING (MITER CORNERS)

CORNER MOLDING (MITER CORNERS)

PLEXIGLAS

LID—LOOKING DOWN

PLYWOOD

INSERT

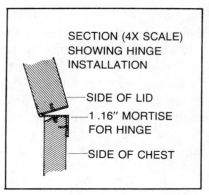

Fig. 6-87. Hinge the lid to the chest (courtesy Stanley Tools).

SECTION (4X SCALE)
SHOWING HINGE
INSTALLATION

—SIDE OF LID

—1.16" MORTISE
FOR HINGE

—SIDE OF CHEST

stock with miter corners. A piece of ½" plywood is placed on the frame and secured, and over this goes the "picture." The sheet of plastic is applied over the insert and held in place by the corner molding. Your decorative insert must be applied over the plywood before you put on the plastic or corner molding.

Make up the basic frame of the lid. These pieces need miter cuts and the over-all dimension of the side pieces is 37" and the end pieces 19". Use your miter box to make the cuts and your miter clamp to hold the pieces together as you secure them with the 6d nails and wood glue. Cover the frame with a

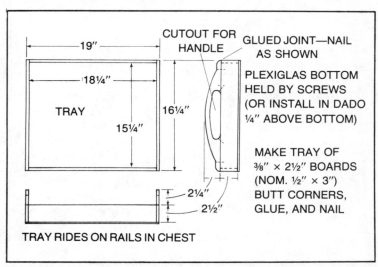

CUTOUT FOR HANDLE

19"

18¼"

TRAY

16¼"

15¼"

GLUED JOINT—NAIL AS SHOWN

PLEXIGLAS BOTTOM HELD BY SCREWS (OR INSTALL IN DADO ¼" ABOVE BOTTOM)

MAKE TRAY OF ⅜" × 2½" BOARDS (NOM. ½" × 3") BUTT CORNERS, GLUE, AND NAIL

2¼"

2½"

TRAY RIDES ON RAILS IN CHEST

Fig. 6-88. Assemble the sliding tray as shown (courtesy Stanley Tools).

sheet of ½″ plywood 19″ × 37″ and nail and glue to the frame. Before you finish the lid, hinge it to the chest.

The sliding tray is easy (Fig. 6-88). Cut two pieces of ½″ × 3″ stock 18¼″ long and two pieces 16¼″ long. Assemble the four pieces with 6d nails and glue. The bottom of the tray is acrylic plastic 1/10″ thick. It should be 16¼″ × 19″ and secured to the bottom of the tray with No. 4 flathead screws ¼″. Drill holes through the plastic for the screws. They will require a countersink so the screw heads will fit flush with the bottom face of the plastic.

The handles of the tray are made of the same size stock as the tray frame and need to be 16¼″ long. Cut the handles to rough size with a coping saw and finish them with your surform tool. You'll get a better match if you clamp the two handles together when doing the final work with the surform tool. Fasten the handles in place with 6d nails and wood glue.

For the bottle rack, cut two pieces 19″ long and two pieces 14 ¾″ long from the 1″ × 4″ stock (Fig. 6-89). Drill the holes for the dowels before assembling these pieces. Clamp each pair of pieces together so that holes can be drilled through both at the same time. This will insure getting exact

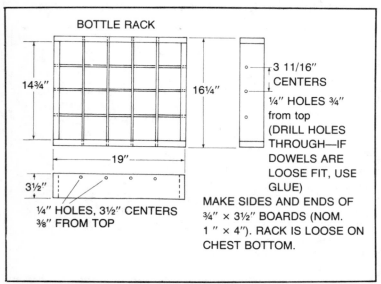

Fig. 6-89. The bottle rack detail (courtesy Stanley Tools).

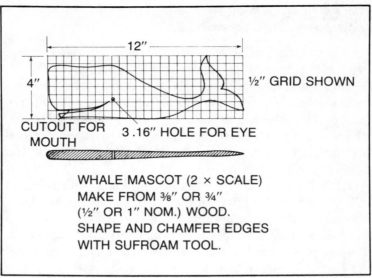

Fig. 6-90. The whale mascot detail (courtesy Stanley Tools).

alignment of the holes. Note that the location of the holes is not the same on the side pieces as for the end pieces. This difference is necessary so that the dowels will overlap properly.

After the holes are drilled, assemble the rack with 6d nails and glue. Cut the ¼" dowels to length. You'll need four pieces 16¼" long and three pieces 19" long. Insert the dowels and if they are loose in the holes, put a spot of wood glue on the ends of each one. Since the bottle rack sits on the bottom of the chest, it doesn't need a bottom. If you plan to use it for some other purpose, though, you can add one. A sheet of ⅜" hardboard will do.

Use the detail with a ½" grid to draw the whale mascot on a piece of 1" × 4" (Fig. 6-90). Cut it out with a coping saw and finish with a surform tool. You can also use the grid to work out a design for some other decorative mascot of your choosing. The mascot can be held in place with 6d finishing nails or just wood glue.

I don't think much comment is needed to convince anyone that a tool cabinet/workbench is a good idea for any home. Today, all of us have to have tools around, for we have passed the stage of being able to afford the prices charged to make home repairs. Keeping them handy and in good shape is easily done with this project from the American Plywood Association (Fig. 6-91). Refer to Figs. 6-92 and 6-93 for materials and plywood parts.

Assemble the 2 × 4 lower shelf framing with glue and nails. Fasten the ¾" plywood shelf to this frame. Set up legs, end cross braces and top rails. Nail and glue the ¼" plywood back and end panels to the 2 × 4s (Fig. 6-94). Glue the two ¾" plywood panels for the top back-to-back, using clamps and weighting them around edges with screws at other points

Fig. 6-91. This complete work bench takes little time to build

MATERIALS LIST
REcommended plywood:
A-C Exterior or A-D Interior APA® grade-trademarked plywood
PLYWOOD

Quantity	Description
2 panels	¾ in. × 4 ft × 8 ft plywood
1 piece	¼ in. × 4 ft × 4 ft plywood. (See your dealer for availability of ½ panel or precut panels.)

OTHER MATERIALS

Quantity	Description
13 lin. ft	2 × 4 lumber (based on 8 ft lengths)
As required	6d and 8d finish nails
As required	8d common nails
As required	Wood screws and tool hooks
As required	Glue (urea resin type recommended) for glue-nail assembly
As required	Fine sandpaper for smoothing cut edges of plywood
As required	Finishing materials, including primer or sealer and two top finish coats
As required	Wood dough or filler for filling countersunk nail holes and any small gaps in cut plywood edges if desired.

Fig. 6-92. Materials needed to build the cabinet-work bench

driven into the underside until the glue sets. Then true the edges of the top, rounding corners slightly, with 1/0 sandpaper or a block plane. Fasten the top to the bench framework with glue and wood screws (Fig. 6-95). Counterbore and plug these screw heads.

PLYWOOD PARTS

Code	No. Req'd.	Size	Part Identification
A	1	34½″ × 58½″	Tool Cabinet Back
B	2	4¾″ × 60″	Tool Cabinet Top, Bottom
C	2	4¾″ × 34½″	Tool Cabinet Sides
D	1	4″ × 34½″	Tool Cabinet Shelf Standard
E	3	4″ × ½″	Tool Cabinet Shelves
F	2	23¾″ × 60″	Work bench Top
G	1	19⅜″ × 48″	Work bench Bottom Shelf
H	2	21″ × 25⅞″	Work bench Sides
I	1	22″ × 44¾″	Work bench Back

LUMBER PARTS (2 × 4's)

4 at 45″
2 at 21″
2 at 18″
4 at 30½·″

Fig. 6-93. Here are plywood and lumber parts

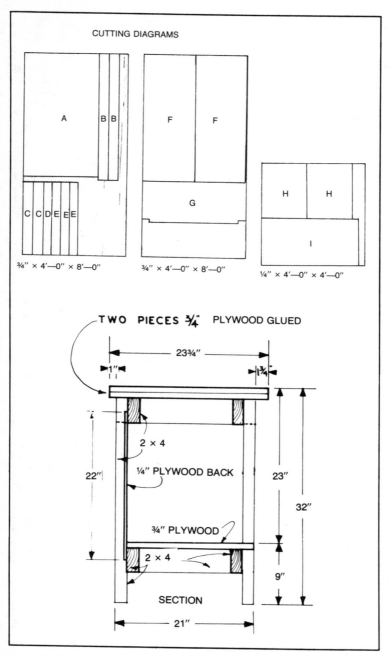

CUTTING DIAGRAMS

¾″ × 4′—0″ × 8′—0″

¾″ × 4′—0″ × 8′—0″

¼″ × 4′—0″ × 4′—0″

TWO PIECES ¾″ PLYWOOD GLUED

23¾″

1″

¾″

2 × 4

¼″ PLYWOOD BACK

22″

23″

32″

¾″ PLYWOOD

2 × 4

9″

SECTION

21″

Fig. 6-94. Cutting diagrams and dimensions for the cabinet-work bench

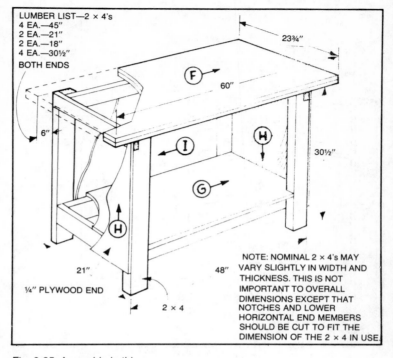

Fig. 6-95. Assemble in this manner

Within the figure:

LUMBER LIST—2 × 4's
4 EA.—45"
2 EA.—21"
2 EA.—18"
4 EA.—30½"
BOTH ENDS

23¾"

F

60"

6"

H

I

30½"

G

H

NOTE: NOMINAL 2 × 4's MAY VARY SLIGHTLY IN WIDTH AND THICKNESS. THIS IS NOT IMPORTANT TO OVERALL DIMENSIONS EXCEPT THAT NOTCHES AND LOWER HORIZONTAL END MEMBERS SHOULD BE CUT TO FIT THE DIMENSION OF THE 2 × 4 IN USE.

21"

¼" PLYWOOD END

48"

2 × 4

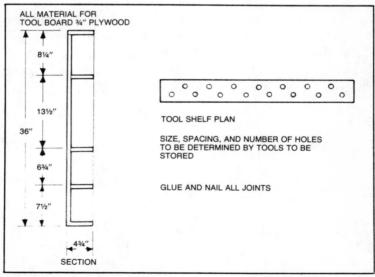

Fig. 6-96. The tool shelf plan

Within the figure:

ALL MATERIAL FOR TOOL BOARD ¾" PLYWOOD

8¼"

13½"

36"

6¾"

7½"

4¾"

SECTION

TOOL SHELF PLAN

SIZE, SPACING, AND NUMBER OF HOLES TO BE DETERMINED BY TOOLS TO BE STORED

GLUE AND NAIL ALL JOINTS

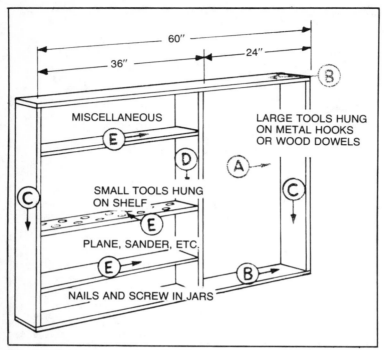

Fig. 6-97. Organize your cabinet like this

To assemble the tool cabinet, glue and nail side and end strips to the back panel (Fig. 6-96). Bore holes for chisels, screwdrivers, etc., in one shelf before fitting the vertical divider and shelving. Countersink nails and fill holes. Sand filler and edges smooth and finish (Fig. 6-97).

Divide a room with shelves and get more than extra wall space against which a chair may be placed (Fig. 6-98). Simply adjust for the ceiling height in your home, and go ahead. This project is quite simple and can be built in just a few short hours. Refer to Fig. 6-99 for materials.

Cut plywood panel in half crosswise and glue the sections back-to-back (Fig. 6-100). Weight the panel down over-all until the glue dries. Locate a wall stud approximately where the divider should go. Plan to position the divider so that the center line of the divider end will be over a stud. Cut out a section of baseboard and ceiling molding to accommodate the divider end 2 × 12. Cut wall-end and center 2 × 12s to floor-to-ceiling height less 1½″, and cut the other end 2 × 12 full height. Cut top 2 × 12 to 68½″ long (Fig. 6-101). Nail top 2

Fig. 6-98. If you must split up a room, do it so that storage space increases with this room divider

241

```
MATERIALS LIST
Recommended plywood:
303® Exterior plywood siding, or decorative
interior plywood, APA grade-trademarked


PLYWOOD
Quantity                        Description
1 panel          ⅜ in. × 4 ft × 8 ft plywood (303 plywood) or
                 5/16 in. × 4 ft × 8 ft plywood (decorative)


OTHER MATERIALS
Quantity                              Description
32 lin. ft    2 × 12 lumber (based on 8 ft lengths) for verticals and top
28 lin. ft    2 × 10 lumber (based on 8 ft lengths) for shelves
As required   10d finishing nails for frame construction (approx ½ lb)
As required   6d or 8d finishing nails for installing plywood (approx ¼ lb)
As required   Finishing materials (see Building Hints)
```

Fig. 6-99. Materials needed for making the room divider

× 12 to wall end 2 × 12. Tilt the assembly up and push it into position. The fit should be snug. Fasten it securely to the ceiling and wall, nailing stud and ceiling joists into the wall where possible. Countersink nails.

Draw shelf locations lightly on 2 × 12s, making sure they are the same distance up from the floor so that the shelves will be level. Check the side view in Fig. 6-102. Slide the middle 2 × 12 into place and toenail it to the top 2 × 12. Insert longer shelves and match them to markings on 2 × 12s. Check for level. Nail through middle 2 × 12 into one end of shelves, and toenail other ends to wall end 2 × 12. Toenail from underneath shelves. Toenail short shelves in position. Nail the screen section to shelves. Space nails about 6″ apart. Fill holes if desired. Finish the screen.

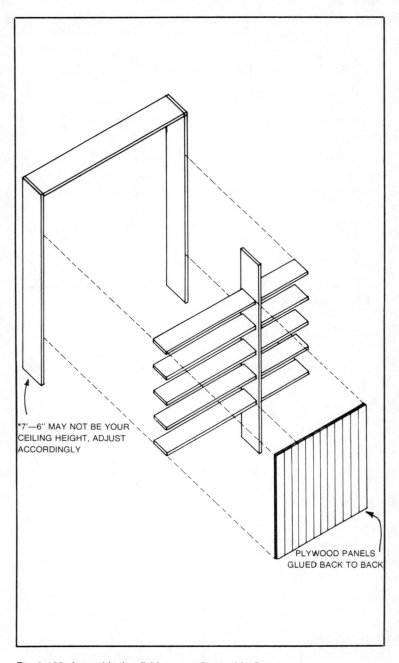

*7'—6" MAY NOT BE YOUR CEILING HEIGHT, ADJUST ACCORDINGLY

PLYWOOD PANELS GLUED BACK TO BACK

Fig. 6-100. Assemble the divider according to this diagram

243

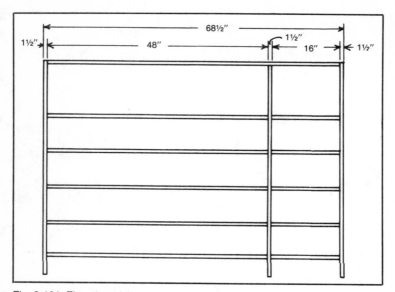

Fig. 6-101. Elevation of the room divider

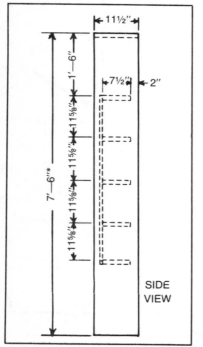

SIDE
VIEW

Fig. 6-102. Elevation of the room divider

244

Have you checked the cost of a new dining room or outdoor table lately? This table will be fine for almost all outdoors plan and many indoor. The only requirement for use

Fig. 6-103. A trestle table is a handy thing to have

MATERIALS LIST

Recommended plywood:
For outdoor or indoor use: A-A, A-B, or A-C Exterior plywood or Medium Density Overlay (MDO). APA grade-trademarked.

For indoor use only: A-A, A-B, B-B, or A-D Interior. APA grade-trademarked.

PLYWOOD

| 1 panel | ¾ in. × 4 ft × 8 ft plywood |

OTHER MATERIALS

Quantity	Description
7 lin. ft	2 × 8 lumber for top frame
7 lin. ft	2 × 2 lumber for top frame
2 ft	¾ in. diameter dowel for pegs
3 dozen	#8 × 1¼ in. flathead wood screws to fasten top frame
½ lb	6d finishing nails to fasten top support to top
As required	Wood dough or other filler such as spackle for filling any small gaps in cut plywood edges
As required	Fine sandpaper for smoothing cut plywood edges and filler
As required	Glue (waterproof for permanent outdoor use)
As required	Finishing materials (stain, paint including primer, or antiquing kit)

Fig. 6-104. Materials for building the trestle table

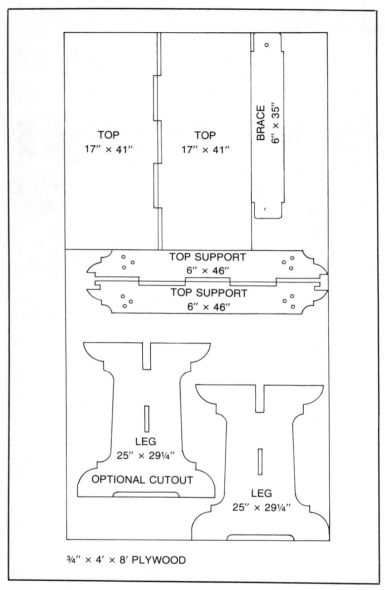

Fig. 6-105. Panel layout for the table

as a formal dining table is more care in finishing. At 3' × 4½' it is large enough for families and even a guest or two (Fig. 6-103). Figure 6-104 lists materials.

Lay out plywood panel for cutting as shown in Fig. 6-105. Cut out pieces and true edges with a coarse sanding block. Plywood edges that will be exposed should be filled with surfacing putty. Allow to dry, then sand smooth. Cut lumber to sizes shown (Figs. 6-106 through 6-108) and rout. Cut six pegs 3″ long, and two pegs 2¼″ long. Assemble top framing lumber around plywood tops by gluing and screwing through lumber and into plywood tops. Then glue-nail top supports to top assemblies (Fig. 6-109). Countersink nails, fill holes, and allow to dry and sand smooth. Assemble the table to be sure all parts fit properly. If parts are snug, sand to allow for additional thickness of finish. Wipe clean and finish.

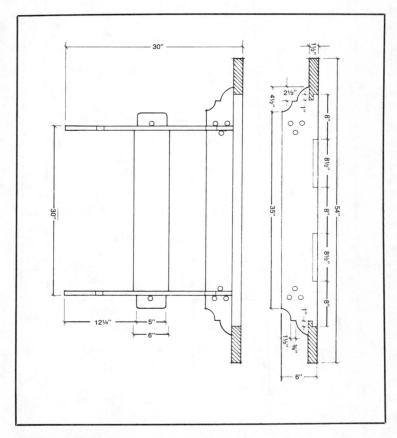

Fig. 6-106. Take pains to measure properly

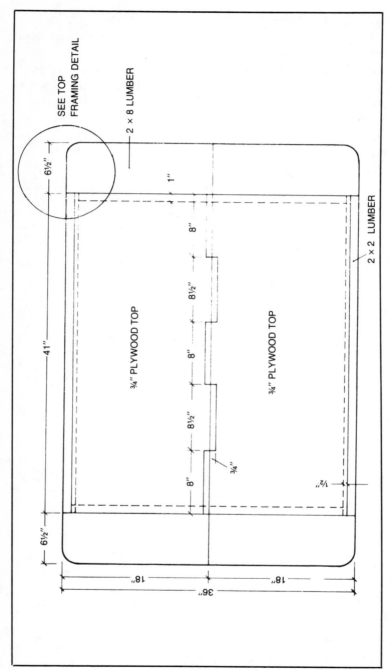

Fig. 6-107. The table top detail

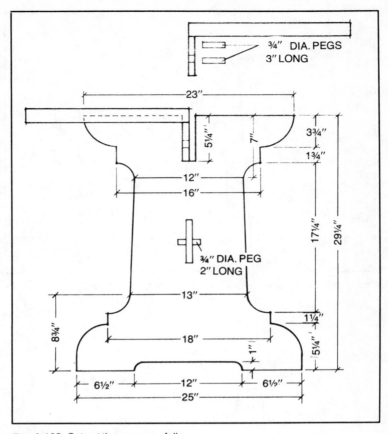

Fig. 6-108. Cut out the pegs carefully

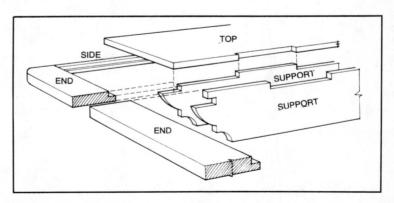

Fig. 6-109. Table top assembly and framing details

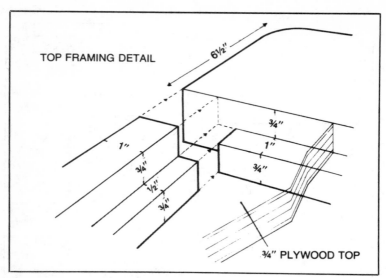

Fig. 6-109. Table top assembly and framing details Continued.

Storage. No matter the kind, there's never enough. Similar to Stanley's "Anything Chest" in some ways, the American Plywood Association's storage chest is a bit fancier, with legs and external trim pieces added (Fig. 6-110). Construction will take a bit longer, but you'll end with exterior dimensions of 24″ × 18¼″, and a very decorative cabinet for use in any room. For a knock-around box, I'd leave off some of the decorative trim and simply use edge sealer on the plywood. Or miter the edge joints instead of butting them. Figure 6-111 lists materials.

Draw parts on plywood (Fig. 6-112). Cut lumber parts (Figs. 6-113 through 6-116). True edges with a sanding block, and fill edges that will be exposed with wood dough or other filler such as spackle. Allow to dry and sand smooth. Glue and nail bottom, sides, back, shelf and front together. Assemble

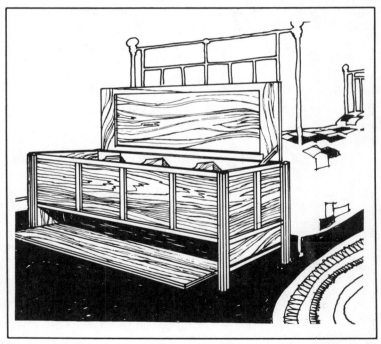

Fig. 6-110. Much can be stored at the ends of the beds in your home if you build this storage chest

MATERIALS LIST
Recommended plywood:
A-B Interior, A-C Exterior, or Medium Density Overlay (MDO) APA grade-trademarked plywood
PLYWOOD

Quantity	Description
1 panel	¾ in. × 4 ft × ft plywood for box parts
1 piece	¾ in. × 4 ft plywood (ask your dealer about availability of half panels or precut plywood) for box parts
1 piece	¼ in. × 4 ft × 4 ft for dividers and trim

OTHER MATERIALS

Quantity	Description
4 lin. ft	2 × lumber for top frame (select grade, if avaiable)
7 lin. ft	2 × 2 lumber for top frame (select grade, if possible)
7 lin. ft	11/16 in. × 1⅝ in. molding (legs) such as WP 229
3 doz.	#8 flathead wood screws 1¼ in. long for top frame and hinges
½ lb	6d finishing nails for glue nail assembly of box
½ lb	3d finishing nails for fastening molding (legs)
½ lb	¾ in. brads to fasten trim, etc.
4	2 in. hinges
1	Door pull
1	Magnetic catch
1	Lid support
As required	White glue for glue nail and glue screw assembly
As required	Wood dough or filler for filling any small gaps in cut plywood edges and countersunk nail holes
As required	Fine sandpaper for smoothing filler and cut plywood edges
As required	Finishing materials

Fig. 6-111. Materials required to build the storage chest

top framing lumber around plywood top by gluing and screwing through lumber and into plywood top (Fig. 6-117). Glue-nail divider supports in place (Fig. 6-118). Then glue-nail molding (legs) and plywood trim to box assembly (Fig. 6-119). Coun-

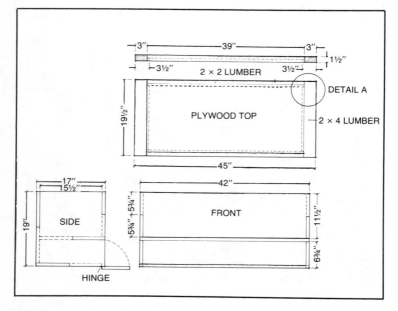

Fig. 6-112. Plywood panel layout for the storage chest

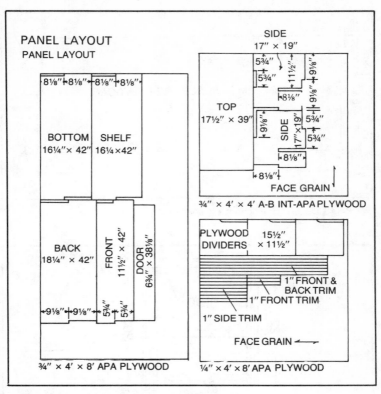

Fig. 6-113. The chest's top, side and front details

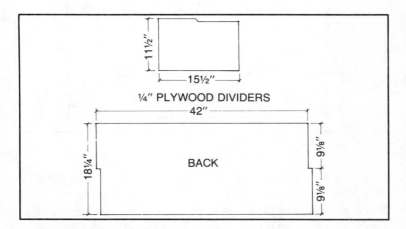

Fig. 6-114. The dividers and back details

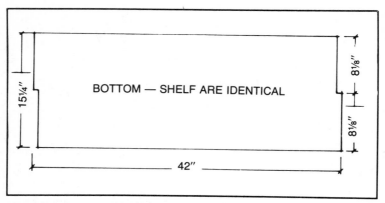

Fig. 6-115. Detail for the bottom and shelf

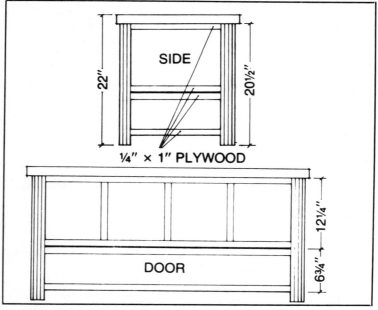

Fig. 6-116. The side and door details

tersink nails, fill holes, allow to dry and sand smooth. Install a
magnetic catch to the bottom of the shelf. Stain or paint the
box assembly, door and top as desired. After the finish is dry,
apply remainder of the hardware. Complete the unit by hinging
door and top to the box assembly.

254

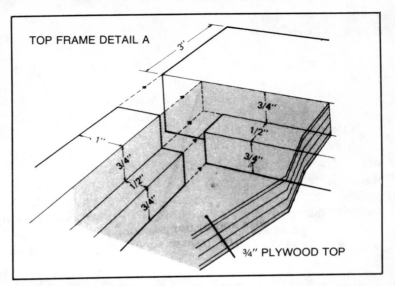

Fig. 6-117. The top frame detail

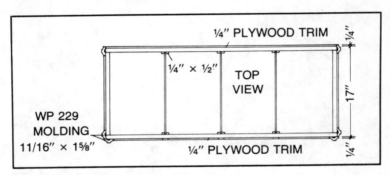

Fig. 6-118. Top view of the chest

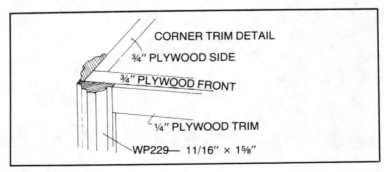

Fig. 6-119. The corner trim detail

255

This one seems to be one of the easiest plans. But be careful to follow directions about laying out those pot lids before doing the final assembly with the dowels or you're going to end up with a lot of wasted space (Fig. 6-120). Refer to Fig. 6-121 for materials.

Lay out your pots, pans and their lids on a rack piece before drilling the dowel holes. Dowel spacing may differ from the placement shown in Fig. 6-122, depending on the size of your pans and lids. Drill the dowel holes for both pieces at once by laying one piece of plywood on top of the other. Notch one end of the pot hanger dowels with a knife or saw to fit the rings on your pot handles so the pots can't be knocked easily off the

Fig. 6-120. These pots are up and out of the way

BUILDING HINTS:

1. Lay out your pots, pans, and their lids on a rack piece before drilling the dowel holes. Dowel spacing may differ from the placement shown here, depending on the size of your pans an and lids.

2. To assure alignment of the assembled rack pieces, drill the dowel holes for both pieces at once by laying one piece of plywood on top of the other.

3. Notch one end of the pot hanger dowels with a knife or saw to fit the rings on your pot handles so the pots can't be knocked easily off the rack.

4. If necessary, adjust the diameter of the half-circles shown on the plan to the size of your lid knobs.

5. If you want the dowels painted, do it before assembling the rack. When all the painted pieces are thoroughly dry, gently pound the dowels in place.

MATERIALS LIST:
Recommended plywood: A-B Interior, A-C Exterior, or Medium Density Overlaid (MDO) APA® grade-trademarked plywood

PLYWOOD
Quantity	Description
⅛ panel	½ in. × 1 ft × 4 ft

OTHER MATERIALS
Quantity	Description
22 linear in.	⅝ in. wood dowel (cut into 6 pieces 3½ in. long)
22 linear in.	⅝ in. wood dowel (cut into 4 pieces 5¼ in. long)
As required	Fine sandpaper
As required	Interior semi-gloss enamel paint
As required	Molly-bolts for fastening the rack to the wall, or wood screws for screwing it into wall studs.

Fig. 6-121. Materials for building the cookware rack

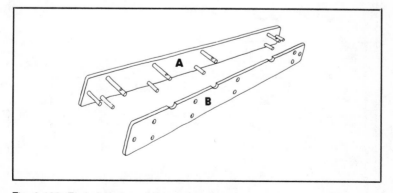

Fig. 6-122. Exploded view of the cookware rack

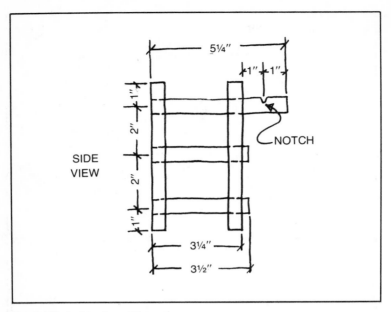

Fig. 6-123. A side view of the rack

rack (Fig. 6-123). If necessary, adjust the diameter of the half-circles shown to the size of your lid knobs (Fig. 6-124). If you want the dowels painted, do it before assembling the rack. When all the painted pieces are thoroughly dry, gently pound the dowels in place.

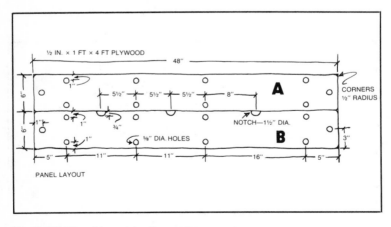

Fig. 6-124. Panel layout for the cookware rack

It's more complex, but this patio cart offers quite a few uses for outdoor entertaining. With very little change, it is adaptable for use indoors. Apply a smoother finish in a more formal color, and you've got an attractive indoor serving cart and tray (Fig. 6-125). Figure 6-126 lists needed materials.

Fig. 6-125. This cart is handy for cookouts

MATERIAL LIST:

Recommended plywood: A-B or A-C Exterior, or Medium Density
Overlaid (MDO) APA® grade-trademarked
plywood

PLYWOOD

Quantity	Description
1 panel	¾ in. × 4 ft × 8 ft

OTHER MATERIALS

Quantity	Description
22 linear in.	1½ in. wood dowel
4 linear in.	¾ in. wood dowel
2	10 in. tricycle spoke wheels (with axle and end caps)
23 linear ft	2 in. wood tape
As required	8d finishing nails
As required	Fine sandpaper
As required	Wood dough
As required	White glue
As required	Exterior semi-gloss enamel paint

Fig. 6-126. Items needed to make the patio cart

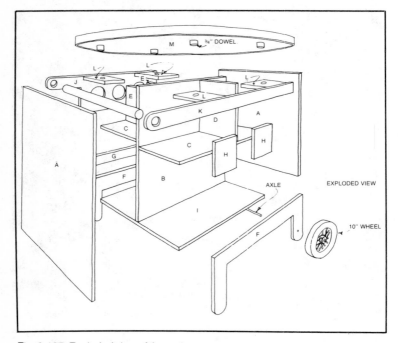

Fig. 6-127. Exploded view of the cart

Figures 6-127 through 6-129 detail cutting and construction procedures.

Before making the circular tray, first cut its rough area (approximately 29″ × 29″) away from the remainder of the panel. Cut the circle carefully and fill the edge with wood dough as needed. Countersink the ¾″ dowels ⅛″ into the underside of the tray. Position the dowels to correspond with the dowel holes in sections L. Glue dowels to the tray bottom only.

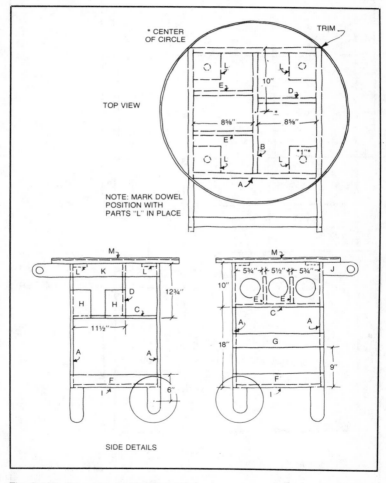

Fig. 6-128. A top view and side details

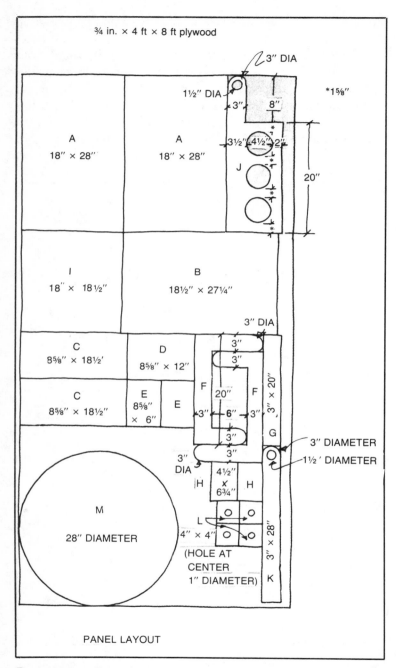

Fig. 6-129. Panel layout for the cart

262

Cut wood tape into three equal lengths. Glue-nail one strip around the circumference of the tray. Since the wood tape is wider than the tray is deep, the tape protrusion should be on the top edge, to form a "lip" along the tray edge. Glue the second layer of wood tape to the first layer, staggering butt joints of the two layers. Apply a third layer of tape, with butt side down and butt joint staggered away from the first two joints. Assemble the interior compartments of the cart. You may wish to paint these pieces before assembling the entire cart. Attach the axle to the bottom of the cart. Assemble the cart, paint remaining areas, and attach wheels.

This sewing center keeps things handy for work (Fig. 6-130). For this project you'll need either a saber saw or a jig saw. The plastic laminate is most easily trimmed with a router, along its edges, but it can also be worked with a knife. Measuring 30″ by 29½″ by 31″ high, this sewing center expands into a combination sewing cabinet—with drop-in well for the machine and 20″ × 30″ work surface—and a supply/storage center. Five drawers hold everything from notions to patterns; at the other end there's storage space for the machine,

Fig. 6-130. If there's a seamstress or budding seamstress in your home, this sewing center will make things easier

plus one deep shelf for fabric and other sewing paraphernailia. Figure 6-131 gives materials. Figure 6-132 covers panel layout. Drawers and the machine's storage area are shown in Fig. 6-133. For a side cutaway view, refer to Fig. 6-134. Figure 6-135 shows drawer detail and traditional overlays. Figure 6-136 depicts tempered hardboard dividers for the drawers. Assembly procedures are detailed in Figs. 6-137 through 6-139. Have fun!

Materials List

Recommended plywood: A-A or A-B Interior, A-C Exterior, or Medium Density Overlay (MDO). Or ask your dealer for alternate APA plywood suggestions.

PLYWOOD

Quantity	Description
2 panels	¾ in. × 4 ft. × 8 ft plywood
1 panel	⅜ in. × 4 ft × 8 ft plywood

OTHER MATERIALS

Quantity	Description
11 linear feet	½ × 1 in. lumber for drawer slides
11 linear feet	¾ × 3 in. lumber for drawer glides
6 linear feet	½ × ¾ in. lumber cleats for pull-outs
4 linear feet	1 in. diameter dowel
3 linear feet	1 × 2 in. lumber for stretcher
¼ sheet	⅛ in. tempered hardboard for notion drawer dividers
30 × 72 in.	laminate for contemporary unit
30 × 45 in.	laminate for traditional unit
5 pr.	drawer stops
15	2 in. #10 wood screws
24	1¼ in. #10 wood screws
4	3 in. rigid casters, such as Faultless Casters #RP
1	24 in. continuous hinge (cutto size)
1 pr.	¾ in. warp-around door hinges
1	magnetic catch
As required	miscellaneous finishing nails and glue (urea-resin-type recommended)
As required	Surfacing putty of filling any small gaps in exposed plywood edges
As required	Fine sandpaper for smoothing and rounding cut edges and surfacing putty
As required	Paint, stain, or antiquing for finishing

Fig. 6-131. Materials required to construct the sewing center

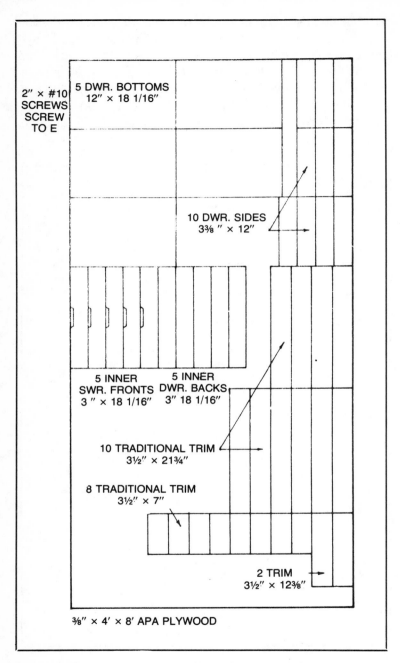

Fig. 6-132. Panel layout for the sewing center

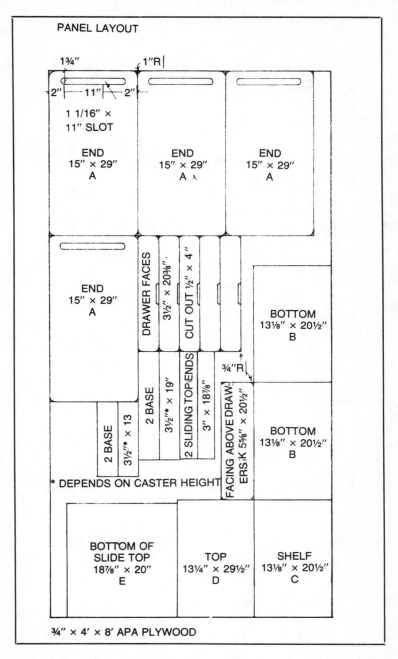

Fig. 6-132. Continued from page 266.

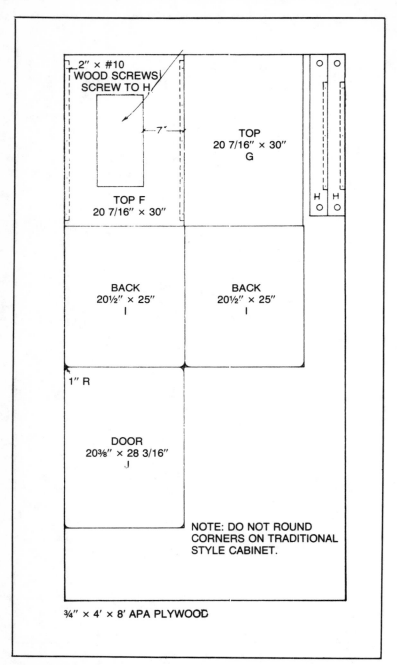

Fig. 6-132. Continued from page 267.

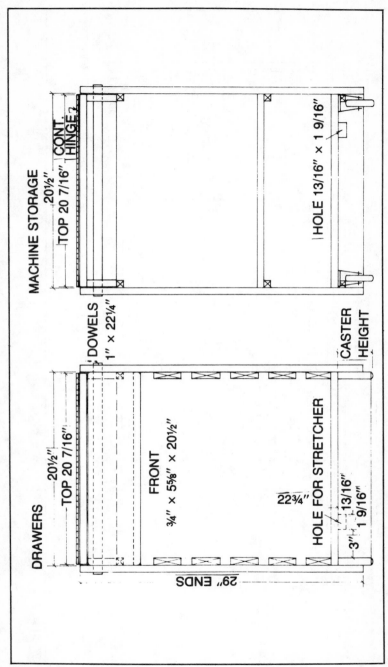

Fig. 6-133. Plans for the drawers and machine storage

269

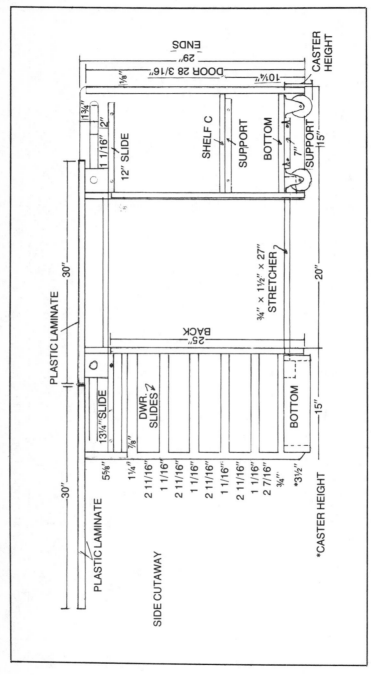

Fig. 6-134. A side cutaway view of the sewing center

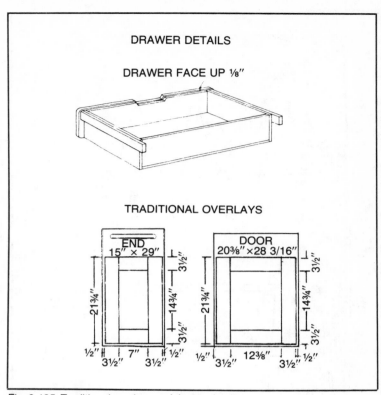

Fig. 6-135. Traditional overlays and drawer details

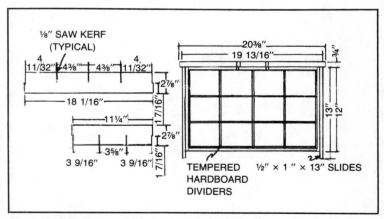

Fig. 6-136. The drawer dividers are made out of tempered hardboard

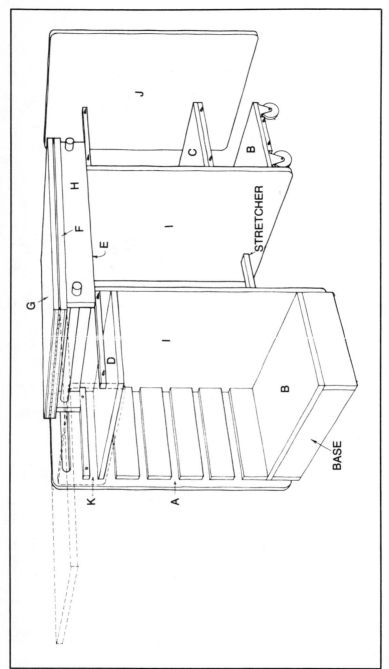

Fig. 6-137. Assemble the cart parts

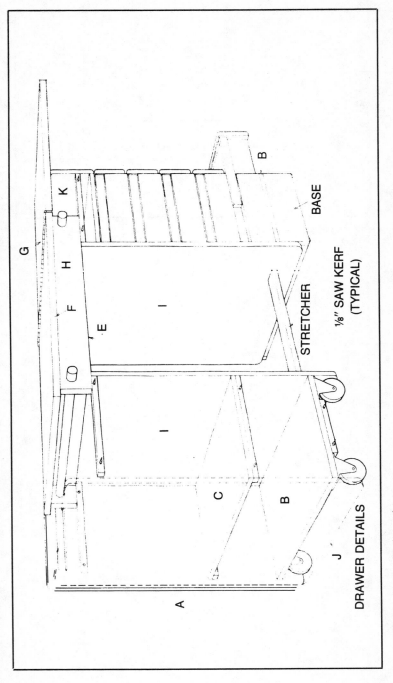

Fig. 6-138. Fasten the wheels as shown

273

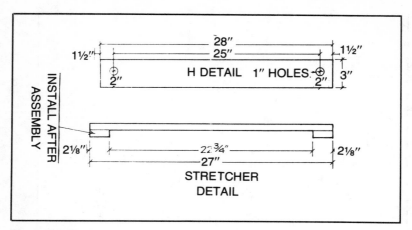

Fig. 6-139. The stretcher detail

Paneling walls adds greatly to the value of most homes and is often much easier than applying wallboard of other types, particularly since finishing is not required. The paneling must be selected with great care. You have to live with it for a long time. Make a scale drawing of the wall or room to estimate how much plywood you'll need (Fig. 6-140). Use plywood from openings to panel over and under windows and above doors.

If you will have any horizontal joints not backed by framing, toenail pieces of 2 × 4 blocking in place to provide a solid nailing base (Fig. 6-141). Install any insulation between studs before plywood is nailed in place. If the wall is an outside one, the insulation foil back or vapor barrier should be toward the room interior, the "warm" side of the wall. If both sides of a wall are to be paneled, put in the insulation after one side of the wall is complete. Mark openings for windows, doorways, etc., on the plywood. For small openings, drill pilot holes in the

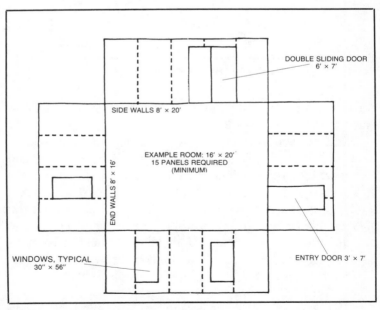

Fig. 6-140. An example of a scale drawing

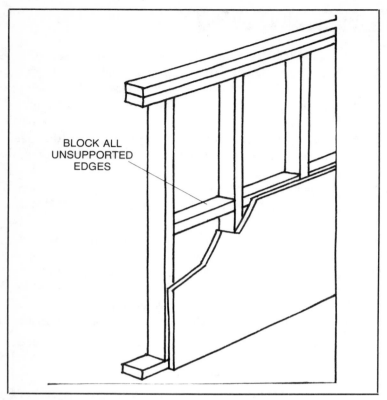

BLOCK ALL UNSUPPORTED EDGES

Fig. 6-141. Add blocking to supply a solid nailing base

corners of each cutout; then use a keyhole or sabre saw to finish the job (Fig. 6-142).

Nail plywood to studs, cross blocking and plates (Fig. 6-143). Space nails 6″ apart along panel ends and edges and 12″ apart into studs behind the panel (Fig. 6-144). Countersink nails and fill the holes with filler. To fit baseboards and moldings, first cut a piece to fit the longest wall. To cut the shorter side pieces, draw the shape of the molding end on the back of the shorter, adjoining molding. Tape the front to prevent splitting, then cut along the lines drawn on the back. The shorter piece will fit over the uncut piece at the corner (Fig. 6-145).

If the molding has an irregular back, cut both inside corner pieces accurately at a 45 degree angle the other direc-

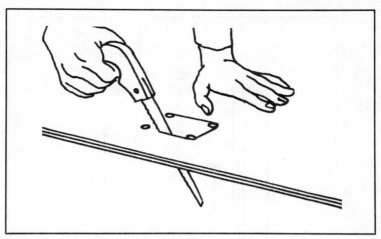

Fig. 6-142. This saw works fine for small openings

FASTENERS	
Plywood Thickness (inch)	Nail size (casing or finishing)
¼	4d
5/16	6d
⅜	6d
½	6d
⅝	8d
¾	8d
Texture 1-11	8d

When using any of the grooved panelings, one may nail through grooves to the stud, where they line up.

Fig. 6-143. Plywood thicknesses and corresponding nail sizes

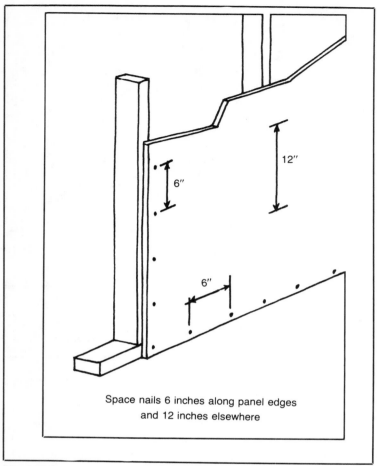

Fig. 6-144. Space nails correctly

tion. At openings that have no molding, you can cap the plywood edges with slim plastic molding manufactured for that purpose. Baseboards at these entries should be trimmed to a 45 degree angle at the opening (Fig. 6-146). Plywood joints may be covered with ornate moldings as well as simple batten strips.

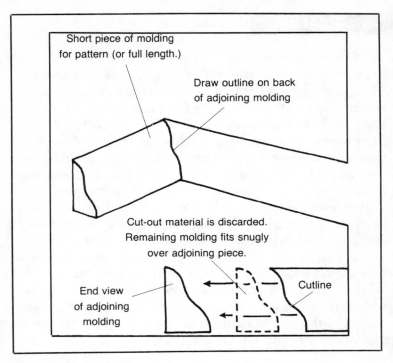

Fig. 6-145. Diagrams of molding

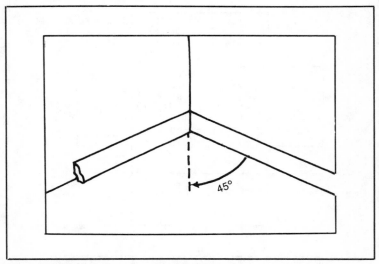

Fig. 6-146. Trim baseboards and molding properly

Determine how much plywood you'll need by making a scale drawing of the wall or room (Fig. 6-147). To see if the wall is flat and even, place a long straight edge against it horizontally or stretch a string from one end to the other. Locate wall studs and make a small mark on the ceiling or floor. Mark openings for doorways, windows and electrical boxes on the plywood. Some electrical hardware has enough surface so you can rub chalk on edges and then press the panel against it to locate openings. Mark on the back side of the plywood if you're using a sabre saw. Mark on the front if you're using a hand saw. For small openings, drill pilot holes in the corners of each cutout. Then use a keynote or sabre saw to finish the job.

If your wall is flat and true, you can glue plywood right over the old wall. Use paneling adhesive, which comes ready to use in applicator containers. Apply a glue bead about ⅜" wide horizontally and vertically every 16" along the top and bottom of the wall and around all openings. Press the panel against the adhesive and drive small finishing nails (3d or 4d)

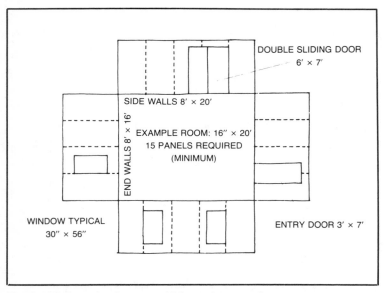

Fig. 6-147. An example room which requires paneling

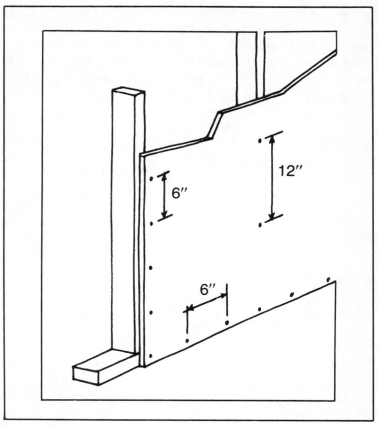

Fig. 6-148. Position nails properly

about halfway in, all along the top edge of the panel at 6″ intervals.

Pull the bottom of the panel out from the wall about 6″ and prop it out with a small block. Wait five or 10 minutes for the adhesive to become tacky. Then push the panel into place. When the glue is set, finish driving nails along the top edge and countersink them. Sometimes a good effect can be achieved by installing molding at the ceiling. Apply finish and replace baseboards and receptacle covers.

Position panels one by one, making sure each fits. Use 3d finish nails or 1″ brads for ¼″ plywood, or 4d finish nails for ⅜″ plywood. Use longer nails if existing walls are lath and plaster. Start nailing along the top edge of each panel. The first nail should be driven near the center of the panel into the underlying framing. Nail from the center toward the edges to prevent nailing a warp into the panel. Space nails every 6" along panel top, bottom and edges and every 12" into studs under the panel (Fig. 6-148). Countersink nails and replace baseboards, moldings and receptacle covers.

Here's one handy for those long football afternoons in the fall. Instead of using metal rod, as suggested, you may well wish to buy commercial metal or wood legs for your TV trays. Select sturdy ones. The tray tops are simply pieces of ¼″ hardwood plywood, 14″ × 16″, of a species to harmonize with the room furnishings. They fit into wood blocks cut from 2″ × 4″ lumber. Metal rods set into the blocks serve as legs. The blocks serve as handles and join the parts. Cut eight 6″ lengths of 2 × 4, two for each of the four trays. Diagonal cuts are made from points ⅞″ in from each side of the block top to the extreme ends of the base. The corners of one face of each block are rounded on a radius of about ⅜″ (Fig. 6-149).

Cut ⅜″ from the rounded face, which is to be the handle side. Extend the cut from the base to ⅝″ from the top; then cut in diagonally from the face at a point ⅜″ from the top (Fig. 6-150). On the reverse face, 1″ from the top, make a ¼″ mortise ½″ into the block. Then drill two ⅜″ holes into the base to a depth of 1¼″. These holes should be centered on the narrow dimension and drilled at an angle paralleling the slanting side, with a space of 7/16″ between the slanting surface

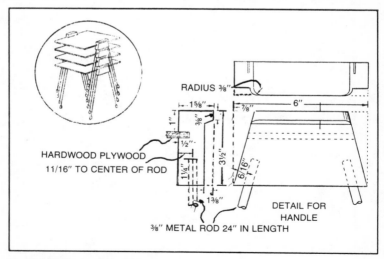

Fig. 6-149. Parts of the TV tray

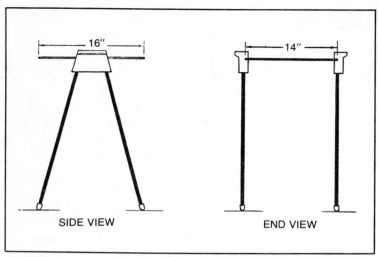

Fig. 6-150. Side and end views of the tray

and the hole. Glue the plywood panels into the mortises and fit 24" lengths of metal rod into the leg holes. Rubber caps should be fitted over the bottoms of the legs. Finish the plywood top.

We'll end the projects with the most complex and expensive of all. Because many new homes are much smaller than ever before, as well as much more expensive, the time comes when more room is essential to a comfortable lifestyle. Hiring someone to erect that extra room may lead to bankruptcy for many of us. Skills developed by working with the other projects, and a bit of common sense, will allow most people to erect these designs, executed for the American Plywood Association by Hobbs/Fukui Associates.

This project requires much thought, care and checking. Check local building codes, foundation depth needs, and look

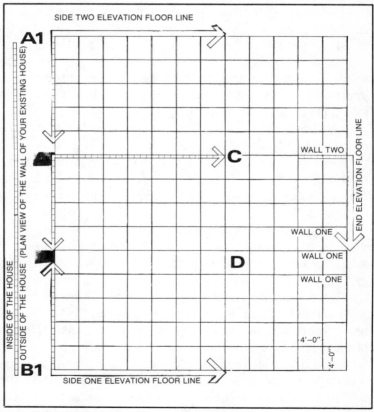

Fig. 6-151. Example of a master worksheet grid

Fig. 6-152. A single story shed roof design

for any other site limitations, as well as basic construction methods. A post and beam home will require somewhat different plans than one made up in more normal 2 × 4 stud construction, 16″ on center. In many newer homes you'll find 2′ × 6 construction, 2″ on center, to allow for more wall insulation and greater energy savings. Cooperate fully with your local building inspector. He's there to help you build a safe addition and not to hinder you.

In terms of zoning considerations, here are a few of the most frequently agreed upon guidelines. Dens go with living rooms or the master bedroom. Family rooms go with kitchens or dining areas. Avoid opening a bedroom onto a kitchen or dining room. Make sure a new bedroom is convenient to existing bathrooms.

Begin your work by locating the important features of your existing house along the wall to which you intend to attach an added room. You might want to copy Fig. 6-151 on grid paper. Let line A1-B1 represent the wall. Indicate important features as precisely as you can by actually drawing them along line A1-B1. Once this is done, it's time to sketch your new room on a tracing paper grid sheet. By rough sketching on blank sheets of ordinary paper laid over the grid, you can get an appreciation of the size of the room you'll need and the possibilities of altering the use of interior rooms to make the new room blend more easily into the plan. It should be a simple matter to sketch out a desirable room size for your addition. Once you're fairly certain what you want, you're ready to lay out the plan view. Line A-B represents the wall between the existing house and the new room. Mark on line A-B the desired length of the new room, and mark a new point B.

Line A-C on your grid sheet represents one wall of your added room. Mark on it the distance you plan to build out from your existing house. (One grid square equals 4'). At the point your wall stops, mark a new point C. Drop a line from your new point C the same length as line A-B and mark that new point D. Connect new point D and new point B with a line. You now have an outline of the floor plan of your new room.

The next step is to relate your new room to the house. The way to do it is to superimpose tracing paper line A-B over line A1-B1. You can find the best connection point by sliding the new room plan up and down along A1-B1. Once you've located the best connection point, trace that area of line A1-B1 onto tracing paper line A-B. You now have a floor plan that shows exactly where you'll attach the added room to the house.

After you've established a floor plan that meets your requirements, the next step is to relate your new room to the exterior lines of the house. The greatest single design influence on your choice of rooflines is the character of your house. The shape and pitch of your new roof should either duplicate the old roof or harmonize with it. Figures 6-152 through 6-159 show typical roof styles and pitches. After you've determined the roof shape for your new room, turn your worksheet one quarter turn clockwise so the words "End Elevation" appear

Fig. 6-153. A shed with clerestory roof design

Fig. 6-154. A gable roof design

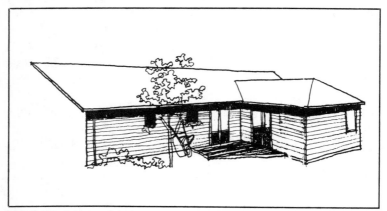

Fig. 6-155. A hip roof design

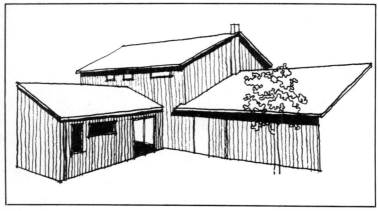

Fig. 6-156. A two story shed roof design

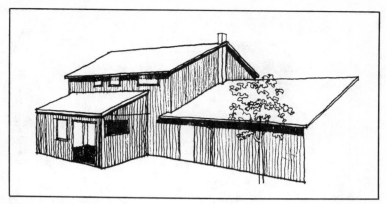

Fig. 6-157. Another two story shed roof design

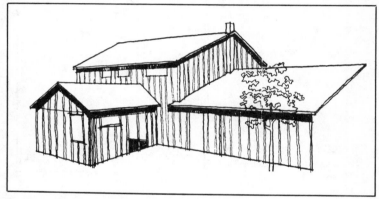

Fig. 6-158. A two story gable roof design

Fig. 6-159. A two story hip roof design

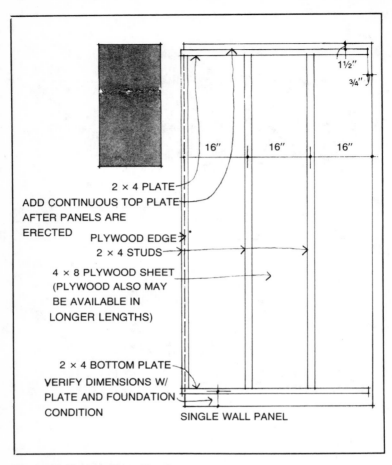

Fig. 6-160. Single wall panel framing

right side up along the floor line. Extend line A-C, filling it in from the end elevation floor line a distance that corresponds with the plate height of your house. The plate height is the height of the inside wall measured from floor to ceiling. To indicate the opposite wall, extend line B-D in the same manner. Next indicate the roof line. If the new roof is to duplicate the old one, you need to know the pitch of your existing roof as well as the plate height. The pitch is the number of inches a roof rises per horizontal inch of span.

The side elevations should be drawn using the same procedure used to draw the end elevation. Turn your tracing paper so the words "side one elevation" appear right side up along the floor line. To determine the length of side one elevation, drop line C-D to the side elevation floor line. The wall height of side one elevation will be the same as wall one of the end elevation. Locate and draw the roof height. Next, turn the tracing paper so the words "side two elevation" appear right side up along the floor line. Extend line C-D to the floor line. The wall height will be the same as wall two of the end elevation. Draw the roof line.

You may find the panelized wall illustrations (Figures 6-160 through 6-165) helpful in visualizing doors and windows. Small windows, high in the wall, provide light, but help pre-

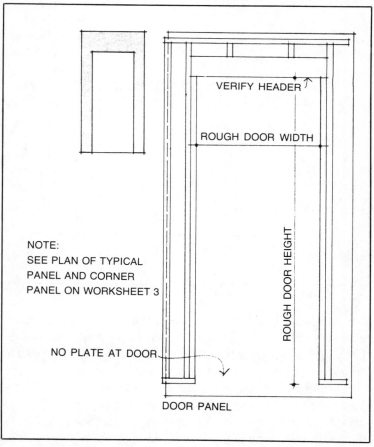

VERIFY HEADER

ROUGH DOOR WIDTH

ROUGH DOOR HEIGHT

NOTE:
SEE PLAN OF TYPICAL
PANEL AND CORNER
PANEL ON WORKSHEET 3

NO PLATE AT DOOR

DOOR PANEL

Fig. 6-161. Door panel framing

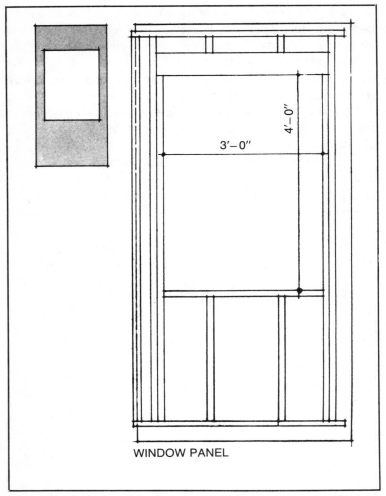

Fig. 6-162. Window panel framing

serve privacy in a bedroom. For a family room or children's playroom, bigger windows that let in more light make sense. Let your house be the basic guide in selecting style and size for windows and doors in the new room.

Building codes, conditions and practices vary widely from area to area. Figures 6-166 through 6-181 represent possible conditions and solutions. All construction details must be verified with your local building code prior to obtaining a building permit.

292

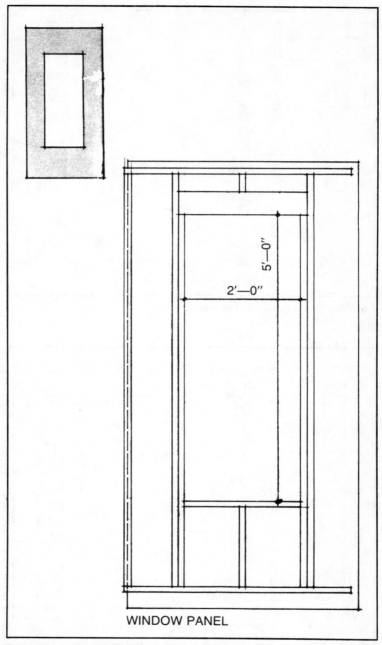

WINDOW PANEL

Fig. 6-163. More window panel framing

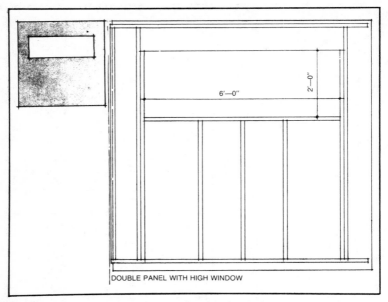

Fig. 6-164. Double panel with high window framing

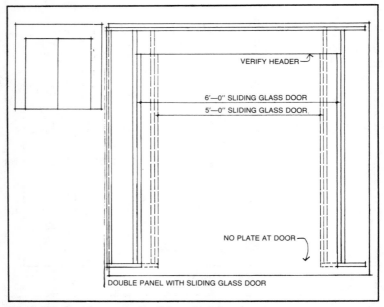

Fig. 6-165. Double panel with sliding glass door

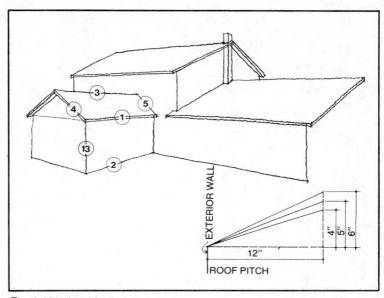

Fig. 6-166. A gable roof pitch diagram

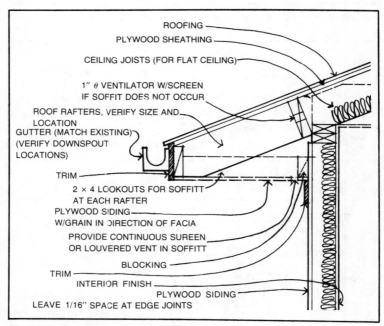

Fig. 6-167. Eave-side wall building details

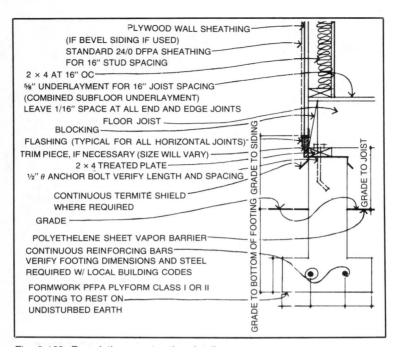

PLYWOOD WALL SHEATHING
(IF BEVEL SIDING IF USED)
STANDARD 24/0 DFPA SHEATHING
FOR 16" STUD SPACING
2 × 4 AT 16" OC
⅝" UNDERLAYMENT FOR 16" JOIST SPACING
(COMBINED SUBFLOOR UNDERLAYMENT)
LEAVE 1/16" SPACE AT ALL END AND EDGE JOINTS
FLOOR JOIST
BLOCKING
FLASHING (TYPICAL FOR ALL HORIZONTAL JOINTS)
TRIM PIECE, IF NECESSARY (SIZE WILL VARY)
2 × 4 TREATED PLATE
½" θ ANCHOR BOLT VERIFY LENGTH AND SPACING
CONTINUOUS TERMITE SHIELD
WHERE REQUIRED
GRADE
POLYETHELENE SHEET VAPOR BARRIER
CONTINUOUS REINFORCING BARS
VERIFY FOOTING DIMENSIONS AND STEEL
REQUIRED W/ LOCAL BUILDING CODES
FORMWORK PFPA PLYFORM CLASS I OR II
FOOTING TO REST ON
UNDISTURBED EARTH

GRADE TO SIDING
GRADE TO JOIST
GRADE TO BOTTOM OF FOOTING

Fig. 6-168. Foundation construction details

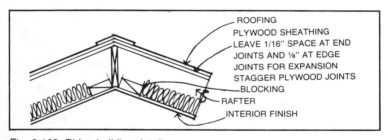

ROOFING
PLYWOOD SHEATHING
LEAVE 1/16" SPACE AT END
JOINTS AND ⅛" AT EDGE
JOINTS FOR EXPANSION
STAGGER PLYWOOD JOINTS
BLOCKING
RAFTER
INTERIOR FINISH

Fig. 6-169. Ridge building details

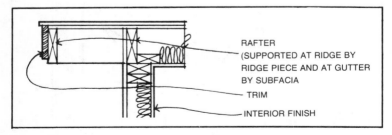

RAFTER
(SUPPORTED AT RIDGE BY
RIDGE PIECE AND AT GUTTER
BY SUBFACIA
TRIM
INTERIOR FINISH

Fig. 6-170. Overhang-end wall building details

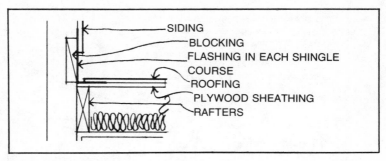

Fig. 6-171. Gable and hip roof connection details

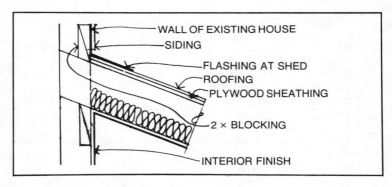

Fig. 6-172. Shed roof connection details

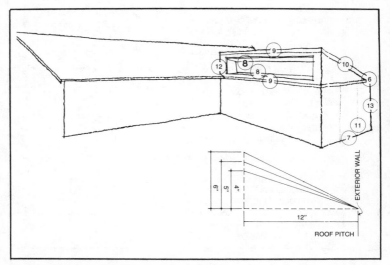

Fig. 6-173. A shed roof pitch diagram

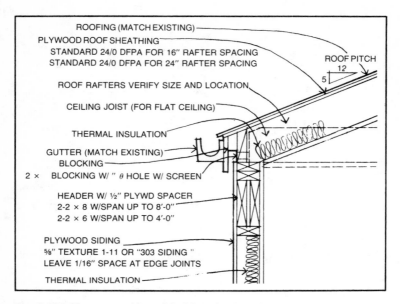

Fig. 6-174. More eave-side wall building details

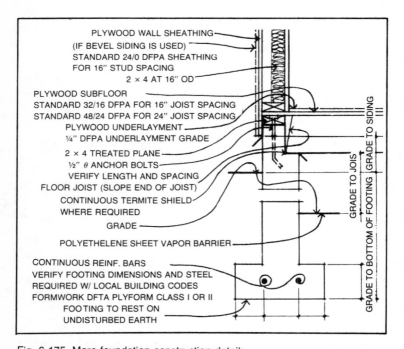

Fig. 6-175. More foundation construction details

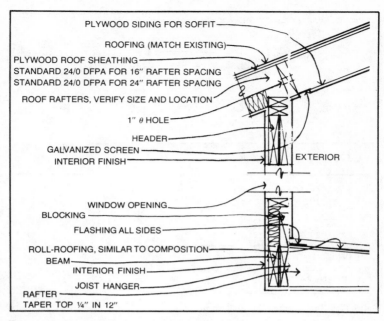

PLYWOOD SIDING FOR SOFFIT
ROOFING (MATCH EXISTING)
PLYWOOD ROOF SHEATHING
STANDARD 24/0 DFPA FOR 16" RAFTER SPACING
STANDARD 24/0 DFPA FOR 24" RAFTER SPACING
ROOF RAFTERS, VERIFY SIZE AND LOCATION
1" θ HOLE
HEADER
GALVANIZED SCREEN
INTERIOR FINISH
EXTERIOR

WINDOW OPENING
BLOCKING
FLASHING ALL SIDES
ROLL-ROOFING, SIMILAR TO COMPOSITION
BEAM
INTERIOR FINISH
JOIST HANGER
RAFTER
TAPER TOP ¼" IN 12"

Fig. 6-176. Recessed clerestory at window building details

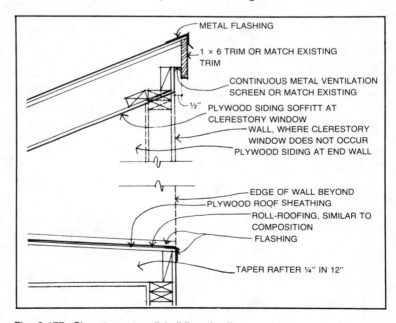

METAL FLASHING
1 × 6 TRIM OR MATCH EXISTING TRIM
CONTINUOUS METAL VENTILATION SCREEN OR MATCH EXISTING
½"
PLYWOOD SIDING SOFFITT AT CLERESTORY WINDOW
WALL, WHERE CLERESTORY WINDOW DOES NOT OCCUR PLYWOOD SIDING AT END WALL

EDGE OF WALL BEYOND
PLYWOOD ROOF SHEATHING
ROLL-ROOFING, SIMILAR TO COMPOSITION
FLASHING
TAPER RAFTER ¼" IN 12"

Fig. 6-177. Clerestory at wall building details

299

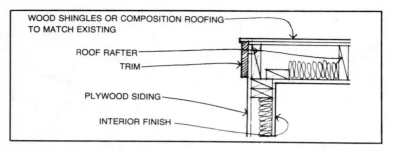

Fig. 6-178. Trim at end wall details

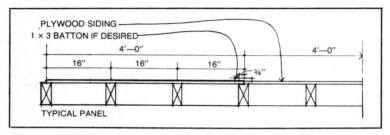

Fig. 6-179. Plan view of the wall panel

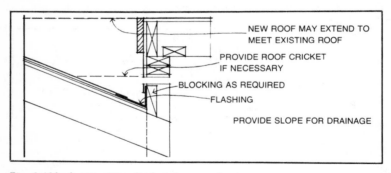

Fig. 6-180. A one story shed roof connection

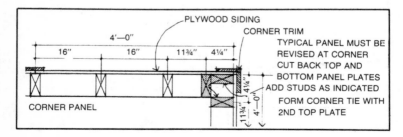

Fig. 6-181. Plan view of wall panels at corner

Plywood Gazetteer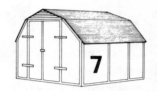

A-A interior—A sanded panel grade described by grades of face (A) and back (A) veneers, with minimum D quality inner plies, bonded with interior or exterior glue. Commonly used in cabinet doors, built-ins, furniture where both sides will show, it can be painted or stained.

> A·A · G·3 · INT·APA · PS 1·74

A-A exterior—A sanded panel grade described by grades of face (A) and back (A) veneers, with minimum C quality inner plies, bonded with exterior glue meeting all the performance requirements of Exterior type plywood. Can be used for fences, built-ins, signs, boats where both sides will show.

> A·A · G·4 · EXT·APA · PS 1·74

A-B interior—A sanded panel grade described by grades of face (A) and back (B) veneers, with minimum D quality inner plies, bonded with interior or exterior glue. Commonly used as an alternate for A-A Interior where the appearance of one side is less important.

A·B · G·4 · INT·APA · PS 1·74

A-B exterior— A sanded panel grade described by grades of face (A) and back (B) veneers, with minimum C quality inner plies, bonded with exterior glue. Can be used as an alternate for A-A Exterior where the appearance of one side is less important.

A·B · G·1 · EXT·APA · PS 1·74

A-C exterior—A sanded exterior panel grade described by grades of face (A) and back (C) veneers with minimum C quality inner plies, bonded with exterior glue meeting all the requirements of Exterior type plywood. Used in siding, soffits, fences. Face is finish grade. Can be painted or stained.

A-D interior—A sanded interior panel grade described by grades of face (A) and back (D) veneers, with minimum D quality inner plies, bonded with interior or exterior glue. A finish-grade face for paneling, built-ins, and backing. Can be painted or stained.

A-D
GROUP 1 (APA)
INTERIOR
PS 1-74 000

acoustical characteristics—Sound absorption and transmission qualities.

acrylic resin— An ingredient of water-base (latex) paints and stains. Synthetic resin with excellent weathering characteristics. Acrylics may be colorless and transparent or pigmented.

adhesive—A subtance capable of holding materials together by surface attachment. A performance specification developed by the American Plywood Association for glues recommended for use in the APA Glued Floor System. AFG-O1 requires that glue applied at the jobsite be strong under many moisture and temperature conditions; be able to fill gaps, and be moisture and sunlight resistant.

aggregate coated panel—A plywood panel coated with stone chips imbedded in a resin coating.

along the grain—In the same direction as the grain. In plywood, the same direction as the grain of the face ply, normally the long (8 foot) dimension. Plywood is stronger and stiffer along the grain (as is all wood) than it is across the grain.

American Plywood Association—A trade organization representing most of the nation's plywood manufacturers. The Association has three main jobs: (1) research to improve plywood performance and products, (2) inspection and testing to make sure plywood quality is consistent and high, and (3) promotion and information service so that the public will know about new products and uses.

APA—Abbreviation for American Plywood Association.

approved agency mark—Plywood that bears the mark of a qualified inspection and testing agency as specified by the plywood product standard. American Plywood Association is an approved inspection and testing agency for softwood plywood.

AWWF—All weather wood foundation.

B-B interior—A sanded panel grade described by face (B) and back (B) veneers; with minimum D quality inner plies

B-B exterior—B-D interior

bonded with interior or exterior glue. It permits circular plugs and is paintable.

> B-B · G-3 · INT-APA · PS 1-74

B-B exterior—A sanded panel grade described by face (B) and back (B) veneers, with minimum C quality inner plies and bonded with exterior glue meeting all the performance requirements of Exterior type plywood. An outdoor utility panel with solid paintable faces.

> B-B · G-1 · EXT-APA · PS 1-74

B-B plyform—A sanded panel grade described by face (B) and back (B) veneers, with minimum C quality inner plies and bonded with exterior glue meeting all the performance requirements of Exterior type plywood. A concrete form grade with a high re-use factor. The surface is mill-oiled unless otherwise specified.

B-B PLYFORM
CLASS I **(APA)**
EXTERIOR
PS 1-74 **000**

B-C exterior—An exterior panel grade described by grades of face (B) and back (C) veneers, with minimum C quality inner plies bonded with exterior glue meeting all the requirements of Exterior type plywood. It is used for utility uses such as farm buildings, some kinds of fences.

B - C
GROUP 2 **(APA)**
EXTERIOR
PS 1-74 **000**

B-D interior—An interior panel grade described by grades of face (B) and back (D) veneers with minimum D quality inner plies and bonded with interior or exterior glue. This is a utility grade with one paintable side. Used for backing, cabinet sides, etc.

back—The side of a plywood panel having the lower grade veneer.

back-priming—Application of a coat of primer to the back of a plywood panel. When plywood is to be used in especially damp locations, siding panels should be back-primed for best results. Cabinet doors also should be back-primed to prevent warping.

batten—A thin narrow strip of plywood or lumber used to seal or reinforce a joint between adjoining pieces of lumber or plywood.

beam, plywood box—A beam built up from lumber and plywood in the form of a long hollow box, which will support more load across an opening than will its individual members alone. Lumber members form the top and bottom (flanges) of the beam, while the sides (webs) are plywood. An example of a box beam is illustrated below. For more information on box beam fabrication write for APA's BB-8; Plywood Design Specification, Supplement 2; and Nailed Plywood and Lumber Beams, Z416.

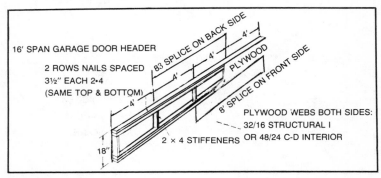

bending—Although plywood is best known as a flat, stiff sheet material, it can be bent, without loss of strength, to form curved surfaces for such uses as walls or concrete forms. Simple curves are easy to form with plywood. A continuous rounded bracing produces best results. When application calls for abrupt curvatures, fasten panel end to shorter radius first. The following radii have been found to be appropriate minimums for mill-run panels of thicknesses shown, bent dry. Shorter radii can be developed by selection for bending of areas free of knots and short grain, and/or by wetting or steaming. (Exterior glue recommended). Panels to be glued should be re-dried first. An occasional panel may develop localized fractures at these radii. To achieve these radii with narrow strips, select for straight grain and freedom from knots.

bevel—To cut plywood edges or ends at an angle to make smooth joints between panels.

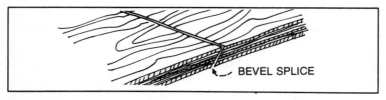

BEVEL SPLICE

blocking—Light lumber strips nailed between major framing members to support edges of plywood panels where they meet.

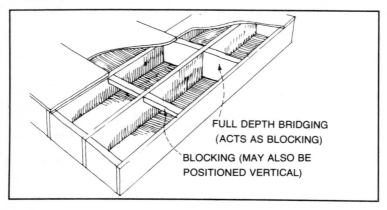

FULL DEPTH BRIDGING
(ACTS AS BLOCKING)

BLOCKING (MAY ALSO BE
POSITIONED VERTICAL)

BOCA—Basic Building Code.

bond—To glue together as veneers are "bonded" to form a sheet of plywood. Pressure can be applied to keep mating parts in proper alignment. Some glues used in plywood manufacture require both heat and pressure to cure properly.

bow—Distortion in a plywood panel so that it is not flat lengthwise.

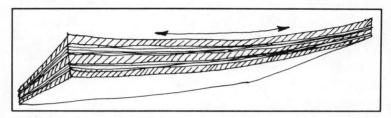

bridging—Short wood or metal braces or struts placed crosswise between joists to hold them in line. Bridging may be solid or may be crossed struts.

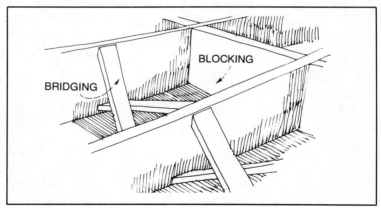

brushed plywood—A manufacturing surface treatment for plywood siding in which softer wood is abraded away so that the harder grain pattern stands in relief, creating a striking panel surface.

bundle—A unit or stack of plywood sheets held together for shipment with metal bands. Stack size varies throughout the industry, with the average stack running about 30 to 33 inches high. A bundle 30 inches high will contain, for example, 120 sheets of 1/4 inch plywood, 80 sheets of ⅜ inch, or 60 sheets of ½ inch plywood.

butt joint—The joint formed when two parts are fastened together without overlapping. For end-to-end joints, use a nailing strip. For corner joints, nail directly into plywood if it is at least ¾ inch thick. If plywood is thinner than ¾ inch, use a reinforcing block as shown by dotted line.

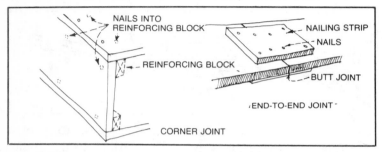

C-C exterior—Exterior unsanded panel grade of face (C) and back (C) veneers with minimum C quality inner plies bonded with exterior glue meeting all the requirements of Exterior plywood. The lowest grade of Exterior plywood, it is used for rough construction that is exposed to weather.

C-C plugged—An exterior panel described by grade of face (C-Plugged) and back (C) veneers, with minimum C inner plies bonded with exterior glue meeting the requirements of Exterior type plywood. The face is plugged with open defects not larger than ¼ inch × ½ inch. Used as pallet bins, boxcar and truck floors, and linings. Touch-sanded. Also called Exterior.

C-D interior—An interior unsanded panel grade described by grade of face (C) and back (D) veneers, with minimum D quality inner plies bonded with interior or exterior glue. Used for sheathing and for structural uses such as subflooring.

CDX—C-D Interior sheathing grade plywood manufactured with exterior glue. Although called CDX in the trade, the term is not an official name. CDX is an Exterior panel and should not be used for permanent outdoor applications.

cantilever—A structural member, such as a beam or truss, which projects beyond a support. Also a bracket-shaped support for supporting a balcony or cornice.

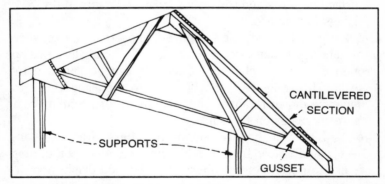

casein glue—Casein glue should be used where only slight resistance to moisture is required. Home craftsmen can use it for many do-it-yourself projects. Sold in powder form, casein glue is mixed with water and applied by spreading on the surfaces to be joined under pressure. It must be allowed time to cure. Casein glue should not be exposed to weather.

caulk—A sealing material to fill joints or seams to make them waterproof. Caulks are made in several forms, including puttys, ropes, or compounds extruded from cartridges.

center—Inner ply of a plywood panel with five or more plies, whose grain directions runs the same way as the face and back plies.

chamfer—The flat surface created by slicing off the square edge or corner of a piece of wood or plywood.

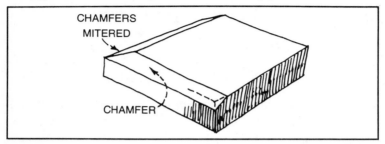

channel groove—A plywood siding shiplapped for continuous patterns. Grooving is typically 1/16 inch deep and ⅜ inch wide, 4 inches o.c. (other spacings are available) in faces of ⅜ inch thick plywood. Channel groove is available in surface patterns and textures similar to Texture 1-11. See sidings for picture.

checking—Plywood that is exposed, unprotected, to severe conditions of moisture or dryness will eventually develop open cracks or "checks." Checking can be reduced by sealing the edges of panels prior to installing them to minimize moisture absorption, and by using a priming coat or resin sealer on the surfaces.

chord—Either of the two outside members of a truss connected and braced by the web members. Also, sometimes refers to perimeter members of a plywood diaphragm.

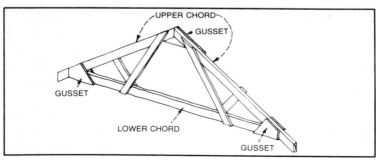

Class 1, 11—Terms used to identify different species-group combinations of Plyform® panels. (See Plywood for Concrete Forming, V345).

Class 1—Faces of any Group 1 species, crossband of any Group 1 or Group 2 species, and centers of any Group 1, 2, 3 or 4 species.

Class 11—Faces of any Group 1 or Group 2 species, and core and centers of any Group 1, 2, 3 or 4 species, or, faces of Group 3 species of ⅛ inch minimum thickness before sanding, crossband of any Group 1, 2, or 3 species, and centers of any Group 1, 2, 3 or 4 species.

See also group species for classification of woods, and plyform.

clear face—Plywood panel with face ply free of knots, knotholes, patches or resin fills. In some cases a few small, well-matched repairs are permitted. Clear face definition varies from mill to mill.

clear span—Distance between inside faces of supports.

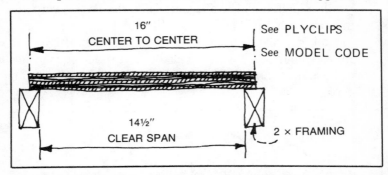

coefficient of thermal expansion—The rate at which a material expands or shrinks when the temperature changes. Plywood expands slightly when heated and contracts when cooled. Because of plywood's cross-laminated construction, however, the change is so small that it is seldom important.

commercial standards—Obsolete term for product standards.

component—As applied to plywood, a term describing a glued or nailed structural assembly of plywood and lumber,

311

such as a box beam or stressed-skin panel. Term also used to describe prefabricated building sections in panelized construction.

concrete form—Mold in which concrete is poured to set. Plywood is used for concrete form-work because it is tough, durable, easy to handle, split resistant, and lightweight. Plywood can be bent for curved forms and liners, and the natural insulating properties help level out temperature variations to provide more consistent curing conditions. Plywood used for concrete formwork is called plyform and is available in two grades: Class 1 and Class 11. Strength and stiffness are greater in Class 1. The choice is determined by loads, framing costs, and nature of job. Both Classes of plyform are also available with High Density Overlay (HDO) and a variety of special-purpose mill-applied coatings. All plywood for concrete formwork is sanded two sides, and (unless otherwise specified) mill oiled.

condensation—Moisture condensation on the surface of a plywood panel should be prevented because it may warp the panel or permit mold to develop. Plywood should be stored in a cool, dry place out of the sunlight and weather. If left outdoors, plywood stacks should be covered in such a way as to provide good air circulation and ventilation between the panels.

construction systems—Plywood roof systems range from conventional installation of roof sheathing over trusses or lumber joists, to preframed and stressed-skin panels, to folded plates. Wall systems provide resistance to wind and earthquake forces, are durable and economical. They include Single Wall, Double Wall, and preframed systems. Floor systems include conventional subfloor and underlayment installation, combination subfloor/underlayment, APA Glued Floor, and plywood stressed-skin floor panels.

continuous beam—A beam supported at three or more points over two or more spans.

core (cores)—Plywood inner plies whose grain runs perpendicular to that of outer plies.

core gap (or center gap)—An open veneer joint extending through or partially through a plywood panel, which results when core (or center) veneer sections are not tightly butted together during manufacture. Product Standard PS 1 specifies that the average of all gaps shall not exceed ½ inch, and that every effort be made to produce closely butted core joints.

corrosion resistance—Ability of metal fasteners (or hardware) to withstand chemical erosion or wearing away. Untreated nails or staples used to apply exterior plywood siding may corrode or rust, staining the surface. Fasteners must be made of, or coated, with, corrosion resistant material. Hot-dip galvanizing is one common coating method.

crawl space—A space about two feet high provided in a building to allow workmen access to plumbing or wiring under a house.

crossband (cores)—In plywood, the veneer layers whose grain direction is at right angles to that of the face plies.

cross lamination—Consecutive layers are placed at right angles to each other (cross-laminated) in plywood manufacture. Cross-laminated construction minimizes shrinkage and produces a strong panel.

cross panel stiffness—Stiffness in the direction perpendicular to (across) the grain of the face ply, normally stiffness in the 4-foot direction.

cup—Distortion of a plywood panel from flatness across the panel.

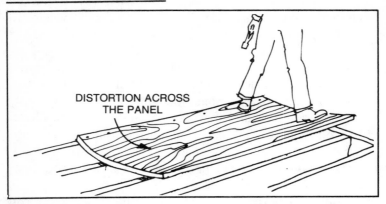

curved panel—Stressed-skin or sandwich panels that are curved to varying degrees. Used in roof construction.

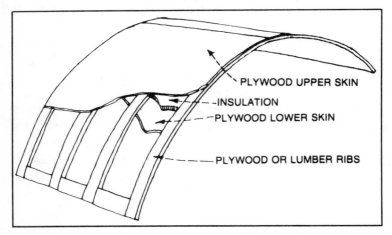

D veneer—The lowest grade of veneer, used for backs or inner plies of Interior type panels.

dado joint—A joint formed by intersection of two boards, in which one is notched with a rectangular groove.

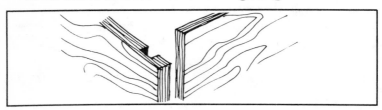

deck, pallet—The horizontal load-carrying plywood surface of a pallet. See PALLET

decking, plywood—Plywood sheathing used for the deck (flat) portion of a roof.

deflection—Downward bending of a plywood panel between supports when a load is applied to it.

delamination—Separation of plies through failure of the adhesive bond.

DFPA—Originally, the Douglas Fir Plywood Association, predecessor of American Plywood Association. One of the marks of the American Plywood Association.

diaphragm—Refers to the thin plywood skin of a building working in combination with the framing to withstand wind and earthquake loads imposed on the structure. See sketch below and APA's Plywood Diaphragm Construction, Form U310, for specific nailing and application instructions.

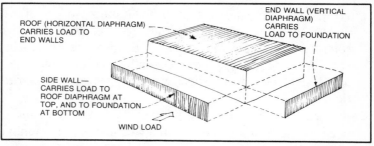

ROOF (HORIZONTAL DIAPHRAGM) CARRIES LOAD TO END WALLS

END WALL (VERTICAL DIAPHRAGM) CARRIES LOAD TO FOUNDATION

SIDE WALL— CARRIES LOAD TO ROOF DIAPHRAGM AT TOP, AND TO FOUNDATION AT BOTTOM

WIND LOAD

dimensional stability—One of the outstanding properties of plywood. Plywood does not swell as much as many other materials when it is wet. In normal construction, ⅛ inch spacing between panel edges and 1/16 inch between panel ends is enough to take care of any expansion. In very wet or humid areas, and in farm buildings, the spacing should be doubled.

drier—A tunnel-like forced-air oven used to dry veneer for plywood to a predetermined level (usually about 3%) before grading and layup.

drilling—To bore a hole using a brace and bit or an electric drill. In drilling plywood with brace and bit, the trick is to use the tool properly. **For large diameter holes** (up to 3 inches), it's important to protect the plywood from splintering. Do this by backing the panel with a scrap of wood clamped behind the area being drilled. This prevents splintering when the bit pierces the panel. Another technique is to bore from one side until the spur (point) of the bit comes through on the opposite side. Then, drill from the opposite side to complete the hole.

Using an expansion bit, you will get better leverage making partial turns with the brace ratchet. Otherwise the resistance of the side cutter tends to tear the wood.

For small diameter holes, such as where fastening must be very close to a plywood edge, either a hand drill or a push drill is preferable. Best results are obtained by holding the drill steady and turning the operating crank evenly, at the same time keeping pressure on the handle. A drill bit slightly smaller than the fastener diameter should be used.

earthquake design—Design of a structure so that it will withstand the forces imposed during an earthquake. Also referred to as "seismic design." Because of its bracing strength and rigidity, plywood sheathing is commonly used in earthquake-resistant shear wall and diaphragm construction.

eased edges—A term used to describe slight rounding of edge surfaces of a piece of lumber or plywood to remove sharp corners.

eaves—The edge of a roof that extends beyond or overhangs the wall. The underside of an eave may form an "open soffit." Textured plywood, applied face down to eave rafters as roof sheathing, gives a decorative finished surface to the open soffit.

edge treatment—Refers to edge finishing method used, such as banding with wood or plastic, or filling with putty or spackling.

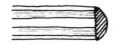

BUTT EDGING. KEEP EDGES SQUARE: USE MATCHING STRIP OF SOLID WOOD.

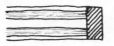

BUTT EDGING. KEEP EDGES
SQUARE: USE MATCHING STRIP
OF SOLID WOOD.

"MITTERED" BUTT EDGING. USE
GLUE AND BRADS TO FASTEN
THE STRIPS ON.

edge sealing—Application of a coating (e.g., sealant, paint)
to the edges of a plywood panel to reduce water absorption
into the panel. Edge seal before painting the panel surface if
panel edges will be repeatedly exposed to wetting and
drying.

edge support—Support, such as Plyclips, or blocking, installed between framing members at plywood panel edges to
transfer loads from one panel to the other across the joint.
Plywood with tongue-and-grooved edges can be used in
many applications without additional edge support.

edge void—A panel defect in which the edge or end of an
inner ply has split or broken away during manufacture,
leaving a gap in the edge of the plywood panel.

embossed plywood—Surface treatment of plywood by heat
and pressure against a master pattern to produce a variety
of textured effects. The texture or design is impressed into
the surface which remains smooth and paintable.

end grain—The end of a piece of wood (plywood or lumber)
that is exposed when the wood fibers are cut across the
grain.

engineered grades—General term for plywood panel
grades designed for structural uses, as opposed to "appear-

Unsanded sheathing grades for wall and roof sheathing, subflooring. Also available with exterior glue. Specify exterior
glue where durability is required in construction delays. For
permanent exposure to weather or moisture, only Exterior
type plywood is suitable.

| **C-D** 32/16 (APA) INTERIOR PS 1-74 000 | **C-D** 32/16 (APA) INTERIOR PS 1-74 000 | STRUCTURAL I **C-D** 32/16 (APA) INTERIOR PS 1-74 000 EXTERIOR GLUE | STRUCTURAL II **C-D** 48/24 (APA) INTERIOR PS 1-74 000 EXTERIOR GLUE |

For underlayment or combination subfloor-underlayment under resilient floor coverings. Also available with exterior glue for use where moisture conditions may be present, for instance, bathrooms or utility rooms. Sanded or touch-sanded as specified.

UNDERLAYMENT
C-C PLUGGED

GROUP 3 (APA)
EXTERIOR
PS 1-74 000

UNDERLAYMENT

GROUP 1 (APA)
INTERIOR
PS 1-74 000

Unsanded grade with waterproof bond for subflooring and roof decking, siding on service and farm buildings, crating, pallets, pallet bins, cable reels.

C-C
32/16 (APA)
EXTERIOR
PS 1-74 000

ance grades," which are usually sanded or textured. Grade-trademarks and uses of typical APA engineered grade plywood are shown below.

epoxy—An ingredient (synthetic resin) used in some paints and adhesives. Selected for its toughness, adhesion, and resistance to solvents.

exterior finishes—Surface coatings such as paints, stains, or sealers that protect plywood from weathering in outdoor exposures and improve appearance.

exterior type plywood—Plywood manufactured for outdoor or marine use. This type of plywood is bonded with 100% waterproof adhesives. Veneers are all grade C or better.

face—The better side of any plywood panel whose outer plies are of different veneer grades; also either side of a panel where grading rules draw no distinction between faces. Example is an A-C Exterior panel the A veneer side is the face of the panel.

face checking—Partial separation of wood fibers in the surface of plywood or wood, caused chiefly by the strains of weathering and seasoning.

face grain parallel (or perpendicular)—Direction of the grain of the outer ply (face) of a plywood panel in relation to the supports. Plywood's greatest strength is parallel to the face grain. Therefore, in construction, run the face grain across supports.

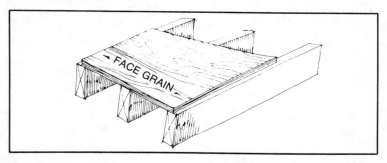

fascia—Wood or plywood trim used along the eave or the gable end of a structure.

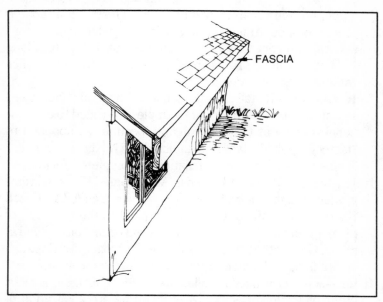

fasteners—Any device, such as a nail, screw, clip, or staple used to hold plywood securely in place of application (e.g., to structural framing). Nail size and type required is determined primarily by thickness and function of plywood. For an even stronger joint, use both glue and nails.

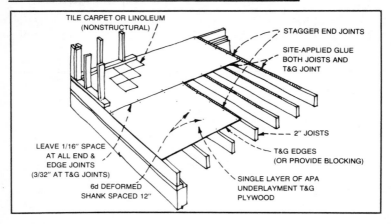

fiberglass reinforced plastic (FRP)—A product made up of glass fibers, used in combination with resins to create a tough, nonscuff coating over plywood. The resulting coated panel (composite) is used in truck and trailer bodies, containers, and concrete forms. Seamless panels 40 feet long and longer can be produced as a sidewall or roof of a trailer without internal framing.

field applied—Installed at the jobsite. Plywood panels used as wall or roof sheathing, for example, are nailed to conventional framing at the construction location, as opposed to "factory applied" where panelized or modular units are finished and ready for installation in completed form.

field gluing—Procedure used in APA® Glued Floor System, in which tough, specially developed glues (See APA's Glued Floor System, Form U405) are applied to the top edge of the floor joists, then the plywood is laid on and also nailed in place. Glue rather than nails carries the load, developing a stiffer floor construction that is virtually squeak-free.

filler—A material used for filling nail holes, checks, cracks or other blemishes in surfaces of wood before application of paint, varnish, or other finishes.

finishing—A finish's primary function is to protect the siding and maintain its appearance. It minimizes the weathering action which roughens and erodes the surface of unfinished wood. Different finishes give varying degrees of protection so the type, quality, quantity and application must be considered to achieve the desired performance.

Exterior finishing: All plywood edges should be sealed with a heavy application of exterior house paint primer if the panels will be painted. If the panel will be stained, edge seal with a water repellent preservative compatible with the finish. Sealing while the panels are stacked is easiest.

Semitransparent Stain: High quality oil base stains are recommended for textured plywood siding. These penetrate the surface and add color without film formation for a durable, breathing finish. Semitransparent stains give maximum grain and color showthrough. A brush-out test is recommended using a siding sample containing color contrasting characteristics. Apply one or two coats, following manufacturer's instructions. Two coats give a greater color tone.

Brush application gives the best performance. This helps work the stain into the surface, giving a uniform appearance. Application with a long napped roller is next best. Spray application is the poorest method and, if used, should be followed by back brushing. The spray must be liberally applied and back brushed to work the stain into the surface and under loose particles, especially on rough sawn surfaces. If the spray is fogged onto the siding, too little is applied. It rests completely on the outer surface on any loose particle, dust or fibers and quickly weathers away.

Opaque Stain: Oil base or latex emulsion opaque stains are highly pigmented and give a solid, even color, hiding all wood characteristics except texture. These stains penetrate the surface and develop a good bond.

Do not use typical shake and shingle paints or stains because they do not penetrate the wood properly. Usually cracks appear and water gets underneath to flake away the finish in a short time.

Paint: Top quality acrylic latex exterior house paint systems are recommended if paint is used on textured surfaces. It is the only finish recommended for untextured plywood. A minimum of two coats, consisting of primer and topcoat, are essential. A primer penetrates the wood, giving a good bond and minimizes extractive staining. Some latex systems use an oil or alkyd primer followed by the latex topcoat. Others use a specially formulated latex primer. In any case use companion products, preferably from the same manufacturer.

The primer should be brushed on for best performance. Use a stain resistant primer with a compatible top coat. Two top coats give much longer life and performance.

Plywood can be expected to check, especially on southern exposures. Checks usually blend with the surface of rough sawn or textured panels. Even when checking occurs, bond and wear characteristics of a good quality latex paint have been found to be completely satisfactory.

Specify Medium Density Overlaid (MDO) plywood for a completely check-free surface. MDO may be painted with any top quality exterior house paint system formulated for wood surfaces. Do not use clear film-forming finishes on plywood exposed outdoors.

Interior finishing: Preparation for interior finish is minimal. Overlaid (MDO and HDO) and textured plywood need no preparation; sanded grades require only touch sanding to smooth filler or spackle applied to fill any openings in the panel face, or to remove blemishes. Always sand with the grain, using fine sandpaper. Do not paint over dust or spots of oil or glue. All knots, pitch streaks, or sap spots in sanded or textured plywood should be touched up with sealer or shellac before panels are painted.

Paints are rolled, brushed, or sprayed on where washability and durability are most important. Generally, these are alkyd resin base enamels, characterized by good hiding properties. Some are self-priming on wood. Flat finish water-base latex paints have some degree of washability. They are easily applied with brush, roller or spray. When using these paints, prime plywood surface with an oil or alkyd compatible primer. Gloss and semigloss enamels (alkyd resin type) are extremely durable, washable finishes. Brush, roll or spray over manufacturer's recommended primer.

Plywood for natural finishes should be carefully selected for pattern and appearance. For the most natural effect, use two coats of clear sealer. Plywood's repairs and grain irregularities can be pleasantly subdued with either color toning or light stain.

Color toning requires companion stains and nonpenetrating sealers. These are combined and applied by brush or spray. After drying and light sanding, a coat of clear finish gives luster and durability. Tones of light gray, brown or tan go well with wood colors and provide best grain masking.

With light stain, the panel is first whitened with pigmented resin sealer or thinned interior white undercoat, then wiped to show grain. Clear resin sealer is applied, allowed to dry, and sanded lightly. Color is added (tinted undercoat, thin enamel, pigmented resin sealer or light stain) and wiped to the proper color depth. A final coat of satin varnish or brushing lacquer provides luster and durability.

For special effects, stipple texture paints can be applied, usually over taping to hide panel joints, after stain-resistant prime coat. Multicolor spatter finish (usually lacquer) achieves a distinctive effect when sprayed over colored or primed panels.

For attractive natural finish textured plywood (rough sawn, patterned surfaces, Texture 1-11, etc.) should be protected against soiling with two coats of a clear sealer or, pigmented stain. If desired, the few repairs and grain irregularities can be subdued by color toning or light stains. For complete finishing information for interior and exterior plywood, write for APA's Paint and Stain on Plywood, Form B407.

Government restrictions on the use of lead and mercury compounds in finishes have resulted in some uncertainty regarding the performance of new paints and stains. Results of tests in progress on new formulations will not be available for some time. APA® finishing recommendations are based on experience with formulations made prior to current restrictions. Check your supplier for interim recommendations.

fire-rated systems—Wall, floor, and roof construction of specific materials and designs that has been tested for conformance to fire safety criteria (e.g., flame spread rate and fire resistance), and rated accordingly. Testing and approval is done by agencies such as Underwriter's Laboratories, Inc. A one-hour rating, for example, means that an assembly similar to that tested will not collapse nor transmit flame or high temperature, for at least one hour after the fire starts. Plywood is an approved material in a number of fire rated designs.

fire retardant treated (FRT)—Chemical treatment of wood and plywood to retard combustion. Fire retardant chemicals mixed in water are deposited in the wood under pressure in accordance with American Wood Preservers Association Standard AWPA C27.

flame spread—Term that relates to spread of flame along the surface of a material. Flame spread ratings are expressed in numbers or letters and are used in describing interior finish requirements in building codes.

flange—Top and bottom longitudinal members of a beam. Plywood box beams are fabricated with lumber flanges (top and bottom) and plywood webs (sides).

floors—In modern wood construction, plywood is nearly indispensable as a floor material. Plywood for floors includes conventional subflooring, underlayment, and 2.4.1®(1-⅛ inch). Underlayment in ½, ⅝ and ¾ inch thickness and 2.4.1® may be used as combination subfloor and underlayment in a single layer (single floor) depending on support spacing.

APA Glued Floor System: APA-developed floor construction system in which structural plywood underlayment is glued with elastomeric adhesives and nailed to wood joists. The bond is so strong that floor and joists behave like an integral unit, which greatly increases stiffness and virtually eliminates squeaks. Joists can sometimes be reduced in size or in some cases, spaced further apart, reducing material costs.

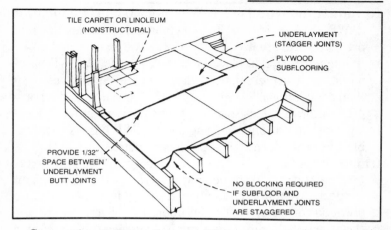

Conventional Floor System: With conventional floor construction, plywood underlayment covers subflooring applied to joists.

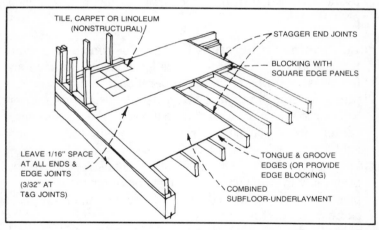

foam core—Center of a plywood "sandwich" panel. Liquid plastic is foamed into all spaces between the plywood panels and serves to insulate as well as support the component skins. Or plywood skins are pressure-glued to both sides of rigid plastic foam boards or billets.

fortified glue—Hot press protein adhesives to which phenolic resin has been added. Used in Interior type plywood. Not suitable for exterior exposure.

foundation wood—All Weather Wood Foundation (AWWF). A residential building foundation system in which pressure-preservative-treated plywood panels and wood framing are used in place of masonry walls. AWWF basements are warmer, tighter, drier, and more leak-resistant than conventional basements. AWWF can be installed on a prepared site in less than half a day in any weather, speeding construction and reducing costs. AWWF is also applicable to crawl-space foundation construction.

frame construction—A type of building in which the structural parts are wood or dependent on a wood framework for support. Commonly, lumber framing is sheathed with plywood for roofs, walls and floor. In building codes, the classification of frame construction remains the same even when masonry covering is applied on exterior walls.

furring—Process of leveling parts of a ceiling, wall, or floor by means of wood strips called furring strips, before adding plywood cover.

gang forming (concrete)—Grouping of lumber or metal-framed plywood panels to create large formwork sections for massive concrete pouring operations.

girder—A large horizontal beam used to support interior walls or joists. Most wood frame houses have a lengthwise center girder that supports the floor joists and plywood subflooring.

glue—In plywood construction, many adhesives are used, preferably in conjunction with nails or other fasteners, to produce strong joints. Type used depends upon purpose and exposure of finished product.

glue-nailed (also nail-glued)—Combination of gluing and nailing plywood joints and connections for stiffest possible construction. For most effective fastening, pieces to be joined should contact at all points. Glue is applied to one or both surfaces according to manufacturer's directions, then surfaces are pressed together and nailed in place. For work such as cabinets or drawers, or whenever possible, joint should be clamped as well as nailed to maintain pressure until glue sets.

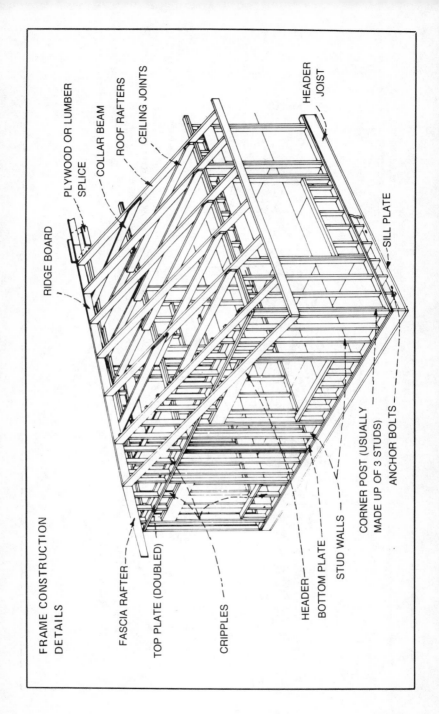

FRAME CONSTRUCTION DETAILS

RIDGE BOARD

PLYWOOD OR LUMBER SPLICE

COLLAR BEAM

ROOF RAFTERS

CEILING JOISTS

HEADER JOIST

SILL PLATE

FASCIA RAFTER

TOP PLATE (DOUBLED)

CRIPPLES

HEADER

BOTTOM PLATE

STUD WALLS

CORNER POST (USUALLY MADE UP OF 3 STUDS)

ANCHOR BOLTS

327

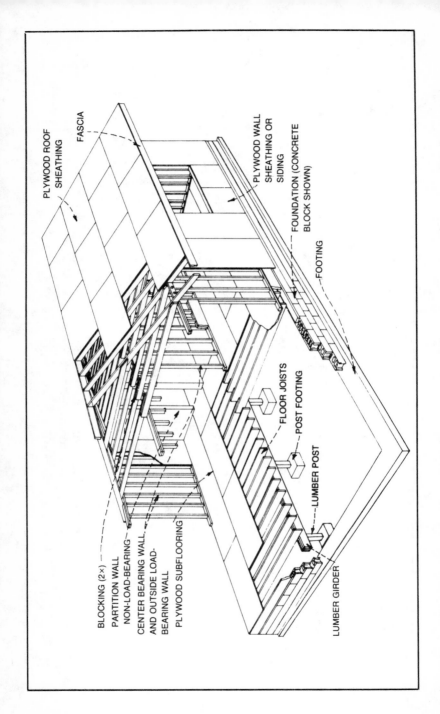

PLYWOOD ROOF SHEATHING

FASCIA

PLYWOOD WALL SHEATHING OR SIDING

FOUNDATION (CONCRETE BLOCK SHOWN)

FOOTING

FLOOR JOISTS

POST FOOTING

LUMBER POST

LUMBER GIRDER

BLOCKING (2×)

PARTITION WALL NON-LOAD-BEARING

CENTER BEARING WALL AND OUTSIDE LOAD-BEARING WALL

PLYWOOD SUBFLOORING

glulam—Short for glued-laminated structural timber, term is used to describe large beams fabricated by bonding layers of specially selected lumber together with strong, durable adhesives. End and edge jointing permits production of longer and wider structural wood members than are normally available. Glulam timbers are used with plywood for many types of heavy timber construction.

good one side—Obsolete term for plywood that has a higher grade veneer on the face than on the back, used in situations where only one side of the panel will be visible. Such panels are properly identified by referring to their face grades, as "A-D" for instance.

grade—Designation of the quality of a piece of plywood. In plywood there are several veneer grades described by letter which calls out the face and back veneers (B-C, etc.) or by intended end use of the grade, for example,

grade-trademark (GTM)—In the plywood industry, a mark stamped on the back or branded into the edge of a panel of plywood, which includes the type and grade of the panel in addition to an identifying symbol.

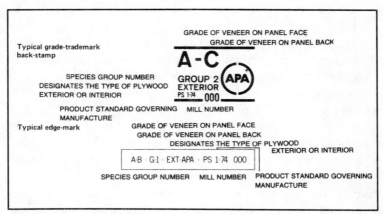

grading rules—Standards of grading for the softwood lumber industry. Grading rules were standardized originally about 1925 and published by the major softwood lumber associations. Current grading rules agree with Product Standard PS 20-70, The American Lumber Standard.

grain—The natural pattern of growth in wood. The grain runs lengthwise of the tree; therefore, the strength is greatest in that direction.

grain direction—In the face and back veneers of a plywood panel, grain usually runs the long dimension making the panel strongest in that direction.

grain raise—The condition resulting on the surface of a plywood panel when the harder or more dense fibers of wood swell and raise above the surrounding softer wood.

groove—One of the surface treatments frequently given to textured plywood, in which a series of narrow parallel channels are cut into the surface of the panel. Grooving is available in a variety of widths and spacings on several surface textures.

growth ring—The growth layer put on a tree in a single year, including springwood and summerwood.

group, species—Plywood is manufactured from over 70 different species of varying strength. These species have been grouped on the basis of strength and stiffness, and, for purposes of the manufacturing standard, PS 1, divided into five classifications: Group 1, Group 2, Group 3, Group 4, and Group 5. Strongest woods are found in Group 1. The group number of a particular panel is determined by the weakest (highest numbered) species used in face and back (except for some siding panels where strength parallel to face grain is not important).

gusset plate—A piece of plywood used to connect lumber members of a truss or other frame structure. Gussets may be applied to one or both sides of the joint. Plywood is used because of its great strength and resistance to splitting.

handy plans—A series of illustrated home projects for the do-it-yourselfer, published by the American Plywood Association. A wide variety of plans is available, from garden and outdoor sports equipment, to toys, furniture, and storage. See APA Form Y630.

hardwood—Wood of the broadleaved trees—oak, maple, ash, walnut—as contrasted to the softwood of the needleleaved trees such as pine, fir, spruce, hemlock. Term has no reference to actual hardness of the wood. Construction and industrial plywood may use either type.

header—A cross member placed between studs or joists to support openings, such as for stairway, chimney or doors.

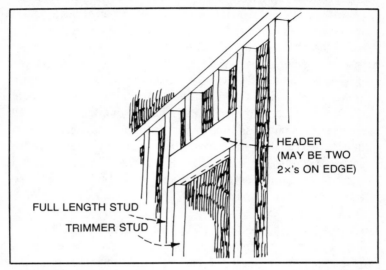

HEADER
(MAY BE TWO
2×'s ON EDGE)

FULL LENGTH STUD

TRIMMER STUD

heartwood—The nonactive core of a tree, distinguishable from the growing sapwood by its usually darker color.

heat, effects of—Because of its glueline durability, plywood performance is not generally degraded by heat. However, plywood should generally not be used where temperatures are to exceed 230°F. Panels subjected to dry heat for long periods naturally will dry out, inviting checking, unless properly finished and protected. Low temperatures do not affect plywood adversely.

heavy timber—A building code designation for a particular type of construction with good fire endurance. Heavy Timber is widely recognized as comparable to one-hour construction. A plywood roof deck of tongue-and-grooved 1-⅛ inch 2.4.1 over 4 inch wide supports meets the Heavy Timber requirements, and provides the same good performance as nominal 2 inch tongue-and-groove lumber decking. See Construction for Fire Protection, Form W305.

high density overlay (HDO)—Exterior type plywood finished with a resin-impregnated fiber overlay to provide extremely smooth hard surfaces that need no additional finishing, and have high resistance to chemicals and abrasion. The overlay material is bonded to both sides of the plywood to become an integral part of the panel faces. Used for concrete forms, cabinets, highway signs, counter tops, and other hard-wear applications.

humidity, effects of—Moisture absorption by wood causes it to swell slightly. Plywood's cross-laminated construction restricts expansion and contraction within the individual plies. From oven-dry to soaking wet, plywood panels swell across the grain less than ⅛ inch. When applying plywood always leave 1/16-inch space between panel ends and ⅛ inch between edges of adjacent panels. If wet or humid conditions are expected (such as in farm buildings), these spacings should be doubled.

I-beam—Beam whose cross-section resembles the letter I. Plywood box beams are constructed much as enclosed I-beams and are used extensively as structural supporting members.

IIC—Impact Insulation Class. IIC values are a measure of the capacity of floor assemblies to control impact noise such as footfalls. FHA codes (and some local building codes) specify minimum acceptable ratings. See APA Form W460, Plywood Construction and Noise Control.

INR—Impact Noise Rating. A technical term for floor assembly sound transmission values. Now being replaced by IIC standards.

INT with exterior glue—Interior type plywood manufactured with exterior glue for greater ability to withstand exposure to moisture. Not suitable for permanent exterior exposure.

identification index—A set of numbers (e.g., 24/O) used in marking sheathing grades of plywood. Numbers relate to species of the panel face and back veneers and to the panel thickness. They describe the panel's strength and stiffness properties. The Identification Index was developed primarily to identify maximum support spacing for plywood in conventional construction. Numbers on the left side of the slash (/) refer to the required spacing of roof framing members (good for 35 pounds per square foot uniform live load or better). Right-hand numbers refer to floor framing spacing requirements. (Maximum uniform live loads vary, but all are at least 160 pounds per square foot; also good for concentrated loads such as pianos, home freezers, water heaters, etc.)

Actual maximum spans for plywood panels are established by local building codes.

impact resistance—Ability to withstand sharp blows or violent contact. Plywood's cross-laminated construction provides great resistance to these blows and distributes the force across both dimensions of the panel.

inner plies—All layers of a plywood panel except face and back.

interior type—Term used to describe plywood intended for inside uses or for construction where plywood will be subjected to only occasional wetting. Interior type plywood is bonded with adhesives that are highly moisture resistant but not necessarily waterproof.

intermediate glue—A glue which can be used in the manufacture of Interior type plywood that is more moisture resistant than interior glue, but not intended for permanent exposure. Panels with intermediate glue are suitable where moderate delays in providing protection are expected, or where high humidity or water leakage may occur temporarily. Check availability before specifying.

joint treatment—Method of covering or sealing space between panels. For subfloor, roof, and wall sheathing, a space of ⅛ inch should be left between sheathing panel edges and 1/16 inch between ends to allow for expansion. **Exterior siding joints** may be sealed with building paper or caulking. Edges may be shiplapped, or horizontal butt joints may be sealed with Z-flashing. Battens may be used with vertically applied sidings to double as decorative finish. In all cases, exterior joints should be backed with solid lumber framing. See APA's Residential Construction Guide, Form Y405 for spacing recommendations.

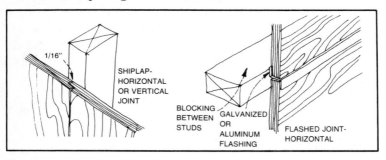

jointed core—Core veneer that has had edges machined square. Gaps between pieces of core shall not exceed ⅜ inch, and the average of all gaps in the panel shall not exceed 3/16 inch.

joist—Horizontal framing members of a floor or ceiling. Plywood is commonly used for subflooring and underlayment over floor joists.

joist spacing—Distances (specified by building codes) between joists. Usually specified as o.c. (on center), which is the distance from the center of one joist to the center of the next joist.

kerf—A slot made by a saw; the width of the saw cut.

kiln dried—A term applied to wood that has been dried in ovens (kilns) by controlled heat and humidity to specified limits of moisture content. Plywood veneers are kiln dried before lay-up.

knot—Natural growth characteristic of wood that occurs where a branch base is imbedded in the trunk of a tree.

knotholes—Voids produced when knots drop out of veneer.

laminate—To produce a product by bonding together a series of layers, as plywood or laminated structural members. Plywood is laminated with grain of layers at right angles to that of adjacent layers for two-way strength.

Structural members, such as beams, are laminated with the grain running the same direction in all layers.

lap—To position so that one surface extends over the other. Term may be used to designate a plywood exterior **lap siding** technique, in which each plywood panel overlaps the edge of the next lower panel. A plywood **shiplap joint** unites two panels when half the thickness of each panel is cut away so that the two pieces fit together with outer faces flush.

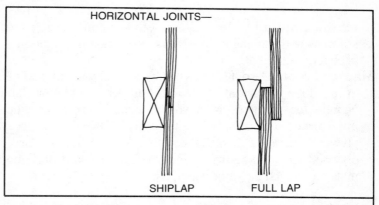

HORIZONTAL JOINTS—

SHIPLAP   FULL LAP

latex paint—Water-base paints which are available for both interior and exterior use, and which have excellent adhesion and blister-resistant characteristics.

layer—A single ply, or veneer, or two or more plies laminated with grain directions parallel.

lay-up—The step in manufacture of plywood in which veneers are "stacked" in complete panel "packages" after gluing and before pressing.

loads—The weight or pressure a structure carries or sustains, which must be considered in planning a building. **Uniform loads** are evenly distributed over a large area, usually the entire surface of a plywood panel. **Concentrated loads** are loads applied over a very small area (for example, by a piano leg). **Dead loads** are stationary, permanent loads; that is, the weight of all the material used in construction of the building (or section). **Live loads** are planned loads the structure must carry under normal conditions, such as people or furniture and equipment, that would be moved on the surface. These loads are generally assigned by the building code for the type of structure; for example, a heavy-equipment storage warehouse, a house, or an office building. Live loads are generally considered to be uniform loads.

lumber core—Plywood construction in which the core is composed of lumber strips. The face and back (outer) plies are veneer.

machine grading—Mechanical method of measuring the stiffness and assigning the stress grade of a material on a production-line basis.

Mansard roof—A roof with two slopes on all four sides. The lower slope is very steep, and the upper one almost flat. Named for Francois Mansard, a French architect who popularized the shape in the early 1600's. Textured plywood makes a handsome finish for mansards. Also, plywood sheathing is used under other mansard finishing materials, such as wood shingles.

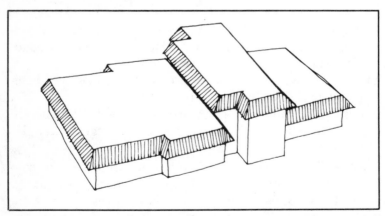

marine grade—Panels manufactured with the same glueline durability requirements as other Exterior type panels but with more restrictive requirements on wood characteristics. The grade is particularly suitable for marine applications where bending is required, as in boat hulls.

mastic—A tacky substance used as a crack filler or sealer that does not completely solidify, but retains some elasticity. Also descriptive of some construction adhesives.

mechanical properties—The strength and stiffness characteristics of plywood affecting its structural behavior in use. These include the following: **Resistance to impact loads,** due to its cross-laminated construction. Grain running crosswise in alternate layers distributes impact forces down the length and width of the panel that would shatter other materials. **Resistance to racking,** the ability to resist forces that would "pull" a plywood panel from its rectangular shape. (Tests prove ¼ inch plywood wall sheathing on a standard stud wall has twice the strength and rigidity of 1 × 8 diagonal board sheathing.) **Stiffness,** strongest and stiffest when panels installed with the face grain across supports. For best results lay panels over 3 or more supports. **Strength in bending,** large panel size with high bending strength make plywood an excellent material for bulkheads, retaining walls and grain bin lining. **Tension and Compression,** plywood splice plates are used to transfer tension (pulling loads) and compression (pushing loads) between skins of stressed-skin panels.

medium density overlaid MDO—Exterior type plywood finished with an opaque resin-treated fiber overlay to provide a smooth surface that is an ideal base for paint. Recommended for siding and other outdoor applications, and for built-ins, signs, and displays.

melamine glue—A type of glue used in scarf-jointing plywood panels. Heat and pressure are required for proper curing. Also used in patching panels and in some coatings.

metal overlaid—Plywood that has a metal face permanently bonded to it. Panels may be metal overlaid on one or both sides. Surface finishes include pebble texture as well as assorted colors (baked-on enamel).

mildew—A mold or discoloration on wood in areas of excessively warm, humid conditions or in areas of poor air circulation. Mildew begins on plywood as dark spots on the surface and spreads in gray, fan-shaped areas. A dark spot usually can be identified as mildew if it disappears when household bleach is applied. To remove mild case of mildew, scrub surface gently with mild detergent, then rinse with household bleach and water. For severe cases, use a stiff bristle brush and a solution of one cup trisodium phosphate (available at drug or paint stores), one cup household bleach, and one gallon warm water. Flush with water and allow to dry.

miter joints—A joint formed by fitting together two pieces of lumber or plywood that have been cut off on an angle.

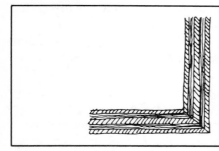

MITERED JOINT

MOD 24 (engineered 24″ framing system)—A building system using plywood over lumber framing spaced 24 inches on center in walls, floors, and roof. The system uses a series of in-line frames—trusses, studs and joists to provide for efficient, less costly utilization of materials and simpler, faster construction. It is recognized by major model codes and the FHA.

model code—A building code developed by a regional federation of building officials. These are continually reviewed and updated by committees of building officials. Model codes in the United States are the Uniform Building Code (UBC), Standard Building Code (BBC) and the National Building Code (NBC).

modular home—A dwelling that is factory-produced as a complete unit, ready to install at the home site on a prepared permanent foundation. Modular homes, constructed of plywood components, are fabricated under factory quality-inspection procedures to provide high quality for lower cost.

moisture content—As applied to wood and plywood, the amount of water held by the wood. It is usually expressed as a percentage of the weight of the oven-dried wood (i.e., a one pound sample of oven-dried wood could absorb 25% of its weight in water and weigh 1-¼ pounds at 25% moisture content.) The plywood product standard limits the moisture content of plywood to a maximum of 18% of the oven-dry weight at the time of shipment from the mill.

NABM—National Association of Building Manufacturers.

NAHB—National Association of Home Builders. A trade organization that represents contractors, builders, and construction firms engaged in home building.

NBC—National Building Code.

NFPA—National Forest Products Association, 1619 Massachusetts Avenue, N. W., Washington, D. C. 20036.

nails—For correct nail spacing, see charts in particular application, such as sidings, underlayment, wall construction.

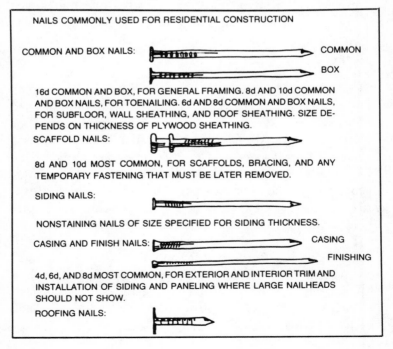

NAILS COMMONLY USED FOR RESIDENTIAL CONSTRUCTION

COMMON AND BOX NAILS: COMMON BOX

16d COMMON AND BOX, FOR GENERAL FRAMING. 8d AND 10d COMMON AND BOX NAILS, FOR TOENAILING. 6d AND 8d COMMON AND BOX NAILS, FOR SUBFLOOR, WALL SHEATHING, AND ROOF SHEATHING. SIZE DEPENDS ON THICKNESS OF PLYWOOD SHEATHING.

SCAFFOLD NAILS:

8d AND 10d MOST COMMON, FOR SCAFFOLDS, BRACING, AND ANY TEMPORARY FASTENING THAT MUST BE LATER REMOVED.

SIDING NAILS:

NONSTAINING NAILS OF SIZE SPECIFIED FOR SIDING THICKNESS.

CASING AND FINISH NAILS: CASING FINISHING

4d, 6d, AND 8d MOST COMMON, FOR EXTERIOR AND INTERIOR TRIM AND INSTALLATION OF SIDING AND PANELING WHERE LARGE NAILHEADS SHOULD NOT SHOW.

ROOFING NAILS:

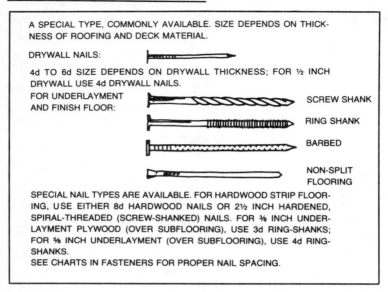

A SPECIAL TYPE, COMMONLY AVAILABLE. SIZE DEPENDS ON THICKNESS OF ROOFING AND DECK MATERIAL.

DRYWALL NAILS:

4d TO 6d SIZE DEPENDS ON DRYWALL THICKNESS; FOR ½ INCH DRYWALL USE 4d DRYWALL NAILS.

FOR UNDERLAYMENT AND FINISH FLOOR:

SCREW SHANK

RING SHANK

BARBED

NON-SPLIT FLOORING

SPECIAL NAIL TYPES ARE AVAILABLE. FOR HARDWOOD STRIP FLOORING, USE EITHER 8d HARDWOOD NAILS OR 2½ INCH HARDENED, SPIRAL-THREADED (SCREW-SHANKED) NAILS. FOR ⅜ INCH UNDERLAYMENT PLYWOOD (OVER SUBFLOORING), USE 3d RING-SHANKS; FOR ⅝ INCH UNDERLAYMENT (OVER SUBFLOORING), USE 4d RING-SHANKS.
SEE CHARTS IN FASTENERS FOR PROPER NAIL SPACING.

nail coatings—Surface treatment, such as galvanizing, to prevent nails from rusting upon exposure to weather, which prevents staining of the siding material. Coatings are also used to color match nails to panels with which they are used.

nail popping—A problem in which nails used in applying the Underlayment sometimes appear to "pop" up so that nail head impressions are visible on the surface of the finished floor covering. The problem is caused by shrinkage of floor joists away from the nails after installation. Unless joists are thoroughly seasoned and dry, counter-sink all nailheads 1/16 inch below the surface of the Underlayment just prior to laying on the floor covering. **Do not fill nail holes.**

nail schedules—Refers to the size and spacing of nails that should be used with various thicknesses of plywood.

nail staining—Staining of a surface (e.g., siding) due to corrosion of the fastener or nail upon exposure to weather.

nail withdrawal—Refers to the resistance of a nail to being pulled out of wood. Ring-shank or spiral-thread nails have much higher nail-holding power than regular smooth-shank nails or coated nails.

340

noise control—Use of materials in construction to reduce sound transmission. Various plywood construction systems have been tested both in laboratories and in buildings, and have been found more than adequate to meet federal standards. To avoid costly mistakes of poor acoustics see APA's Plywood Construction and Noise Control, Form W460.

nominal thickness—Full "designated" thickness. For example, a nominal 2 inch × 4 inch stud may be 1-½ inch × 3-½ inch when dry. It is a commercial size designation, subject to acceptable tolerances.

noncertified—Term that refers to plywood not included in the Product Standard PS 1 and which may bear the mark of the manufacturer rather than one of the recognized testing agencies, such as APA.

O.C.—On-center spacing, meaning the distance from the center of one structural member to the center of the adjacent member, as in the spacing of studding, joists, rafters, nails, etc.

O&ES—Oiled and edge sealed. The surfaces of concrete form panels are lightly coated with oil, and the edges sealed if specified.

one-hour rating—A fire rating.

open defects—Irregularities such as splits, open joints, and knotholes that interrupt the smooth continuity of plywood veneer.

overhang—Projection of a roof or upper story of a building beyond the wall of the lower part, as the overhang of a roof.

overlaid plywood—Plywood panels with factory applied resin-treated fiber faces on one or both sides. Term may also be applied to metal overlaid plywood and other composites.

PRF—Plywood Research Foundation. An affiliate of the American Plywood Association, made up of APA members and associate members engaged in plywood-related activities, such as manufacturers of adhesive equipment, and chemicals.

PSF—Pounds per square foot. Measure of loads distributed over a square foot of surface. Used in determining allowable spans for subfloor and roof sheathing and floor framing.

PSI—Pounds per square inch. Measure of loads distributed over a square inch of surface.

P&TS—Plugged and touch-sanded face of a plywood panel.

pallet—A portable platform designed for storage, handling or movement of packages and materials in warehouses, factories, or vehicles.

pallet bin—A box-type storage container with bottom construction for handling by fork-lift. Plywood pallet bins can absorb sharp blows with little or no damage, can withstand exposure to weather, and offer low-weight high-capacity ratios. Bins may be large or small, demountable (fold flat for storage), and designed for two- or four-way forklift entry.

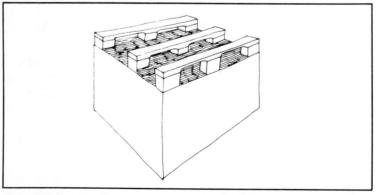

panel faces—Outer veneers of a plywood panel.

panel grades—Appearance or structural grade of a plywood panel, determined by the veneer grades used for the face and back of the panel.

panel patch—A repair installed in the face or back veneer of a panel after lay-up and pressing of the panel.

panel spacing—The gap left between plywood panels when they are installed in a structure. A space should be left between panels in floor, wall or roof deck construction to allow for expansion due to changes in moisture conditions. Space conventional plywood subfloor ⅛ inch at edges and 1/16 inch at all end panel joints. Provide 1/32 inch space between underlayment butt joints over subfloor construction. Space conventional sheathing ⅛ and 1/16 inch. When wet or humid conditions can be expected, double these spacings for sheathing and subfloor panels.

paneling—Wood panels joined in a continuous surface, especially, decorative panels for interior wall finish. Textured plywood in many varieties is often used as interior paneling either in full wall sections or for accent walls. See sidings for texture plywood used as paneling.

panelized construction— Building components fabricated in the form of wall, floor, ceiling, etc., sections, that will be assembled into the completed structure at the building site. Panelized construction cuts on-site labor charges through rapid erection. It offers the high quality available through controlled factory production and inspection procedures.

patch—An insertion of sound wood in veneers or panels for replacing defective areas. Patches may be in a variety of shapes. Most commonly used are "boat" patches, oval shaped with sides tapering to points or small rounded ends; "router" patches with parallel sides and rounded ends; and "sled" patches, rectangular in shape with feathered ends.

peel—To cut wood into thin sheets of veneer in a lathe by rotating the log against a long knife. **Peel quality** refers to smoothness of the veneer.

Penta (Pentachlorophenol)—A type of preservative that gives long-lasting protection against termites, rot, mold, and mildew. Penta-treated plywood is noncorrosive, fairly clean to handle and does not produce skin burn, and may be used for exterior exposure.

permeability—As applied to plywood, the readiness with which water vapor moves through the plywood panel thickness. To prolong the life of finishes, a vapor barrier should be installed on the warm side of the wall and ceiling construction. Vapor transmission is also a factor in construction of the All Weather Wood Foundation System, and must be controlled through use of a vapor barrier.

phenol resorcinol—A synthetic-resin-compound adhesive used in manufacture of plywood and plywood components, in scarf joints, and for Exterior type plywood panel patching. Also called modified resorcinol.

physical properties—The characteristics of plywood as a material other than those relating to strength. Physical properties include: **Thermal conductivity:** Under normal room temperature and humidity conditions, plywood is a natural insulator. **Electrical conductivity**: At low moisture content, plywood is a normally classified as an electrical insulator (dielectric); however, its resistance to passage of current decreases as moisture content increases. **Reaction to chemical exposure:** Plywood behaves much like solid wood with good resistance to chemical exposure. MDO & HDO plywoods have very high resistance to chemicals. **Vapor transmission:** Plywood has good resistance to moisture passing through it; however, for best construction install with a vapor barrier such as polyethylene film. **Acoustics:** Thicker plywood panels are better sound insulators than are thin panels.

pitch streak—A localized accumulation of pitch in wood cells in a more or less regular streak.

planing—To smooth or shape a wood surface. Planing plywood edges with a plane or jointer is not often necessary if the saw cut has been made with a sharp saw blade. If planing is necessary, work from both ends toward the center to avoid tearing out plies at the end of the cut. For best results, use a hollow ground blade and make very shallow cuts.

plate—In wood frame construction, the horizontal dimension lumber member placed on top and/or bottom of the exterior wall studs to tie them together and to support the joists and rafters.

plug—Sound wood of various shapes including, among others, circular or dog bone shapes, used in plywood manufacture to replace defective portions of veneers (see patches). Also synthetic fillers of fiber and resin to fill openings and provide a smooth, level, durable surface.

ply—A single veneer in a glued plywood panel.

plyclips®—American Plywood Association trade name for special aluminum H-clips used as an economical substitute for lumber blocking in roof construction.

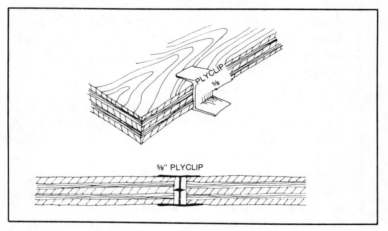

plyform—American Plywood Association trade name for a concrete form panel.

plywood sizes—Although the most common panel size is 4 × 8 feet many manufacturers produce 4 × 9 and 4 × 10 panels. Other sizes are available on special order. Tongue-and-groove panels are usually 4 × 8 overall, or about 47-½ inches wide, plus or minus ⅛ inch on the face. See APA Directory: Members, Products, Services, Form Y815.

plywood systems—A general term to describe a method of construction that incorporates plywood as a major structural material. Plywood construction systems include APA

Glued Floor System, APA Sturd-I-Wall, and All-Weather Wood Foundation System.

prefabricated—To construct or fabricate all parts, as of a house, at the factory, so that final construction consists only of assembling and uniting of standards parts at the jobsite.

prefinished—A panel that has a factory-applied primer or undercoat so that the panel is ready for use.

preframed—Construction term for panelized building, in which the wall, floor, or roof sections are complete; that is, they are framed and sheathed at the factory.

preprimed—A panel that has a factory-applied primer or undercoat so that only the final finish need be applied after the panel is in place.

preservatives—Any of a number of treatments to prevent plywood or wood from deteriorating due to exposure to weather, adverse moisture conditions, or insect attack. Treatments range from chemical impregnation under pressure, as for wood foundation or reservoir cover use, to any of the many paints, stains, or sealers.

press, hot—In the plywood industry a press that utilzes both heat and pressure to bond plywood veneers into panels. All Exterior type plywood is manufactured in hot presses. Hot press may also be used to refer to Interior type plywood that has been manufactured in a hot press.

product standards—Industry manufacturing product specifications promulgated through the U.S Department of Commerce. American Plywood Association grade-trademarks on a panel are positive identification by the manufacturer that the plywood has been produced in conformance to U.S. Product Standard PS 1 for Construction and Industrial Plywood.

puncture resistance—Ability to withstand damage when sharp or extremely heavy objects are dropped on the surface. Plywood is extremely puncture resistant because of its cross-laminated structure, which distributes the impact forces.

purlin—Subframing whose major purpose is to support the roof decking, where larger beams are main structural supports.

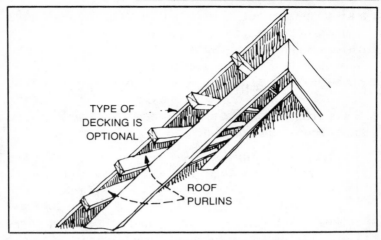

TYPE OF
DECKING IS
OPTIONAL

ROOF
PURLINS

quality testing program—Testing program, administered
by APA and designed to assure quality levels equal to or
exceeding that prescribed by the product standard. The
program is based on a scientific random sampling process.
Plywood quality in every American Plywood Association
member mill is checked in frequent unannounced calls by
trained inspectors. The program includes provisions for
withdrawal of grade-trademark privilege if quality levels are
not maintained.

rabbet joint—A joint formed by cutting a groove in the
surface or along the edge of a board, plank, or panel to
receive another piece.

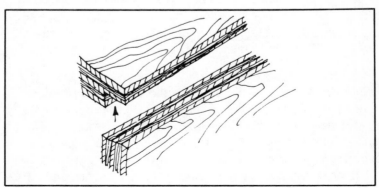

racking resistance—The ability of plywood to resist forces that would pull a panel from its rectangular shape.

rafters—Supporting members immediately beneath the roof sheathing.

refinishing—Application of new surface treatment (paint, stain, or sealer) to renew the appearance and prolong the life of the plywood. Refinishing is necessary only if original finish shows signs of deterioration.

For previously stained plywood, remove surface dust and finish chalk using a mild detergent solution followed by thorough rinsing. (If surface fibers are loose, remove with light bristle brushing before cleaning.) If opaque stain was original finish, remove any loosened film using a water blaster (available from equipment rental agencies).

For previously painted surfaces, remove all loose paint, surface dirt and chalk. On textured plywood, use a stiff brush or water blaster. On sanded plywood, use moderate sanding, a stiff-bristle brush, or power tools. Feather edges of remaining paint by sanding. Wash and rinse off surface dirt and dust and allow to dry. If plywood has checked, fill checks with a pliable patching compound before repainting.

For MDO plywood, remove loose paint by brushing with stiff-bristle brush or use chemical paint remover, using caution so as not to damage the overlay surface. Then clean, rinse, and dry.

For mildewed surfaces, scrub lightly with mild detergent, rinse with household bleach, rinse with clear water, and dry. New paint or stain finish should be applied to prepared surface according to recommendations given in finishing. APA's Paint and Stain on Plywood, Form BA407, for complete details.

repair—Any patch, plug, or shim in a plywood panel.

resawn—Rough sawn. A decorative treatment normally provided by scoring the surface of a panel with a saw after manufacture, which imparts a rough, rustic appearance.

resilient floor covering—Any of the vinyl or asphalt-base floor coverings (tile or sheet) that has a certain amount of "give" to it, to resist deformation such as denting as a result of impact of dropping objects. Resilient floor coverings installed over plywood subflooring and underlayment provide smooth, stiff floors for comfortable walking.

reverse board and batten—One of the surface patterns for plywood siding. Deep, wide grooves give deep, sharp shadowline.

ridge beam—The top horizontal member of a sloping roof, against which the ends of the rafters are fixed or supported.

rigid frame—Structural member in which the studs and rafters are joined together with plywood gussets, so that they act together like an arch. Rigid frame construction eliminates the need for ceiling or tie members.

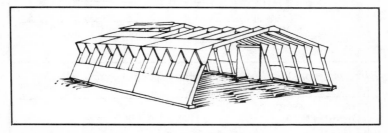

ripping—In woodworking, the sawing of wood with the grain.

rise—The distance through which anything rises, as the rise of a stair or the rise of a roof.

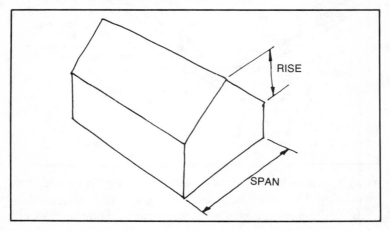

roofs—Plywood provides a tight roof deck with no wind, dust or snow infiltration and high resistance to racking. Roof systems include plywood roof sheathing under conventional shingles, preframed and folded plate systems. (See Plywood Commercial/Industrial Construction Guide Y300).

Folded plate roof

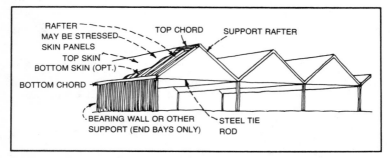

Plywood roof sheathing with conventional shingle roofing

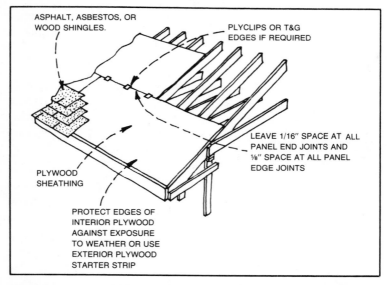

rough sawn—A decorative treatment normally provided by scoring the surface of a panel with a saw after manufacture which imparts a rough, rustic appearance. Same as resawn.

SBC—Standard Building Code

SFPA—Southern Forest Products Association, P.O. Box 52468, New Orleans, Louisiana 70152

STC—Sound Transmission Class. A measure of the ability of a wall or floor assembly to reduce noise transmission. See APA Form W460, Plywood Construction and Noise Control.

Sanding—Smoothing the surface of wood with sandpaper or some other abrasive. With plywood, sanding should be confined to edges. Normally all grades with N, A, or B faces are sanded smooth in manufacture—one of the big timesavers in its use—and further sanding of the surfaces merely removes soft grain. After sealing, sand in direction of grain only. A sanding block will prevent gouging. See APA Form V605, How to Book.

sandwich panels—Sections (as of walls) of layered construction made up of high-strength plywood faces, or "skins" attached to both sides of low-density core materials, such as plastic foam or honeycomb paper fillers.

sapwood—The living wood of pale color near the outside of a log. Under most conditions, sapwood is more susceptible to decay than heartwood.

sawing—In hand-sawing plywood, use a 10 to 15 point (teeth per inch) crosscut saw. Support panel firmly with face up. Hold saw nearly flat to the panel face to score the surface with forward strokes only, then cut through with saw held at normal angle. For power sawing, a plywood blade gives best results, but a combination blade may be used. Place panel face down for hand power sawing; panel face up for table power sawing. With first cuts reduce panel to pieces small enough for easy handling. Use a piece of scrap lumber underneath panel, clamped or tacked securely in place to prevent splintering on back side. Plan to cut matching parts with same saw setting. Use a fine tooth coping saw for curves. If available, you may use a jigsaw, sabre saw or bandsaw for curved parts; just be sure blade enters face of panel. When planning the project always allow for material lost in saw kerfs. See APA's How To Book, Form V605.

scarf joint—An angled or beveled joint in plywood where pieces are spliced together. The length of the scarf is 5 to 12 times the thickness.

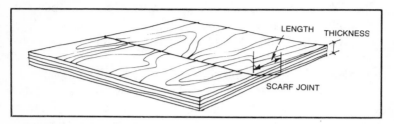

seasoning—Removal of moisture from wood to improve its serviceability, usually by: Air drying—drying by exposure to air without artificial heat; and Kiln-drying—drying in a kiln using artificial heat. Plywood veneers are seasoned before lay-up and gluing into panels.

secondary glueline—The glue joint formed in gluing together wood and plywood and plywood parts in an assembly such as a component. The glueline between veneers in a plywood panel is called the "primary glueline."

seismic design—Construction designed to withstand earthquake forces.

sheathing—The structural covering, usually of plywood or boards, on the outside surface of the framing. It provides support for construction, snow, and wind loads and backing for attaching the exterior facing material such as wall siding or roof shingles. C-D Interior or C-D Interior with exterior glue are recommended as sheathing products.

shelf—Both in commercial and residential applications, plywood is an excellent shelving material because of its inherent stiffness and rigidity. See APA's How To Book, Form V605, and Plywood Design Manual-Shelving, Form S210.

shingles—Thin pieces of wood (or other material) rectangular in shape used for covering roofs or walls. Plywood sheathing under shingles provides a tight deck sealing out wind, dust, or snow and gives the structure high resistance to racking. Plywood may be used under asphalt, asbestos, or wood shingles with excellent results. Shingles should always be installed according to manufacturer's recommendations.

shiplap—A method of jointing in which the ends or edges are milled rectangularly so that they overlap.

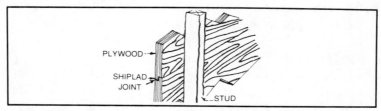

shop cutting panel—Panel rejected as not conforming to the grade requirements defined in the Product Standard. Panel identification, a separate mark that does not mention the Standard, reads: "Shop Cutting Panel—All Other Marks Void." Normally a "shop" panel may be cut up for use in smaller pieces, and the defect eliminated.

siding—Term applied to boards or plywood panels used for the finish covering of the outside walls of frame buildings. Plywood sidings include a group with attractive textured surface finishes, achieved through sawing, sanding, grooving, etc., after the panel has been completed. See nailing and spacing data below.

soffit—The underside of the roof overhang. Plywood is often used as a finishing material for soffits. See APA Residential Construction Guide, Y405.

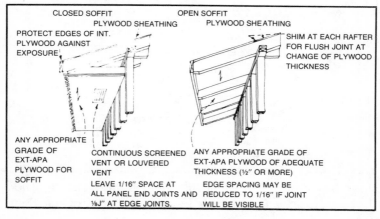

softwood—The general term for trees that have needle-like or scale-like leaves and bear cones. Also the wood produced by such trees. The term has no reference to the actual hardness of the wood.

solid core—Inner ply construction of solid C-Plugged veneer pieces. Gaps between pieces of core should not exceed ½ inch per the Product Standard PS 1. Also defined as plugged core in the Product Standard.

sound transmission (control)—Passage of sound through a panel or construction assembly. Plywood is excellent for "quiet" construction. Large panel size reduces the number of joints and cracks that can leak airborne noise. Plywood is also a superior base for resilient coverings that cut impact noise. For more information see Plywood Construction and Noise Control, APA Form W460. Sound Transmission Class (STC) and Impact Insulation Class (11C) rated assemblies are illustrated below.

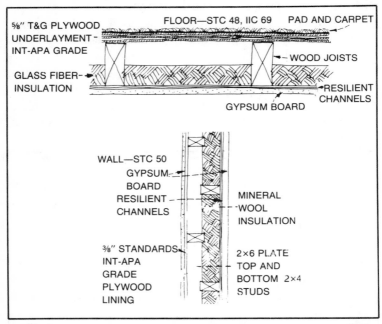

spacing—Small spaces should be left between plywood panels to allow for expansion. Normal spacing for sheathing

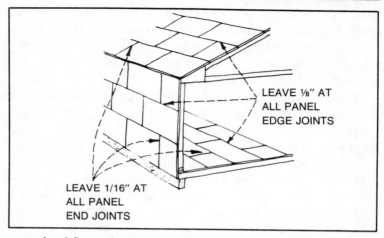

LEAVE ⅛" AT
ALL PANEL
EDGE JOINTS

LEAVE 1/16" AT
ALL PANEL
END JOINTS

and subfloors is shown below. For areas of high humidity, double these spacings.

span tables—A list of allowable spans for plywood. That is, maximum spacing for roof and floor framing under various thicknesses and grades of plywood, along with allowable loads. See APA Residential Construction Guide Form Y405.

special overlay—An overlay similar to high or medium density overlay, which does not exactly fit the product standard description, but which meets the glueline durability requirements of PS 1 and is overlaid for special uses. One example is acrylic overlay plywood used in such applications as highway signs.

splice plate—A piece of wood, often plywood, used to attach lumber members end to end.

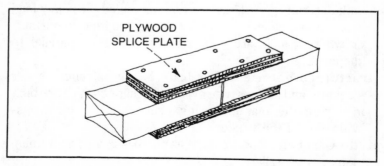

PLYWOOD
SPLICE PLATE

split—A separation of wood fibers.

split resistance—Grain running crosswise in alternate layers allows no line of cleavage for splitting in plywood.

staple—A fastener for applying plywood sheathing.

strength—An outstanding characteristic of plywood, created by cross-laminating veneers and gluing them together, to distribute wood's high along-the-grain strength in both directions.

stressed skin panel—An engineered structural flat panel for roof deck or floor applications built up of plywood sheets glued to framing members. The assembly covers quickly with greater combined load carrying capacity than its individual members would have if installed separately.

striated—A texture in plywood siding characterized by closely spaced shallow grooves or striations which form a vertical pattern.

stringer—A lumber supporting member for a series of cross members. Frequently applied to stair supports.

stripping—Removing plywood forms after pouring. Plywood is a widely used concrete forming material because it is tough, durable, and provides many reuses.

structural 1 & 11—These terms are used with letter grades on certain structural grades of plywood. They mean that the plywood can be made only from particular species of wood, and that they must meet special requirements of veneer grade and workmanship. Any STRUCTURAL 1 panel must use all Group 1 veneers throughout. STRUCTURAL 11 panels allow veneers of species Groups 1 through 3. All STRUCTURAL 1 and 11 panels are made with exterior glue. They are recommended for heavy load applications, especially where shear strength is important, or where panels are applied with face grain parallel to supports.

structural properties—Durability, bending strength, shear strength, and stiffness are plywood qualities which are built in during the manufacturing process with the cross-lamination of the veneers.

stud—Generally, 2 × 4's used as the basic vertical framing members of walls.

stud spacing—The distance between the upright members of a wall's framework, traditionally 16 inches on center. Sometimes placed at 24 inches on center when using plywood for structural stability as in the Engineered 23″ Framing System.

subflooring—Plywood applied directly over floor joists which will receive an additional covering such as underlayment, if tile is to be applied. Plywood is used for strength and to reduce the number of floor joints. For application, see UNDERLAYMENT.

swelling—Expansion of wood caused by the absorption of water. In normal construction, ⅛ inch spacing between panel edges and 1/16 inch between panel ends is enough to take care of expansion. In very wet or humid areas, and in farm buildings, the spacing should be doubled.

synthetic repairs—Used to repair defects in plywood. In APA plywood, they must pass rigid qualifying tests.

303® specialty sidings—A grade designation covering APA proprietary plywood products for siding, fencing soffits, wind screens and other exterior applications. Panels have special surface treatments including rough sawn, striated and brushed. May be grooved in different styles. Check the grade-trademark on the panel for proper support spacings, i.e. 16 inch o.c. or 24 inch o.c. See SIDING for some sample patterns.

T-beam—Beam whose cross section resembles a "T." Several T-beams side by side, if acting as a unit, might form a floor. This is the principle which accounts for the increased stiffness of the APA Glued Floor System.

tanks—Plywood is used for liquid tank construction because of its workability, strength, insulating value, acid resistance, and economy. While wood itself is sufficiently resistant to water and many other solutions, so that unlined plywood tanks are used extensively, plywood tanks are easily coated or lined when use dictates.

telegraphing—Show-through on the surface of the grain or defects in the material beneath it.

termites—Wood-destroying insects. Panels may be treated with pentachlorophenol to increase their resistance to these pests.

testing agency—An organization whose function is continuous testing of random samples of plywood from the plywood mills to assure the product meets applicable standards. The American Plywood Association is such an organization.

testing and inspection (APA)—APA mill supervisors may enter member mills on an unannounced basis to inspect the quality of plywood production and to take random samples. The samples are then sent to APA laboratories for extensive glueline-quality tests. Mills must maintain their high standards of quality or lose their APA grade-trademarking privileges.

texture 1-11—APA trade name for a special 303 siding panel 19/32 or ⅝ inch thick with ⅜ inch wide vertical grooving spaced 2, 4, or 8 inches on center. Panels have shiplapped edges to maintain pattern continuity when installed.

textured plywood—Panels with many different machined surface textures. Available in Exterior type with fully waterproof glueline for siding and other outdoor uses and for interior wall paneling.

thickness—Plywood panels, range from ¼ inch through 1-¼ inches thick and are made up of three, four, five, six, seven or more veneers.

tongue-and-groove joint—A system of jointing in which the rib or tongue of one member fits exactly into the groove of another. A specially designed American Plywood Association tongue-and-groove plywood edge joint is particularly efficient in transferring the load across the joint. T & G panels measure 48 inches overall, or about 47-½ inches ± ⅛ inch, on the face.

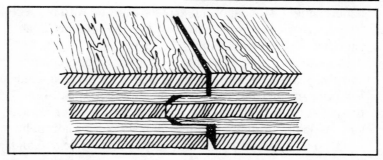

touch-sanding—A sizing operation consisting of a light surface sanding in a sander. Sander skips are admissible. Normally applied to C-Plugged faces.

truss—A combination of members usually arranged in triangular units to form a rigid framework for supporting loads over a span. Parallel chord trusses are also used for floor and roof supports.

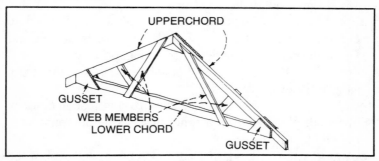

type—Classification of plywood into Interior and Exterior panels based on glueline and veneer grades.

UBC—Uniform Building Code.

U.L.—Underwriter's Laboratories, Inc. Plywood marked with the UL fire hazard classification label has been treated according to required fire-retardant specifications.

underlayment—A material applied directly below nonstructural finish flooring such as tile or carpeting. Plywood is available in UNDERLAYMENT grade for use in underlayment and in combination subfloor-underlayment. Write for APA's Residential Construction Guide, Form Y405. Apply underlayment with panel end joints staggered with respect to each other and offset from all joints in the subfloor. Space panel ends and edges about 1/32 inch.

Unless joists are thoroughly seasoned and dry, countersink nail heads 1/16 inch below surface of the underlayment just prior to laying finish floors to avoid nail popping. Countersink staples 1/32 inch. Fill any damaged or open areas, such as joints or splits. Do not fill nail holes. Thoroughly sand any surface roughness, particularly at joints and around nails.

unsanded plywood—Sheathing grades of plywood are left unsanded for greater stiffness, strength and economy.

urethane—A synthetic resin used in the manufacture of protective coatings and insulation.

values, nail—Resistance of nail to load; varies with nail size, wood type and quality, and use.

vapor barrier—A material (such as plastic film) used to control moisture transmission through walls and floors. Often used in combination with insulation to control condensation. A vapor barrier should be installed on the warm side of the wall and ceiling.

veneer—Thin sheets of wood, laminated in manufacture of plywood, glued to form a panel that is split-and puncture-resistant.

veneer grades—Standard grades of veneer used in plywood manufacture. The six grades are described as follows:

N Special order "natural finish" veneer. Select all heartwood or all sapwood. Free of open defects. Allows some repairs.

A Smooth and paintable. Neatly made repairs permissible. Also used for natural finish in less demanding applications.

B Solid surface veneer. Circular repair plugs and tight knots permitted.

C Knotholes to 1". Occasional knotholes ½" larger permitted providing total width of all knots and knotholes within a specified section does not exceed certain limits. Limited splits permitted. Minimum veneer permitted in Exterior type plywood.

C Improved C veneer with splits limited to ⅛″ in width, and knotholes plugged and borer holes limited to ¼″ by ½″.

D Permits knots and knotholes to 2-½″ in width, and ½″ larger under certain specified limits. Limited splits permitted.

vinyl—Thin plastic floor covering in tile or sheet form used over plywood subflooring and underlayment.

WWPA—Western Wood Products Association, 1500 Yeon Building, Portland, Oregon 97204

wainscot—The wooden lining of the lower part of an interior wall.

waler—Horizontal timbers used in concrete form construction to brace the section. See APA Plywood for Concrete Forming, Form V345.

wall construction—Plywood systems for building walls. See APA's Residential Construction Guide, Form Y405.

APA Sturd-I-Wall Construction: Plywood panel sidings attached directly to studs. 303 plywood siding bearing the designation "303-24 o.c." on the grade-trademark may be

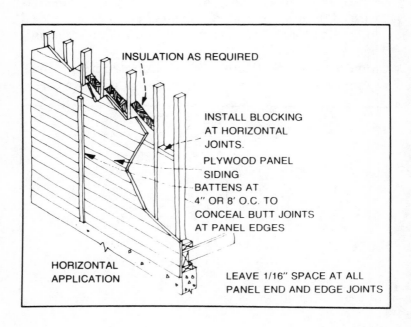

INSULATION AS REQUIRED

INSTALL BLOCKING AT HORIZONTAL JOINTS.

PLYWOOD PANEL SIDING

BATTENS AT 4″ OR 8′ O.C. TO CONCEAL BUTT JOINTS AT PANEL EDGES

HORIZONTAL APPLICATION

LEAVE 1/16″ SPACE AT ALL PANEL END AND EDGE JOINTS

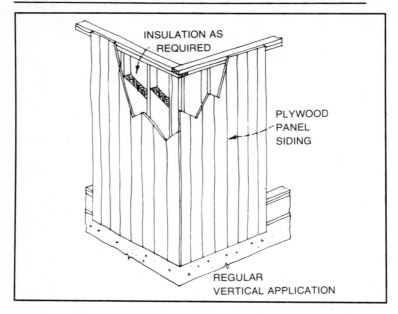

INSULATION AS REQUIRED

PLYWOOD PANEL SIDING

REGULAR VERTICAL APPLICATION

applied vertically directly to studs spaced 24 inches on center. 303-16 o.c. may be used vertically over studs spaced 16 inches on center. Either designation may be used on studs 24 inches o.c. when applied with face grain horizontal.

Conventional or Double Wall Construction: Uses plywood siding over sheathing applied to wood framing.

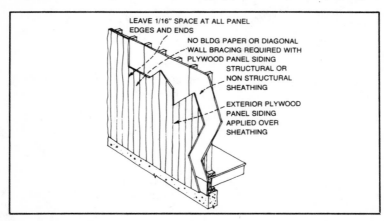

LEAVE 1/16" SPACE AT ALL PANEL EDGES AND ENDS

NO BLDG PAPER OR DIAGONAL WALL BRACING REQUIRED WITH PLYWOOD PANEL SIDING STRUCTURAL OR NON STRUCTURAL SHEATHING

EXTERIOR PLYWOOD PANEL SIDING APPLIED OVER SHEATHING

wall sheathing—Plywood nailed to the studs which acts as a base for the siding application.

warping—To bend, twist, or turn from a straight line. A piece of lumber, when improperly seasoned and exposed to heat or moisture may warp. To reduce the possibility of warping, avoid exposing plywood panels to dampness or moisture. Painting and water-repellent dips will minimize moisture absorption. Also, sealing all edges and back-priming will reduce the chances of warping in cabinet doors.

water repellents—Wood preservatives, with water-resistant properties.

watertight—A term applied to any construction that is waterproof.

wicking—The tendency of wood to draw moisture up through the cells in the direction of the grain.

"Z" flashing—A Z-shaped piece of galvanized steel or aluminum or plastic used at horizontal joints of plywood siding to prevent water from entering wall cavity.

 # Appendix

Table A-1. Minimum bending radii

Panel Thickness	Across Grain	Parallel to Grain
1/4''	2'	5'
5/16''	2'	6'
3/8''	3'	8'
1/2''	6'	12'
5/8''	8'	16'
3/4''	12'	20'

Table A-2. Concrete form plywoods

Use these symbols when you specify plywood *	Description	VENEER GRADE	
		Faces	Inner Plies
B-B PLYFORM Class I & Class II**	Specifically manufactured for concrete forms. Yields many reuses. Smooth, solid surfaces. Mill-oiled unless otherwise specified.	B	C
HDO PLYFORM Class I, & Class II**	Hard, semiopaque resin-fiber overlay, heat-fused to panel faces. Smooth surface resists abrasion. Yields up to 200 reuses. Light oiling recommended after each pour.	B	C Plugged
STRUCTURAL I PLYFORM**	Especially designed for engineered applications. Contains all Group 1 species. Stronger and stiffer than Plyform Class I & II. Especially recommended for high pressures where face grain is parallel to supports. Also available with HDO.	B	C or C Plugged
* Commonly available in 5/8 inch and 3/4 inch panel thickness (4 x 8 foot size). ** Check dealer for availability in your area.	SPECIAL PANELS** Special Overlays, proprietary panels, and MDO plywood specifically designed for concrete forming. Panels produce a smooth uniform concrete surface. Generally mill treated with form release agent. Check with manufacturer for design specifications, proper use, and surface treatment recommendations for greatest number of uses. Check dealer for availability in your area.		

Table A-3. A nail to plywood thickness chart

Plywood Thickness (inches)	Common Nail	Finish Nail
3/4	8d	8d
5/8	8d	8d
1/2	6d	6d
3/8	6d	4d

Table A-4. A screw and drill size to plywood thickness chart

PLYWOOD THICKNESS	SCREW LENGTH	SCREW SIZE	DRILL SIZE FOR SHANK	DRILL SIZE FOR ROOT OF THREAD
3/4" 5/8"	1½" 1¼"	#8	11/64"	1/8"
1/2" 3/8"	1¼" 1	#6	9/64"	3/32"
1/4"	1	#4	7/64"	1/16"

Table A-5. Exterior finish applications

Exterior Applications

TYPE OF FINISH		RECOMMENDED FOR	APPLICATION
PAINT	Acrylic Latex	Medium Density Overlaid, striated, or regular plywood panel or lap siding. Also Texture 1-11 and rough sawn	Apply recommended primer plus two finish coats, or follow manufacturer's recommendations
	Oil-Alkyd	Medium Density Overlaid	Apply with zinc-free primer, using two or three coats (including primer).
STAIN	Semitransparent	Textured plywood	One or two-coat systems as recommended by the manufacturer.
	Opaque	Textured plywood	One or two-coat systems as recommended by the manufacturer.

Table A-6. Interior finish applications

Interior Applications

TYPE OF FINISH	RECOMMENDED FOR	APPLICATIONS
Oil—flat paint, semi-gloss or gloss enamel	Medium Density Overlaid, regular plywood, striated, embossed.	Apply over primer or may be self-priming.
Latex emulsion	Regular and textured plywood, Medium Density Overlaid.	Apply over oil or stain-resistant primer.
PAINT Texture, multicolor, spatter	Regular plywood, Medium Density Overlaid, Texture 1-11.	Use oil base or stain-resistant primer.
STAINS, SEALERS	Regular plywood, textured.	Apply stains with companion sealer or over sealer separately applied. Where sealer alone is desired, use two coats.

Table A-7. Glue application chart

TYPE OF GLUE	DESCRIPTION	RECOMMENDED USE	PRECAUTIONS	HOW TO USE
UREA RESIN GLUE	Comes as powder to be mixed with water and used within 4 hours. Light colored. Very strong if joint fits well.	Good for general wood gluing. For work that must stand some exposure to dampness, but is not completely waterproof.	Needs well-fitted joints, tight clamping, and room temperature 70° or warmer. Some require heat to cure.	Make sure joint fits tightly. Mix glue and apply thin coat. Allow 16 hours drying time.
LIQUID RESIN (WHITE) GLUE	Comes ready to use at any temperature. Clean-working, quick setting. Strong enough for most work, though not quite so tough as urea resin glue.	Good for indoor furniture and cabinetwork. First choice for small jobs where tight clamping or good fit may be difficult.	Not sufficiently resistant to moisture for outdoor furniture or outdoor storage units.	Use at any temperature but preferably above 60°. Spread on both surfaces, clamp at once. Sets in 1½ hours.
RESOR- CINOL (WATER- PROOF) GLUE	Comes as powder plus liquid, must be mixed each time used. Dark colored, very strong, completely waterproof.	This is the glue to use with Exterior type plywood for work to be exposed to extreme dampness. Good for farm buildings, boats.	Expense, trouble to mix and dark color make it unsuited to jobs where waterproof glue is not required. Needs good fit, tight clamping.	Use within 8 hours after mixing. Work at temperature above 70°. Apply thin coat to both surfaces; allow 16 hours drying time.

Table A-8. Unsanded grades identification

| Thickness (inch) | C-D INT - APA C-C EXT - APA | | |
	Group 1 & Structural I	Group 2* or 3 & Structural II*†	Group 4**
5/16	20/0	16/0	12/0
3/8	24/0	20/0	16/0
1/2	32/16	24/0	24/0
5/8	42/20	32/16	30/12†
3/4	48/24	42/20	36/16†
7/8	....	48/24	42/20

NOTES:

* Panels with Group 2 outer plies and special thickness and construction requirements, or STRUCTURAL II panels with Group 1 faces, may carry the Identification Index numbers shown for Group 1 panels.

** Panels made with Group 4 outer plies may carry the Identification Index numbers shown for Group 3 panels when they conform to special thickness and construction requirements detailed in PS 1.

† Check local availability.

Table A-9. Plywood subflooring identification

Panel Identification Index (1)(2)(3)	Plywood Thickness (inches)	Maximum Span (4) (inches)	Nail Size and Type (common)	Nail Spacing (inches)	
				Panel Edges	Intermediate
30/12	5/8	12 (5)	8d	6	10
32/16	1/2, 5/8	16 (6)	8d (7)	6	10
36/16	3/4	16 (6)	8d	6	10
42/20	5/8, 3/4, 7/8	20 (6)	8d	6	10
48/24	3/4, 7/8	24	8d	6	10
1-1/8" Gps 1 & 2	1-1/8	48	10d	6	6
1-1/4" Gps. 3 & 4	1-1/4	48	10d	6	6

(1) Applies to STRUCTURAL I and II grades, C-D Interior sheathing, and C-C Exterior grades only.

(2) Identification Index appears on all panels, except 1-1/8" and 1-1/4".

(3) Special conditions may impose heavy concentrated loads requiring subfloor construction in excess of these minimums.

(4) Spans limited to values shown because of possible effect of concentrated loads.

(5) May be 16" with 25/32" wood strip flooring at right angles to joists.

(6) May be 24" with 25/32" wood strip flooring at right angles to joists.

(7) 6d common nail permitted if plywood is 1/2".

Table A-10. Here are maximum allowable uniform live loads for plywood roof decking. Five pounds per square foot load is assumed. Live load is applied load, like snow. Dead load is the weight of plywood and roofing

Panel Identification Index	Plywood Thickness (inch)	Max. Span (inches)	Unsupported Edge—Max. Length (inches)(4)	Allowable Roof Loads (psf) (5) Spacing of Supports (inches center to center)									
				12	16	20	24	30	32	36	42	48	60
12/0	5/16	12	12	150									
16/0	5/16, 3/8	16	16	160	75								
20/0	5/16, 3/8	20	20	190	105	65							
24/0	3/8	24	20	250	140	95	50						
	1/2		24										
32/16	1/2, 5/8	32	28	385	215	150	95	50	40				
42/20	5/8, 3/4, 7/8	42	32		330	230	145	90	75	50	35		
48/24	3/4	48	36			300	190	120	105	65	45	35	
48/24(6)	7/8						225	125	105	75	55	40	
2·4·1	1-1/8	72	48				390	245	215	135	100	75	45
1-1/8 Group 1 & 2	1-1/8	72	48				305	195	170	105	75	55	35
1-1/4 Group 3 & 4	1-1/4	72	48				355	225	195	125	90	65	40

(1) These values apply for C-D INT-APA, C-C EXT-APA   STRUCTURAL I and II C-D INT-APA and STRUCTURAL I and II C-C EXT-APA grades only. Plywood continuous over 2 or moe spans; grain of face plies across supports.

(2) Use 6d common smooth, ring-shank, or spiral-thread nails for ½ inch thick or less and 8d common smooth, ring-shank, or spiral-thread for plywood 1 inch thick or less. Use 8d ring-shank or spiral-thread or 10d common smooth-shank nails for 2-4-1, 1⅛ inch and 1½ inch panels. Space nails 6 inches at panel edges and 12 inches at intermediate supports, except that where spans are 48 inches or more, nails shall be 6 inches at all supports. Space panel ends 1/16 inch, and panel edges ⅛ inch. Where wet or humid conditions prevail, double these spacings.

(3) Special conditions, such as heavy concentrated loads, may require constructions in excess of these minimums.

(4) Provide adequate blocking, tongue-and-grooved edges or other suitable edge support such as Plyclips when spans exceed indicated value. Use two Plyclips for 48 inch or greater spans and one for lesser spans.

(5) Uniform load deflection limit: 1/180th span under live load plus dead load, 1/240th under live load only.

(6) Loads apply only to C-C EXT-APA, STRUCTURAL I C-D INT-APA, and STRUCTURAL I C-C EXT-APA.

Table A-11. A chart showing exterior plywood lap siding over sheathing

Exterior plywood lap siding over sheathing Recommendations apply to all species groups.

Plywood Siding			Max. Stud Spacing (inches)			Nail Size (Use nonstaining box, siding or casing nails)	Nail Spacing (inches)	
Type	Description	Nominal Thickness (inches)	Face Grain Vertical	Face Grain Horizontal			Panel Edges	Intermediate
Lap Siding	MDO EXT-APA	19/32 & 3/8	—	16[1]		6d for siding 3/8" thick or less; 8d for thicker siding. (2)	4" @ vertical butt joints; one nail per stud along bottom edge	8" @ each stud, if siding wider than 12".
		1/2 & thicker	—	24				
	303–16 o.c. Siding EXT-APA	5/16, 19/32, or 3/8	—	16[1]				
	303–16 o.c. Siding EXT-APA 303–24 o.c. Siding EXT-APA	7/16 & thicker	—	24				

(1) May be 24 inches with plywood or lumber sheathing.

(2) Use next larger nail size when sheathing is other than plywood or lumber, and nail only into framing.

Table A-12. A table showing exterior plywood panel siding over sheathing Recommendations apply to all species groups.

Exterior plywood panel siding over sheathing

| Plywood Siding | | Nominal Thickness (inches) | Max. Stud Spacing (inches) | | Nail Size (Use nonstaining box, siding or casing nails) | Nail Spacing (inches) | |
Type	Description		Face Grain Vertical	Face Grain Horizontal		Panel Edges	Intermediate
	MDO EXT-APA	19/32 & 3/8	16[1]	24	6d for panels ½" thick or less;	6	12
		1/2 & thicker	24	24	8d for thicker panels.		
Panel Siding	303—16 o.c. Siding EXT-APA (including T1-11)	5/16 & thicker	16[1]	24			
	303—24 o.c. Siding EXT-APA	7/16 & thicker	24	24	(2)		

(1) May be 24 inches with 1/2 inch plywood, or lumber sheathing, if panel is also nailed 12 inches o.c. between studs, provided panel joints fall over studs.

(2) Use next larger nail size when sheathing (other than plywood or lumber) is thicker than 1/2 inch.

Table A-13. Shown is information regarding interior plywood paneling

Interior plywood paneling Recommendations apply to all species groups.

Plywood Thickness[1] (inch)	Max. Support Spacing (inches)	Nail Size and Type	Nail Spacing (inches)	
			Panel Edges	Intermediate
1/4	16[2]	4d casing or finish	6	12
3/8	24	6d casing or finish	6	12

(1) Leave 1/32 inch spacing at all panel edge and end joints.
(2) Can be 20 inches if face grain of paneling is across supports.

Table A-14. Recommendations for plywood siding direct to studs

Type	Plywood Siding		Max. Stud Spacing (inches)		Nail Size (Use nonstaining box, siding or casing nails)	Nail Spacing (inches)	
	Description	Nominal Thickness (inches)	Face Grain Vertical	Face Grain Horizontal		Panel Edges	Intermediate
Panel Siding	MDO EXT-APA	19/32, 3/8	16	24	6d for panels ½" thick or less; 8d for thicker panels.	6	12
	MDO EXT-APA	1/2 & thicker	24	24			
	303–16 o.c. Siding EXT-APA (including T1-11)	5/16 & thicker	16	24			
	303–24 o.c. Siding EXT-APA	7/16 & thicker	24	24			
Lap Siding	MDO EXT-APA	19/32, 3/8	—	16	6d for siding 3/8" or less; 8d for thicker siding.	4" @ vertical butt joints; one nail per stud along bottom edge.	8" @ each stud, if siding wider than 12".
	MDO EXT-APA	1/2 & thicker	—	24			
	303–16 o.c. Siding EXT-APA	5/16, 19/32, or 3/8	—	16			
	303–16 o.c. Siding EXT-APA 303–24 o.c. Siding EXT-APA	7/16 & thicker	—	24			

Table A-15. A recommended minimum stapling schedule for plywood

Recommended Minimum Stapling Schedule For Plywood All values are for 16 gauge galvanized wire staples having a minimum crown width of 3/8 inch.

Plywood Thickness	Staple Leg Length	Spacing Around Entire Perimeter of Sheet	Spacing at Intermediate Members
A. Plywood wall sheathing/Without diagonal bracing			
5/16"	1-1/4"	4"	8"
3/8"	1-3/8"	4"	8"
1/2"	1-1/2"	4"	8"
B. Plywood roof sheathing			
5/16"	1-1/4"	4"	8"
3/8"	1-3/8"	4"	8"
1/2"	1-1/2"	4"	8"
C. Plywood subfloors			
1/2"	1-5/8"	4"	7"
5/8"	1-5/8"	2½"	4"
D. Plywood underlayment			
1/4"·(1)	7/8"	3"	6" each way
3/8"	1-1/8"	3"	6" each way
1/2"	1-5/8"	3"	6" each way
5/8"	1-5/8"	3"	6" each way
E. Asphalt shingles to plywood/Staples to have crown width of 3/4" min.			
5/16" and thicker	3/4"	According to shingle manufacturer.	

(1) 18-gauge staples with 3/16 inch crown width may be used for 1/4 inch underlayment.

NOTE: The International Conference of Building Officials recognizes several types of special mechanical fasteners. They are covered in ICBO Report No. 2403.

Table A-16. A table for plywood underlayment. For maximum stiffness place grain across supports and end joints over framing

Plywood Grades and Species Group	Application	Minimum Plywood Thickness	Fastener Size (approx.) and Type (set nails 1/16'')	Fastener Spacing (Inches)	
				Panel Edges	Inter-mediate
All Groups: UNDERLAYMENT INT-APA (with interior or exterior glue), or UNDERLAYMENT EXT-APA(3)	over plywood subfloor	1/4''	18 Ga. Staples or 3d ring-shank nails (1)(2)	3	6 each way
	over lumber sub-floor or other uneven surfaces	3/8''	16 Ga. Staples (1)	3	6 each way
			3d ring-shank nails (1)(2)	6	8 each way
Same Grades as above, but Group 1 or STRUC-TURAL I Only	over lumber floor up to 4'' wide. Face grain must be perpendicular to boards.	1/4''	18 Ga. Staples or 3d ring-shank nails	3	6 each way

Table A-17. A subfloor underlayment chart

| Plywood Species Group | 2-4-1 | | Nail Size and Type | Nail Spacing (inches) | |
	Plywood Thickness (inches)	Maximum Spacing of Supports c to c (inches)		Panel Edges	Inter-mediate
Groups 1, 2, and 3	1-1/8	32(2x joists)	8d ring-shank recommended or 10d common smooth-shank (if supports are well seasoned)	6	10
		48(4x girders)		6	6

Table A-18. A combined subfloor-underlayment chart

Plywood Grade[3]	Plywood Species Group	Maximum Support Spacing[1][2]						Nail Spacing (inches)	
		16" o.c.		20" o.c.		24" o.c.		Panel Edges	Inter-mediate
		Panel Thickness	Deformed Shank Nail Size	Panel Thickness	Deformed Shank Nail Size	Panel Thickness	Deformed Shank Nail Size		
UNDERLAYMENT INT-APA (with interior or exterior glue) or UNDER-LAYMENT EXT-APA (C-C Plugged)	1	1/2"	6d	5/8"**	6d	3/4"**	6d	6	10
	2 & 3	5/8"*	6d	3/4"**	6d	7/8"	8d	6	10
	4	3/4"**	6d	7/8"	8d	1"	8d	6	10

*May be 19/32" **May be 23/32"

(1) Plywood edges shall be tongue-and-grooved, or supported with framing.

(2) In some nonresidential buildings, special conditions may impose heavy concentrated loads and heavy traffic requiring subfloor-underlayment constructions in excess of these minimums.

(3) For certain types of flooring such as wood block or terrazzo, sheathing grades of plywood may be used.

Index

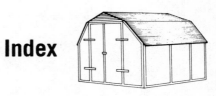